# ON MICHAEL HANEKE

CONTEMPORARY APPROACHES TO FILM AND TELEVISION SERIES

*A complete listing of the books in this series can be found online at wsupress.wayne.edu*

*General Editor*
Barry Keith Grant
Brock University

*Advisory Editors*
Robert J. Burgoyne
Wayne State University

Caren J. Deming
University of Arizona

Patricia B. Erens
School of the Art Institute of Chicago

Peter X. Feng
University of Delaware

Lucy Fischer
University of Pittsburgh

Frances Gateward
Ursinus College

Tom Gunning
University of Chicago

Thomas Leitch
University of Delaware

Anna McCarthy
New York University

Walter Metz
Southern Illinois University

Lisa Parks
University of California–
Santa Barbara

JOHN DAVID RHODES

# ON MICHAEL
# HANEKE

EDITED BY BRIAN PRICE AND

**WAYNE STATE UNIVERSITY PRESS  DETROIT**

© 2010 by Wayne State University Press, Detroit, Michigan 48201. All rights reserved. No part of this book may be reproduced without formal permission.

14 13 12 11 10     5 4 3 2 1

Library of Congress Cataloging-in-Publication Data
On Michael Haneke / edited by Brian Price and John David Rhodes.
p. cm. — (Contemporary approaches to film and television series)
Includes bibliographical references and index.
ISBN 978-0-8143-3405-8 (pbk. : alk. paper)
1. Haneke, Michael—Criticism and interpretation. I. Price, Brian, 1970–
II. Rhodes, John David, 1969–
PN1998.3.H36O52 2010
791.43023'3092—dc22
2009051052

*Typeset by Maya Rhodes*
*Composed in Adobe Garamond and News Gothic Std*

# Contents

*Acknowledgments* vii

Introduction 1
BRIAN PRICE AND JOHN DAVID RHODES

## PART 1. VIOLENCE AND PLAY

Brigitte Peucker
Games Haneke Plays: Reality and Performance 15

Brian Price
Pain and the Limits of Representation 35

Tarja Laine
Haneke's "Funny" Games with the Audience (Revisited) 51

Michael Lawrence
Haneke's Stable: The Death of an Animal and the Figuration of the Human 63

## PART 2. STYLE AND MEDIUM

John David Rhodes
The Spectacle of Skepticism: Haneke's Long Takes 87

Hugh S. Manon
"Comment ça, rien?": Screening the Gaze in *Caché* 105

Fatima Naqvi and Christophe Koné
The Key to Voyeurism: Haneke's Adaptation of Jelinek's *The Piano Teacher* 127

CONTENTS

Mattias Frey
The Message and the Medium: Haneke's Film Theory
and Digital Praxis   153

Meghan Sutherland
Death, with Television   167

Bert Rebhandl
Haneke's Early Work for Television   191

PART 3. CULTURE AND CONFLICT

Christopher Sharrett
Haneke and the Discontents of European Culture   207

Rosalind Galt
The Functionary of Mankind: Haneke and Europe   221

Scott Durham
Codes Unknown: Haneke's Serial Realism   245

Patrick Crowley
When Forgetting Is Remembering: Haneke's *Caché*
and the Events of October 17, 1961   267

*Contributors   281*
*Index   285*

# Acknowledgments

Earlier versions of the essays by Mattias Frey, Brian Price, John David Rhodes, and Christopher Sharrett were published in a dossier on Michael Haneke in *Framework* 47, no. 2 (2006).

The editors would like to thank Rosalind Galt and Scott Krzych for their help with the preparation of this manuscript. We would also like to thank Jane Hoehner and Annie Martin of Wayne State University Press for their unflagging support and commitment to this project.

*Benny's Video* (1992): The view from Benny's camera as it records his parents' discussion about what to do with the body.

Brian Price and John David Rhodes

# Introduction

We are tempted to consider the cinema of Michael Haneke with what might be the too-convenient discourses supplied to us by the accidents of his birth, the arc of his work and life, and the facts of the age—his age and ours. His most fully realized work for the cinema began to appear toward the tail end of the last century, at exactly the moment that the cinema celebrated—or marked, in any case—its first one hundred or so years. His most recent films (we write in 2009) have been singled out as some of the most puzzling, disturbing, rewarding, and controversial works of art of the new century. His cinema, in many ways, seems to be both the beginning and the end of something. Haneke's own birth year (1942) and birthplace (Austria) would seem to offer us a rather convenient, possibly overdetermined, context for thinking about his cinema's meditation on human violence and historical trauma. His student engagements with literature and philosophy and his movement from the theater to the moving image (televisual and cinematic) describe the familiar contours of a distinctively European school of auteur, while his early focus on a national (Austrian) literary, linguistic, and cultural context and his eventual movement toward a polyglot, transnationally funded and acted cinema map neatly onto the radical political, cartographic, and demographic redefinition of Europe during the years of his (ongoing) productivity. In many senses, Haneke's career is consubstantial with its era: his works are immersed in the antinomies and agonies of the contemporary world, and they also provide a profound critical distance or remove from the same.[1]

And yet the neatness of periodizing Haneke's work, the convenience of understanding its relevance and congruence with the world we understand ourselves to inhabit, should also cause us some concern. Haneke is certainly the most rigorous and in many senses the neatest of cinematic formalists. However, the philosophical problems raised by his films, the way in which his films seem to ask us to think forward and backward in time, the sense in which he seems at turns obeisant to and contemptuous of the traditions (cinematic and otherwise) out of which his work extends—these problems and questions are also impossibly messy and obscure. How to entertain and to probe both Haneke's clarity and his opacity is the challenge for those who wish to think about his work.

This collection extends out of this challenge. We believe that, like the work of filmmakers such as Robert Bresson or Pier Paolo Pasolini before him, Haneke's body of work is discomfiting, impatient, and sometimes as infuriating as it is infuriated. He carries on one of the most important modes of intellectual and artistic production in modern and contemporary culture: that of art cinema. At its best, art cinema (a mode initially identified with Europe but now perhaps most forcefully embodied in films produced in Asia, Africa, and Latin America) figures a serious mode of aesthetic, philosophical, and political inquiry in which the filmmaker assumes that there might be an audience—perhaps even a mass audience—for whom such inquiry matters. Art cinema devotes itself in equal measure to a profound skepticism toward and an extravagant indulgence in the image. It regards the cinematic image as much as a mode of thought as a mode of picturing, and it is, moreover, dedicated to picturing thought and to picturing as a mode of thought. Such a regard and such dedication mean that the art cinema must risk seriousness, at the expense of being charged with hubris or obscurity. And yet fitting Haneke comfortably into the history of the global art cinematic auteurs may also tell us less than we want. While Haneke obviously inserts himself into this tradition, this mode, his films, if we follow them to what seem to be their conclusions, would seem to suffer us to witness the implosion of this very same mode of practice.

We turn to Haneke in this collection because, yes, he makes unforgettable, precise, and provocative films. We turn to him, moreover, because these films provoke us into thinking about images, into thinking about how we and others have thought about images, and into thinking about the world of which such images constitute a crucial and critical dimension.

## Introduction

It would be all too easy—and, perhaps, far too comfortable—to understand Haneke's work as constituting a moral diagnosis of and tonic for the social ills of our time, a cure for what Guy Debord so famously and so accurately described as the "society of the spectacle." After all, Haneke's production is nothing if not obviously concerned with our own relation to images. Why else with such frequency are we made to encounter in Haneke's work images of the most degraded nature: images of pornography, sequences from slasher films, footage of Michael Jackson's Neverland or of Jennifer Rush bellowing "The Power of Love"? Why else does his work ask us to bear so many bloody images of Bosnia and Rwanda, of decapitated chickens and suicidal North Africans? Haneke's images of violence seem especially to press in on us. The image of violence is so often understood as the cause of violence, the cause of our inability to be moved by violence in the real world. Haneke's work might seem to affirm that that Jean Baudrillard was right all along: the image has replaced the territory in the screen of our consciousness and has done so in the service of further violence.[2] Always, the image produces violence and subjects both immune to and productive of further violence.

If Haneke's career is an unusual one—unusual in its force and unusual in the constellation of issues the films present to us—let us ask ourselves to approach Haneke in somewhat less familiar terms. Let us, by way of introduction—as the introduction to the collection of essays you are holding—consider *Benny's Video* and its representation of violence in and through the image. Doesn't *Benny's Video* tell us that the image produces violence or even is constitutive of violence itself?[3] Isn't this what Haneke "means" when he shows us Benny, the teenage videophile, murder a young girl with whom he has just tenderly shared a plate of microwaved pizza? Benny murders his victim, you will recall, with the same pneumatic gun featured, in the most uncomfortable way, in the opening of the film itself in which we see the gun being used to kill a pig on a farm. In the opening we see Benny's very own amateur video footage of the slaughter; the animal's movement seems to evince a stubborn exhaustion and fatal resignation to its own slaughter. Benny lingers, by way of rewind and remote control, on the instant of the pig's death. It all seems clear. Benny exhibits the telltale symptoms of the sociopath: a fascination with the moment of death, with the power of decision, and with the pleasure that might be had upon its revisitation in the form of the image. He is, in other words, desensitized. Following Benny, we might point to names and places forever linked by such acts of violence in our time: Dylan Klebold and Eric Harris and Columbine; Seung-Hui Cho and Virginia Tech, Blacksburg; Osama Bin-Laden and the Twin Towers, New York City. Synonyms, in other words. Or neologisms. We might implicate our own idle pleasures—video games, horror films, pornography, celebrity gossip, football—and vow to get better, to *be* better. We will have seen in Haneke and elsewhere just what images can do.

But if this is what Haneke's films do, ask, ask us to think about, or ask us to do, then we wouldn't really need Haneke at all. We could just dig out a copy of *Natural Born Killers* if all we needed was a dose of moralizing on the image through the image. Initially, Haneke's work would seem a brilliant affirmation of Debord's theory of the spectacle: that it is a set of relations between images. Both Debord's spectacle and Haneke's cinema are preoccupied by and serve as forces of mediation. For Debord, understandably, life under advanced capitalism—the organization of our lives in and through the spectacle—is understood and evoked in the most acerbic of terms. Haneke, however, asks for us to read spectacularity as a description and not a condemnation: yes, the world is mediated—even governed, perhaps—by images and their relation to one another. Mediation, however, is a force that can both reconcile and divide (to mediate is to divide—at least—in two), and that can stir reaction as well. For Haneke, unlike for Debord, the image is not only a two-dimensional condensation of capital. It is something, in a sense, more simple: it is an *image*—that is, it is a picture, a representation of the world, of something in the world, or of something than can be imagined. What the image pictures may force us to draw conclusions as bitter as Debord's, but its efficacy and necessity in doing so keeps alive its claims on our attention, our thought, and our criticism. The problem with the image does not cohere in the fact that it is an image. In other words, the image is not the problem at all. The image is a radically neutral medium—and by medium we do not intend any specific technological means of materializing an image. The image can be that thing that binds us *and* makes us strangers to every other. In these terms, then, we see that Haneke's work in film and television asks different questions and demands different responses than the call and response familiar to us from many of the most powerful and intransigent ethical critiques of the image.

The image that Benny reviews again and again, for instance, is overdetermined, a lure designed to cue our moral certainty about how we understand our own relation to images. Once Benny has invited the girl home and revealed to her and to us his video apparatus (the camera, the monitor, the entire system of surveillance) and the gun, we wait for him to position the girl before the camera, gun to head, and pull the trigger. That is, we expect him to imitate what we have seen him obsess over in the opening sequence. We expect there to be a causal relation between images and actions. He kills her, of course, and with the gun, but not in the way we have expected, and not even on camera, certainly not in the center of the frame. Nor, for that matter, do we see Benny look at the footage of the girl's murder in the same rapt and repetitive mode that he watches the pig's death. He will watch this footage only when, in making his affectless confession, he inexplicably plays it for his unsuspecting parents. Benny's motives remain opaque, to his parents and to us. Faced with the decision of whether to turn his son in or dispose of the body and carry on, the father seeks assurance from Benny that he has, in fact, revealed to him all of the details: who Benny has talked to, whether the girl has been spoken of since, a full a itinerary of Benny's weekend. The father is assured, and the family tacitly agrees—or so it appears to the spectator—to dispose of the body. The father's insistence on truth is, ultimately, what will also bring about his ruin and foreclose the possibility of his own ethical response to the event itself.

In an excruciating conversation in which the father and mother decide to protect Benny and dispose of the corpse, we witness the father's dawning awareness that his wife will not be hearty enough to join him in the act of the intimate dismemberment necessary to keep this murder a secret. The father decides it best to send mother and son away for a few days while he carries out his gruesome task. We see Benny and his mother at the travel agency, buying tickets to Egypt, a desultory destination chosen only on the basis of the expediency of leaving as soon as possible. And then, for an extended period of time, the film follows Benny and his mother on their Egyptian holiday. We see them eating their continental breakfast on the hotel terrace, visiting the pyramids, watching television in their hotel room. This long foray into the Nile River Valley is, like most vacations, leisurely and pointless. We nearly run the risk of forgetting that this visit to the most spectacular of vacation spots is remarkable for what it denies to us. The images of this visit to Egypt negatively materialize the dismemberment going on at the same time in the family's state-of-the-art chrome and steel kitchen back in Vienna. Another of Benny's videos reminds us of this absence. Benny talks into his video recorder and says, "I wonder if he's managed to do it." This video diary he concludes with a wave and a "Ciao, Papa," as if this were a video postcard intended for the offscreen patriarch-cum-vivisector.

In other words, the image discloses violence through the absence of violence in the image. Neither the violent image nor the image of violence is the image of which we should be the most suspicious. The image is neutral. It has no essential relation to violence. The images of Egypt do not constitute a site of repression of the images of the charnel house offscreen. Rather, the absence of violence onscreen embodies a proposition: that we should not depend on the image *as* image to give us the truth of the event or to diagnose the pathology of image production and reception. The ethical dynamic at work here exists instead in the relay between the images we see and the images we do not see or, more accurately, between the images we see and the activities that have not been represented as images. The image, therefore, becomes a site of relay and of deferral—not a site of a lack in a Lacanian sense, but a mode of deferral in which we are pointed to another site, one that could nevertheless at any moment be rendered obscenely, pornographically. The sequence is not one more instance of Benny's inability to experience the world as anything other than an image; rather, it asks us to consider the relation between cultural tourism, violence, and secrecy. The image of the father back home hovers as a potentiality during the time the film spends in Egypt. However, the violence he performs offscreen must remain absent as an image; otherwise we would risk understanding the relation between Vienna and Egypt in strictly temporal terms: *meanwhile, back in Vienna.* To grant us the vision of the father's violence would be to privilege and restrict our understanding of violence to this gross corporeal display. By rendering Egypt in its isolation, Haneke asks us to consider violence in more nuanced terms, even to understand how cultural tourism itself—the desire to produce a picture of oneself in a culture not one's own—is itself an act of violence. Haneke asks us to consider this in relational terms. While an image is just an image, an image is not reducible to what it pictures. Haneke's visual reticence is not evidence of prudishness or art cinema obliqueness; we see more than enough pain inflicted on bodies across the trajectory of his work. The withholding of the image that we experience in Haneke is better understood as an assertion that there is no such thing as "an image"; rather, there are only relations between and among images, and between people and images—images being objects as other as every other. The relations that bind these images one to another are indistinguishable from the relations (those of kinship, property, the nation-state, and so on) that bind people one to another and to the social world they inhabit. In this sense, then, to speak

*Introduction*

of Haneke's images is to speak about much more than the image and the totalizing hold it exerts on us.

For this reason, many of the terms of media theory and criticism seem to us to be insufficient in making sense of Haneke's work, and of violence more generally. Moreover, Haneke's work suggests to us the insufficiency of theories of the image that tend predominantly to questions of medium specificity and the cognitive and moral effects of the moving image, the effects of media *as* media. Haneke's work is replete with images of images and images of image production. These images of images, however, are not merely instances of Platonic skepticism. If the notion of medium is at all appropriate to Haneke's work, it will need to be broadly expanded, allowed a wider berth in which we might come to understand the term not simply as a set of properties unique to any one art or mode of communication but also as something that *stands between*. We might, for instance, speak of the family itself as the constitutive medium of violence. Haneke's work, in other words, forces us into a recognition that to speak about an image is not just to speak about an image but is rather to speak about the world, its inhabitants, the violence they suffer, and the violence of which they are capable.

The essays we have collected here work with but also move beyond or behind many of the canonical discourses of film and media theory that would seem, on first glance, to lend themselves so readily, but perhaps too easily, to the analysis of Haneke's work. To be certain, we do not recommend the jettisoning of film theory for understanding Haneke's work. Rather, we caution against the use of film theory in relation to Haneke's work as a means of reducing his concerns to a set of pious ethical imperatives about images as such. As long as Haneke continues to use the long take, André Bazin will hover nearby. But if Bazin needs be consulted, we will not expect or desire him to direct us back to questions of ontology or the priority or inaccessibility of the real. Reading with and against Haneke's own statements on image making, we interpret his theatricalization of a preoccupation with the image to be the mark of an exhaustion of many of the questions that media theory has asked about images. In most cases, these questions have been simply about whether images are good or bad for us.

We hope that this volume will open up larger questions about Haneke and about the questions his work raises. These questions, as many of the essays will make clear, are often philosophical. We take Haneke seriously as someone invested in philosophical inquiries about the relation between violence and play, representation and sensation, and autonomy and commodity culture and about globalization, notions of recurrence, and the relation between animals and mankind. We also understand Haneke's work, here, in terms of world politics and political philosophy. As an Austrian-born filmmaker who works across, is funded by, and makes films about all aspects of European culture, Haneke speaks to the most pressing issues facing the European Union today: immigration, terrorism, and cultural identity. That is to say, Haneke is not just concerned with the image—certainly not in the way that we have come, within film studies, to regard Alfred Hitchcock as a filmmaker who so thoroughly and consistently raised questions about the image through the image. If Hitchcock's films presented for so long the terms by which film theory came to understand the social, psychic, and aesthetic effects of the medium of cinema through the terms and concepts most boldly on display there—voyeurism, masochism, sadism, identity—then Haneke's films suggest something very important for film and media theory in our time. The expanded conception of medium one encounters in Haneke's work can provide us with some of the most pressing questions facing theorists today, especially those of us who are eager to take seriously a more philosophical theory that is beholden neither to medium-specific conceptions of cinema nor to a fear of representation, more broadly. The project of *Caché*, a film that demands a full consideration—in historical and philosophical terms—of that which goes missing in the frame but that is sensible only through the frame as frame, proves that any inquiry into the film that is governed by a belief in either the inherent plenitude or paucity of the image will not get us very far. Many of the essays collected here take up the challenge of Haneke's work in these terms and offer new theories of culture and the image that speak to questions that must be answered by way of philosophy as much as or more than they must be answered by way of film theory. Finally, we also take Haneke to be one of the most innovative filmmakers of this or any other moment in film history. This volume works not only to identify the nature of Haneke's intervention in world film culture but also to think about stylistic innovation in expressly political and philosophical terms, in, that is to say, the very terms provided by the films themselves.

To do this, we have commissioned essays by a group of scholars well suited to the very challenging and itself unusual task of reckoning with the difficult historical issues that Haneke raises about violence at a philosophical and stylistic register. That is, we have commissioned work from

*Introduction*

scholars whose own work is informed by a mutual understanding of the relatedness of history, philosophical inquiry, and close formal analysis. In many respects, Haneke's work makes abundantly clear that the divisions we have honored in the humanities for so many years—ones that understand history, theory, and criticism as necessarily opposed practices—will no longer suffice. As a result, the authors who appear here are ones whose own practices, much like Haneke's, work to address historical problems with the abstract complexity that they require, theoretical questions with the force and clarity they deserve, and close formal analyses that tend to the distinction of Haneke's style.

Part 1 of *On Michael Haneke*, "Violence and Play," features essays by Brigitte Peucker, Brian Price, Tarja Laine, and Michael Lawrence, all of which concern themselves with the insistent and seemingly opposed relation one detects in Haneke between violence and playfulness. Taken together, this group of essays constitutes a meditation on the possibilities that follow from the unusual conjugation of violence and play. The sign itself—whether as an image, a sound, or text—is something that can produce a free play of both meaning *and* violence. In this sense, we can say that Haneke's films raise a provocative question for poststructural theory, which often understands the free play of the signifier as the solution to domination and violence, or as evidence of the final untethering of the real—a masking of the real by the image. However, as these essays also make clear, the solution to violence is not the reinstallation of the one-to-one correspondence and a metaphysics of presence. What these essays provoke instead—and all in very different terms—is precisely a need to complicate our notions of media, representation, and moral conceptions of violence altogether. For instance, Peucker—noting the many instances of violent play in Haneke—raises the harrowing and ludic possibility that masochism and bloodletting are in some sense fundamental to representation, no matter how paradoxical the conjunction might seem. Laine similarly pursues questions about the reflexive playfulness surrounding violence that we see in *Funny Games,* and the difficulty we should have in trying to make clear moral claims about violence, given the complex structure of identification that Haneke presents to us in that film. While playfulness is not at the core of Price's analysis of *Funny Games,* what comes forward is a reminder of the ways in which the logic of torture—which is articulated in *Funny Games* as play—is itself closely related to the act and process of representation more generally, especially as representations come to us as beautiful or true. Lawrence's essay considers Haneke's interest in the figuration of animal death, the scenes of animal slaughter that punctuate and, in Lawrence's terms, "puncture" the surfaces of Haneke's fictions. In Lawrence's understanding, the presentation of animal slaughter opens up a way of understanding Haneke's representation of human violence and historical trauma.

Part 2 of the book is devoted to questions of style and medium. Essays by John David Rhodes, Hugh Manon, Fatima Naqvi and Christophe Koné, Meghan Sutherland, Mattias Frey, and Bert Rebhandl all tend to one of the most central aspects of Haneke's production and thinking, namely, stylistic innovation and questions of medium specificity. Haneke is often recognized for the stylistic distinctiveness of his films—the ways in which he can be seen as indebted to previous traditions and filmmakers (Italian neorealism, Hitchcock, Michelangelo Antonioni, Bresson). However, Haneke's stylistic innovations are understood here in relation the larger questions that they pose for our understanding of the image itself and its relation to being—not only what an image allows us to see (or to be seen by), but how the material specificity of the image itself may or may not secure a particular relation between us and the world, between us and every other. Rhodes considers Haneke's obvious affiliation with the cinema of neorealism, particularly his use of long-take cinematography, to reevaluate the ethical and epistemological imperatives at work in Haneke's cinema. Manon examines the long takes in *Caché* as a way of reopening and intensifying discussions of the gaze in and for film theory, offering a theory of the gaze that will be central, like Haneke's film, to the way that we understand the concept today or in any other time. Naqvi and Koné explore the formal, thematic, and theoretical preoccupation with voyeurism in *The Piano Teacher*. In paying special attention to the relation between the film and its source, the novel by Elfriede Jelinek, Naqvi and Koné propose that both novel and film might help us beyond some of the ocular models that have dominated psychoanalytic theory. Frey traces the discourse and practice of medium-specificity in Haneke's production and argues for the crucial importance of understanding the role that the "desubstantiated" digital image plays in Haneke's most recent work. Sutherland's analysis of the representation of television in Haneke's films likewise complicates our understanding of the medium as something that simply has a negative effect on culture, presenting instead an innovative theory of television as a socially productive form of mise-en-abyme. Finally, Rebhandl's essay details Haneke's work for television, which has been largely out of circulation and thus largely absent from the growing conversation about Haneke.

*Introduction*

Part 3 of the book brings together four essays that all occupy themselves with questions of culture and conflict. Haneke's concern with play, violence, representation, style, and medium is not for its own sake—as is clear in every instance. Rather, Haneke's questions—philosophical and art historical—are all situated in a Europe in transition and in conflict. With essays by Christopher Sharrett, Rosalind Galt, Scott Durham, and Patrick Crowley, Haneke's work is considered in relation to the historical problems the films both evoke and, as Galt's essay suggests, exacerbate. These essays offer keen insights into the cultural and historical problems suggested by the films but also provide models for thinking about the relation between culture and film style. Sharrett's analysis of Haneke's frequent use of music borrowed from "high" (or "serious") European tradition reveals the complicated status of European culture in the director's work. While European culture often seems to offer a counterpoint to the degraded, homogenizing forces of postmodern media culture, Haneke makes it brutally clear that this tradition's promises of redemption are tenuous at best. Galt bracingly criticizes Haneke's own posturing as a specifically European auteur and in doing so reveals a strain of conservatism that runs through Haneke's enlightened cosmopolitanism. Durham offers a unique theory of the seriality of the image, as it develops in Haneke's practice, as a way of beginning to understand the nature of what he calls "postmodern sociality." The massacre of unarmed Algerians on October 17, 1961, is explicitly referenced in *Caché;* however, how, why, and to what extent this context matters is in no way clear. Crowley's essay argues that the film is not "about" this event or the larger subject of French colonialism but that the event crucially frames the film's investigation of the politics of memory, forgetting, and guilt.

The essays gathered together in this collection, we believe, embody the qualities of experiment, rigor, and critique, qualities they share with Haneke's films themselves.

## *Notes*

1. For a fuller account of the details of Haneke's biography, see Mattias Frey's entry in the Great Directors section of *Senses of Cinema:* http://archive.sensesofcinema.com/contents/directors/03/haneke.html.

2. We have in mind Baudrillard's vastly influential *Simulacra and Simulation,* trans. Sheila Faria Glaser (Ann Arbor: University of Michigan Press, 1995).

3. Jean Luc Nancy has suggestively reversed these terms: "Violence . . . always completes itself in an image." Nancy, "Image and Violence," in *The Ground of the Image,* trans. Jeff Fort (New York: Fordham University Press, 2005), 20.

# Part 1

## VIOLENCE AND PLAY

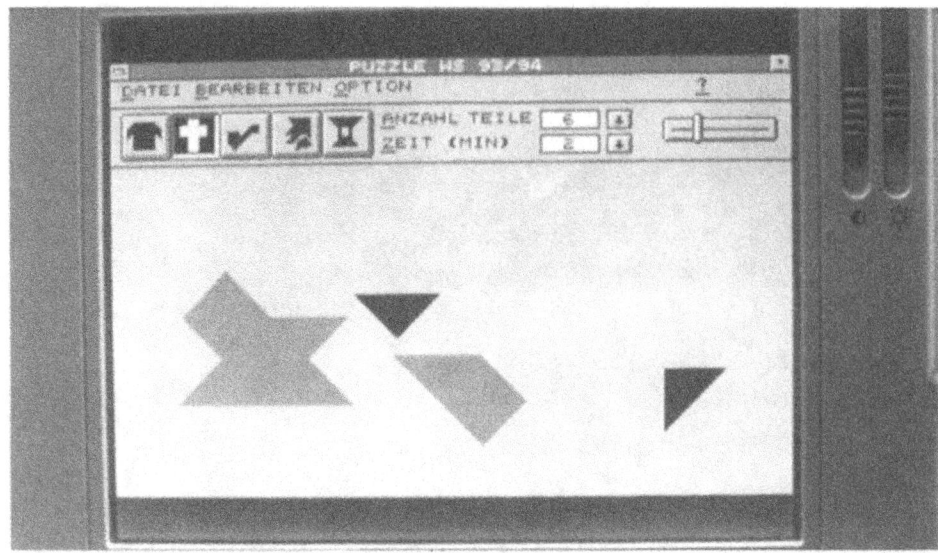

*71 Fragments of a Chronology of Chance* (1994): The playful violence of the part/whole relation.

Brigitte Peucker

# Games Haneke Plays
## Reality and Performance

### *Breaking the Code?*

*Code Unknown* (*Code inconnu,* 2000) repeatedly subsumes an impulse toward realism within modernist concerns, substituting a perceptual realism situated in the spectator for the Bazinian realism of the image that it calls into question. Games with reality and illusion are its dominant strategy for achieving this end, and sometimes they are emblematized by actual game structures. In *Code Unknown,* the moments of undecidability that punctuate Michael Haneke's films tend to be located in performances; in German, the word for playing, *spielen,* is identical to the word for acting. Charades of a special kind bracket the film: its pretitle sequence records a frightened little girl who moves awkwardly toward an empty backdrop as a shadow falls over her cowering form. She does not speak or cry out. It is only when she reaches the wall that the shadow is revealed to be her own, only then that this austere white wall proves to mark the boundary of a performance space. The little girl's cowering movements constitute a performance, as it turns out, and it is witnessed by a diegetic audience. While we are relieved that the child's pain is mimed, our discovery that deaf and dumb children are her audience renews our discomfort. As the children guess at the import of her charade, they pose their questions in sign language; after each question, the little girl shakes her head "no." The game that is being played is didactic—part of a school curriculum, we surmise—its goal to teach the deaf and dumb to speak through and read the body. But while sign language relies on images, on a combination of gestures and letters that, in other words, has a code, this game of charades resorts to pantomimed actions that serve as clues to a word that "solves" the puzzle. Such actions are not signs in an established code; they suggest a wide range of significations. As we the film's audience come to understand, the word that provides the key to the child's performance will remain unavailable to her diegetic audience—and to us. Need we add that the words of the film's title are overdetermined?

For the spectator two sets of questions are generated by this sequence, and they are at the crux of *Code Unknown*. One of these is how images can be understood without the benefit of language, a question central to writing on the ontology of the photograph, evoking especially Roland Barthes's analysis of its uncoded and coded aspects in "The Photographic Message" (1961) and "Rhetoric of the Image" (1964). The other question is this one: what is the boundary between real emotion and mimed emotion, between life and performance, between reality and illusion? The film's movement from what appears to be reality—in this case, a frightened little girl—to its acknowledgment as a diegetic performance is a strategy central to Haneke's film. Time and again *Code Unknown* presents us with sequences that promote confusion between the diegetic reality of the film and a performance within it, sequences that promote the spectators' uncertainty about the status of the image. Since the action of such sequences always involves emotional pain, the sequences promote strong affects in the film's audience, feelings followed by relief that such actions are doubly distanced from the diegetic real, that even in the fictional reality of the film the sequence is "only a performance." Clearly, the spectators' relief is not unqualified; it is tempered, rather, by the knowledge of having been manipulated. For the moment, we are wary, distanced, wondering whether the scenes that unfold before us will stand revealed as diegetically "real" or "performed." How should we read this undecidability, other than as a spectator trap?

The ludic strategy of *Code Unknown* recalls D. W. Winnicott's claim in *Playing and Reality* that the "inherently exciting" nature of play derives from "the precariousness that belongs to the interplay in the child's mind of that which is subjective (near-hallucination) and that which is objectively perceived (actual, or shared reality)."[1] While the function of play for the child will ultimately be to delineate these areas clearly, Winnicott contends, for the adult their confusion finds a place in art.[2] In moving between illusion and diegetic truth, *Code Unknown* provokes in its spectator an uncertainty that is decidedly disturbing: its ludic dimension crosses over into sadistic tricking. But then the film's compelling images catch us up again—at least until we play the spectator game of assembling its narrative fragments, until we try to decipher the film's governing code. This code too remains unknowable.

Tellingly, the subtitle of *Code Unknown* is "Incomplete Tales of Several Journeys," and its structure—one that interlards several tangentially and randomly connected narratives—takes us back to an earlier film of Haneke's, to *71 Fragments of a Chronology of Chance*.[3] Although the attenuated narratives of *71 Fragments* eventually merge in a horrific act of violence in which four people die, our desire to read this earlier film as a whole is consistently thwarted as well. In *71 Fragments* games have a central role to play—indeed, games in this film are the very figure for undecidability. Two games are centrally featured—a set of puzzle pieces and a game of pickup sticks—and they purport to shape our act of reading. Repeatedly in this film puzzle pieces are manipulated into the shape of a cross, but the question of how this overdetermined image signifies is left open. Two students vie with each other to create figures out of these pieces. After the actual game is transposed into a computer game, reality becomes virtual, but the point of the game remains unchanged. Whereas the goal of the puzzle is to create a whole out of fragments—seventy-one, perhaps—the game of pickup sticks aims at the dismantling of random arrangements, the figures created when the sticks are dropped. While the opposition set up between the games is rather pat, no answer is provided to the question of which activity—the construction of forms or the deconstruction of random arrangements—is more relevant to Haneke's film. The modernist interest in the relation of the fragment to the whole and its implied connection to Robert Bresson (Haneke's self-acknowledged mentor) through the image of the cross (the final image of Bresson's *Diary of a Country Priest*) is couched in a worldview predicated on design, not randomness. But the pickup sticks focus chance as determining their arrangements. Does the significance of the one game cancel out the other? At the end of the film, its stories come together in an act of violence that ironizes this question.

In *Code Unknown*, made six years later than *71 Fragments*, the "tales of incomplete journeys" do not culminate in an act of violence, but they do emerge from a random act of hostility. In keeping with the multiethnic identity of contemporary Paris—the film's setting—three stories are told: a French New Wave–style romance, a Romanian story, and an African story, their multiple fragments separated by abrupt cuts, as in *71 Fragments*. The film is a social collage that emphasizes its acts of cutting, illustrating the experiences of a spectrum of characters, with each tale presided over by a modernist belief in selfhood. Like *71 Fragments*, *Code Unknown* is a "chronology of chance": a French actress meets her boyfriend's teen-aged brother on the street and buys him a pastry, a seemingly insignificant act. But when he throws the pastry wrapper into the lap of a Romanian beggar, the teenager captures the outraged attention of a young African who defends the honor of the Romanian woman, demanding an apology from the teenager. When the teenager refuses, the African's irate shouting comes to the attention of the police, who predictably take the African to the police station and, as we later discover, deport the Romanian woman. One of these stories ends in Africa, with the father of the young African—having abandoned his family, either temporarily or permanently—driving through a marketplace. Only the man's family is hurt by his return to his homeland; the people in the marketplace are not his target, although it is a clear indication of his distance from his culture that he negotiates this space by car. The Romanian story is equally unresolved, since the woman, Maria—urged on by her daughter—returns to Paris to beg, only to find herself displaced from her street corner by two Arabs. The film leaves her seeking another space, confirming her narrative entrapment in circularity and repetition. The French story, with its overtones of New Wave relationships and malaise, is resolved when the actress's lover is prevented from entering her apartment building because she has changed the door's security code, an ironic and deflating comment on the film's title. As a conclusion to their love affair, the woman's move is deflating as well. Her lover commits no acts of violence after having been locked out; he merely looks for a cab to take him away. The seemingly failed emigration and return to one's place of origin, the cyclical narrative of expulsion and return, the abrupt dénouement of the love story—these divergent ways of structuring narrative supplement one another. But insofar as these stories are susceptible to interpretation, it is grounded in the family dynamics that shape these melodramas. The family as cornerstone of the bourgeois social order remains the center of Haneke's attention in all of his films.[4]

While a modernist self-consciousness characterizes *Code Unknown* at the level of style, Haneke's interest in the bourgeois family is suggestive of a lingering realism in his filmmaking. Interestingly, another kind of code comes into play here. On one level, *Code Unknown* supports Fredric Jameson's contention concerning a different code—his contention that realism is "the restricted code of the bourgeoisie" and that its "peculiar object" is "the historically specific mode of capitalist production."[5] If, qua Jameson, bourgeois realism is currently being undermined by the "small group codes in contemporary film," this possibility is merely gestured toward in the case of the marginalized groups represented in Haneke's film; the Romanian and African tales are shaped primarily by the family relations within a capitalist order that, in Jameson's understanding, structure realism.[6] The Romanian woman's family is building a fine new house in Romania and chooses to believe that she holds a job in Paris, while the African man who seeks relief from family troubles owns his own taxi. Both of these families operate within realism's "restricted code," then, a code centered in and determining the bourgeoisie, a code that structures a world governed by the marketplace.[7] Although neither the Romanian nor the African narrative is brought to closure, neither of them breaks out of a familiar pattern into a new kind of narrative. The circularity that structures the Romanian tale undermines hope, and the return to the African homeland is not a happy one—there is no doubt that a politics obtains in these stories. But while its political text points to the mutually reinforcing entrapments of family, consumerism, and racism, Haneke's film makes no effort to suggest a solution to these conundrums of contemporary life. (Insofar as the film does offer a solution, it seems to suggest that immigrants are better off at home.) Further, the fragmentation that structures *Code Unknown* undermines the political outcome it might otherwise have by also situating the film within the tradition of modernism, with its pronounced interest in form.

## *Games with Illusion*

It is the French New Wave–style story that enables the film's meditation on the boundaries of the performed and the real by way of its main characters: a film and stage actress, Anne, and her live-in partner, Georges, a photojournalist. Proceeding from and elaborating the situation of the film's opening scene with the cowering child engaged in a game of charades, performance *of* and *as* torture appears in a variety of guises in the film's French story. The first such scene shows Anne in a blood-red empty room in which a disembodied voice announces that she has been locked in and that she will "never get out." Fritz Lang's *The Testament of Dr. Mabuse* looms large in this citation of a disembodied, commanding voice reverberating within a closed room.[8] But to what end, other than to serve as an example of the elision of Lang's directorial identity with that of the notoriously controlling, destructive character of Dr. Mabuse? Although this male voice has asked Anne whether it should read the "other part," almost from the first the boundary between performance and diegetic reality here is murky. The spectator soon takes Anne's terrified and frantic questions for filmic "reality," since the camerawork in this sequence is uncharacteristically dominated by the handheld effects of the horror genre. (In some sense too, the red room literalizes a word in Stanley Kubrick's *The Shining*, where the inscription "redrum" is the mirror image of "murder.") The disembodied male voice claims to like Anne, claims that she has simply fallen into his trap. What the voice demands of her is to show "her true face," to show him "a true expression." Whose voice is this? Is it that of a psychopath? Is it the diegetic director's voice, reading a role for the sake of an audition? Or is this the director of *Code Unknown*—speaking, perhaps, in his own voice? Although it is suggested that the scene represents a screen test for a movie role, not Anne's imprisonment by a maniac, this is only confirmed retrospectively, in the manner of Alfred Hitchcock. In the meantime, the scene's ambiguities are sustained, and our desire to know is frustrated. How and why the film camera is co-opted by the conventions of horror is never explained, although I will offer an explanation later.

After it is established that Anne has a role in a film about a serial killer, *Code Unknown* includes two takes of a scene in which her character is terrorized, but each is obviously a movie shoot, with the actors surrounded by lighting equipment and subjected to the gaze of the camera. Bits and pieces of information about this thriller in the making emerge later: during dinner at a restaurant, Anne remarks that, in the plot of this film, the inspector can solve the crime because his personality resembles that of the murderer—a convention of some detective stories. Minutes later in this very Parisian restaurant scene—and very briefly—we catch a glimpse of Haneke himself, barely in frame, his surprising presence left uncommented upon. Is there a connection? While Haneke's appearance is not a cameo in the usual sense, it evokes Hitchcock's insertion of a costumed self into his films. Like the reference to Lang, the oblique reference to Hitchcock is to a controlling director, one noted for his cruelty to actors. Another sequence features Anne at an audition, this time for a role in *Twelfth Night*. In this scene Anne is on stage alone, uncostumed, a spotlight blinding her while the rest of the theater is in semidarkness. At the end of her monologue, Anne awaits a reaction from figures we only dimly perceive, whose whispers we barely hear. Anne stops speaking, hesitates, then asks: "Is there anyone there, perhaps?" Yet another unseen director has generated fear in a performer.

Two additional sequences center on Anne's performances, this time in a film within the film, where she plays one member of a self-involved couple who discovers that their child is about to fall from their balcony to the street below. Once again there are images of cruelty to children: terrified by the threat of their son's death, his parents use physical violence against him and banish him from their presence. Again it is only retrospectively clear that what we are watching is footage from an interior film, this time when the two stars record the soundtrack for the film as they watch its images. While the actors try to recapture the intense emotions they acted in the film, the temporal gap between shooting and dubbing problematizes the affects generated for and by the images they—and we—are viewing. The film asks whether the images of a traumatic scene can evoke in its actors the intense emotions they once played. At first, the only sounds the images generate are their embarrassed giggles.

What is at stake in this sequence, a sequence that exposes the actors' performance as performance? Is it merely the question of whether the emotions evoked by the film images they watch are real or simulated? Or does this scene serve another purpose? Perhaps it asks questions about the screen presence of the actor—especially about Juliette Binoche's presence—in this film.[9] Does Binoche's centrality to Haneke's film—her appearance both in sequences coded as diegetic "reality" and those exposed as performance—serve as an anchor for the film's several layers of fictionality? One significant boundary-crossing between reality and performance in *Code Unknown* is surely Binoche's pregnancy during the shooting of this film, mostly camouflaged by clothing but incorporated into the narrative when Anne taunts Georges about whether or not she is pregnant, whether or not she has had an abortion.[10] Georges—like the spectator—remains unsure of the "truth." Does the actor's ontologically identical presence in scenes of performance and in scenes of diegetic reality make sequences coded as diegetic reality more real-seeming or less real-seeming in comparison? The stable presence of the actor's body in the oscillation between diegetic "reality" and performance would seem to diminish their difference, to muddy the epistemological waters.

In conversation, Anne mentions that the thriller in which she is acting is tentatively titled *The Collector*. But it is not the 1956 William Wyler film of that title from which the interior film—and *Code Unknown*—essentially borrow. That film, rather, is Michael Powell's *Peeping Tom* (1960). In Powell's film the central character's sadomasochistic project is to capture on film the quintessential image of (female) fear, "the true expression" of fear; as you will recall, this is what the psychopath—or director—wants from Anne. *Peeping Tom* is a famously self-reflexive film that, like *Code Unknown*, blurs the boundaries between "reality," "performance," and their filmic images several times over. Its central character, Mark, turns his film camera into a murder weapon whose assaultive eye projects outward literally in the form of a phallic dagger that kills the women who are the object of its gaze.[11] As the dagger approaches them, the women's faces are distorted by a convex mirror in which they view themselves and by the terror Mark seeks to capture on film. Their fear in turn terrifies Mark. The relation between perpetrator and victim is a reciprocal one that plays out a dynamic Powell's film anchors in childhood experience.

As the story goes, Mark's father, a behaviorist who studies the reactions of the nervous system to fear, filmed his son's every move—especially the child's expressions of terror when awakened at night. From an early age, Mark's life is continuous with its representation. As cameraman and murderer, Mark reenacts the role of his sadistic father; as the one who is terrified by the face of fear, Mark masochistically identifies with the position of his female victim. At the end of the film Mark commits suicide by means of his own camera, producing what he calls the "end of a documentary," the film of his life begun by his father. Here too the epistemological waters are muddied, and the confusion between life and art in the diegesis of the film—and in the psychotic mind of its protagonist—encompasses the life of its director, Michael Powell, as well. What the film may have meant to Powell can only be conjectured, but since he cast his son Columba in the role of Mark as a child and himself in the role of Mark's father, *Peeping Tom* must have held autobiographical significance for him. Powell remarks in his autobiography that "art is merciless observation, sympathy, imagination, and a sense of detachment that is almost cruelty."[12] But our impression that the detached, cold tone of Powell's film is not merely the result of objectivity is reinforced by the appearance of the Powells—father and son—in a film about a sadomasochistic bond between father and son played out by way of a film camera. Like Powell's, Haneke's film art seems detached and cruel.[13] Might there be other correspondences as well? Performance, cruelty, and game playing—imbricated in the little girl's charade mentioned at the beginning of this essay—are harnessed together in other Haneke films as well. An attitude of game playing and theatricality is imposed upon acts of violence most centrally in *Funny Games*. (Haneke's films share this attitude with two great landmarks of filmic modernism—with Kubrick's *A Clockwork Orange* and Michelangelo Antonioni's *Blowup*.) In *Funny Games*, the late-adolescent murderers Peter and Paul base their acts of torture on children's games—hot and cold, cat in the sack, and a version of eeny, meeny, miny, moe. The murderers' adoption of game structures for their acts of torture is partly cued by one of their victims, Anna, who resorts to a common expression regarding her German shepherd's wild barking: "He just wants to play." "Funny game," says one of the torturers in response. The acts of torture prepared by Peter and Paul theatricalize violence as they adapt a variety of plots and structures, including clowning or mime (the egg game) and the imitation of pulp fiction plots (Anna is to act the "loving wife" while she watches her husband's brutal murder).[14] In *Funny Games,* games and performances provide the structure for acts of torture from which the spectator is not excluded. As we have said, the German word for playing, *spielen,* is the same as the word for acting, and they are closely related in Haneke's film. Peter and Paul construct scenarios of inexplicable violence, scenarios they observe with detached—and aesthetic—pleasure. "Here are the Rules of the Game," they tell their victims in a barely veiled allusion to Jean Renoir.

The director has a game to play as well, and it is cat and mouse. Recalling the many references to self-reflexivity in Haneke's interviews and to the mobilization of spectatorial response, we may wonder whether it is in this light that we are to read the efforts at distanciation in *Funny Games.* Media consciousness permeates this film: we find it in the aliases adopted by the murderers—Tom and Jerry, Beavis and Butthead—and we find it distressingly present at the moment in which it seems that at least one of Haneke's characters, Anna, is able to break through the "no exit" structure of the deadly games to which she has fallen prey. Seizing a rifle, Anna shoots and hits Peter, presumably killing him. But if the spectator feels relief at her action, it is momentary only, for Paul simply picks up the remote and rewinds the action, which then continues on its deadly and predictable course. Games of violence, Haneke would have us know, may be played by the director as well. Manipulating the narrative as if the film were a video and he its spectator, Haneke makes it abundantly clear that he is in control.

## *Uncoded Images*

True to its centrality for Bazinian realism, photography struggles against the duplicity of performance in *Code Unknown.* (Antonioni's *Blowup* comes to mind with respect to this issue as well.) The photographic impulse is narratively embodied in the figure of the photojournalist Georges, who seeks to convey the "truth" of political events in Kosovo and Drenica in his photographs of wartime atrocities. Unable to remain long in Paris—where he is required to interact with others—Georges repeatedly plunges himself into dangerous settings where he can relate to people indirectly, as observer and camera eye. Haneke's film displays Georges's wartime photos in full screen in conjunction with a letter read by this character in voice-over. But Georges's aural letter is not "illustrated" by the photographs on screen; rather, it moves evasively from political events to Georges's difficulties in the personal realm. Is the point here that the mute photographic images cannot fully communicate? Or that they communicate something incomprehensible? The static images depict the bodies of the dead, and the moments they record remain enigmatic, illegible. The paradox of the photograph is that what it connotes must be "developed on the basis of a message without a code"—the denoted message based on the photographic analogue, suggests Roland Barthes in "The Photographic Message."[15] Insofar as we read photographs, however, we also derive from them a second-order, connoted message based on a linguistic code. A purely denotative meaning is possible only in the rare instances of traumatic images, those that record moments for which no connotative message is possible—moments when language is blocked, suspended. Their code remains unknown. Georges's images of the dead are traumatic images, images of the Real, of that which is insusceptible to meaning, bereft even of "analogical plenitude."[16] As Georges admits in conversation, these photographs do not represent a "reality," even for him.

Defeated by his subject and scarred by his experiences, Georges opts for another kind of photography and takes candid portraits of random strangers in the Paris Métro. This turn represents a retreat into aestheticism. Haneke's film marks this set of images even more clearly as photographic: they are not shown in full screen, as the wartime photographs are, and they are not in color. The black-and-white images appear as portraits against a black background that suggests unexposed film stock: against this background, they are doubly coded as art. There is a romantic residue in Georges's attempt to record the human face—even the multiethnic faces of today's Parisians—and it dominates over whatever aspirations to documentary are still latent in his project. Even the photographic act of registration—Georges displays his camera but hides the cord that operates it—is problematic, voyeuristic, manipulative. These photographs neither reveal Atget's urban spaces nor exhibit the cataloging intention of August Sander. The topography of the faces Georges records remains as enigmatic as the landscapes with their dead in the wartime photos. Interpretive access is not provided by the images themselves; nor is it provided by the voice-over of yet another letter spoken by Georges. Indeed, the Bressonian separation of the narrative of Georges's capture by the Taliban from his portrait shots of the face is designed to shock. If Georges was incapable of narrativizing his photographs of wartime atrocities—and if, as traumatic images, they are insusceptible to language—he now narrates his experience of capture and terror against images whose connection to his story remain oblique at best. What do these dissonances, these chasms between word and image, have to say about film? While *Code Unknown* asserts its interest in the photographic imaginary of film, it is unclear whether it undermines or supports Georges's assertion that talk about the "value of the nontransmitted image" comes cheap, his claim that "what matters in the end is the result."

But Haneke's film does not read Georges's photos "without a message" as "flat anthropological fact," as Barthes puts it in "Rhetoric of the Image."[17] In the later *Camera Lucida*, Barthes takes a different stance toward the nature of the photograph's effect: in response to a photograph by André Kertész, he waxes lyrical about the image of a dirt road whose "texture gives me the certainty of being in Central Europe; . . . I recognize with my whole body the straggling villages I passed through in my long-ago trips to Hungary and Rumania."[18] Thus, even denotation ultimately bears connotation within. Is it possible that the scene captured by Kertész—a blind, old violinist led over a dirt road by a child—is conjured up in Haneke's film by the Romanian woman and her grandson, walking along a dirt road enveloped in dust? Haneke's film also seems to revel in the affective charge of the photographic, the filmic image—indeed, in any kind of image at all, the digital included. Thus, even if the filmic image is without explanatory power, it nevertheless has the power to move us. Like Barthes, Haneke's films ensure that the spectator will experience the image "with his whole body." It is by means of spectatorial affect that the real of the body is reintroduced into the experience of film. And here is where another aspect of the connection to Powell comes in: Haneke's films are linked to *Peeping Tom* not only by the questions they ask about the possibility of reading the face and body, not only by an appearance of the director that at least figures his involvement in the diegesis, and not only by the violence that occurs in performance spaces but also by their questions about the relation of the film image to the real of affect.

## *Playground Realities*

Affect perforates the formalist surface of Haneke's films, and it often arises from the sight of pain. As I have suggested elsewhere, in all of Haneke's films there is a recurrent interest in the pain of children. Middle-class parents induce their daughter to join them in suicide in *The Seventh Continent*, a young girl is cruelly murdered in *Benny's Video*, a little girl who has been promised adoption is passed over for another in *71 Fragments of a Chronology of Chance*, a young boy is tortured and killed in *Funny Games*, and so on. As we have noted, the camera's direct gaze at deaf-mute children opens and closes *Code Unknown*, but that is just the beginning: since Anne could not bring herself to intervene, the abused daughter of Anne's neighbors is killed by her parents; the little boy in one of the films within the film nearly falls twenty stories to his death, then is punished by his parents for frightening them; Amadou's younger brother Demba is the victim of playground racism and extortion; and finally, there is the child with which Anne may or may not be pregnant, which she may or may not have aborted. But pain is not only inflicted on those least able to defend themselves. As I have argued, there is also a pervasive interest in forms of emotional manipulation that especially dominate the space of performance.[19] Ironically, the message of Anne's audition for *Twelfth Night* may reside in two lines she speaks from the maid's monologue: "I know my lady will strike him—if she do, I know he'll take it as a great favor." Rendered innocuous by comedy, the dynamic these lines describe is that of sadomasochism, suggesting that the metaphor of the puppet master and his puppet mentioned by Haneke with reference to *Code Unknown* has something significant to say.[20] And it may also have something to say about a dynamic in his films that *is not* confined to performance spaces.

Once again *Peeping Tom* looms large. Powell's film is more than a gloss on Haneke's films, serving as a possible source both for their mini-narratives of child abuse and for a modernist fascination with self-reflexivity and form. As mentioned earlier, the narrative of Powell's film is notable for its realist impulse to see and record the "true expression," as well as for the sadistic filmmaker whose films stage real violence. Does it also serve to model the masochistic child who resides in that director and who equates punishment with love, as in *Peeping Tom*? Watching the films of his aestheticized murders, *Peeping Tom*'s Mark commits suicide by means of the same camera with spike he used to murder his victims. But his suicide also marks the fulfillment of his desire for his father. Perhaps the dynamic most central to Haneke's film work lies in the simultaneous "acting out" of his "mastery" over "puppets" *and* the inclusion of scenarios of abuse and pain in which a vulnerable childhood self is figured as puppet as well.

This is certainly the case in *Time of the Wolf*, in which the director as puppet master deploys his puppets at will. *Time of the Wolf* resembles *The Castle* (1997) in representing the victims of a powerful force that is unnamed and disembodied and whose agenda is not understood. Suffering is simply endured, again with children among its most poignant victims. *Time of the Wolf* begins with the murder of a father, a murder that empties the paternal space as though to occupy it with a more abstract power. The victims of the generalized suffering represented in this film do not know the reason for their pain, nor do they know its source, but they grow to accept their condition, struggling to survive within the framework of possibilities left to them. Like Haneke's characters, we spectators are aware that the rivers and lakes of this landscape are polluted and that animals are dying of thirst. Is there a widespread drought? Has there been an ecological disaster? Is this the scene of some biblical plague? Is some malevolent deity visiting an obscure punishment upon all? An aged grandmother selfishly drinks the milk needed by a dying child. The young child dies of fever and dehydration. A young woman commits suicide. *Time of the Wolf* has a ship-of-fools, Noah's ark structure, with multiethnic families gathering at the railroad station of some unknown town, waiting for a train—for Godot?—to release them from their suffering. Whether the unspecified malevolent power is an invisible divinity, the paternal function as penetrating camera (as in Powell), or embodied in a hostile state (as in Kafka), the source of human suffering is never specified by the film. Its spare landscape suggests an undisclosed allegory; the source of its devastation remains unknowable. Once again an act of violence involving a child is central to understanding a Haneke film: when the boy Benny hears talk of "the Just"—an elect whose acts of self-sacrifice guarantee that God will watch over the rest of mankind—he threatens to throw himself onto a self-styled funeral pyre.

Fortunately Benny is saved, not sacrificed. But as the film comes to a close there is a long traveling shot of a lush, green landscape—or so the soundtrack suggests—from the window of a moving train. It is a paradigmatic moment of modernist cinematic self-reflexivity, for the long take of the (seemingly) moving landscape through the train window engages film history in a way that makes such scenes stand in for cinema itself. Redemption would seem to be at hand. "It's enough that you were ready to do it," says the man who saves him to Benny. The uncannily disembodied view from the train suggests that it is cinema itself—or some god of cinema, a director—who, moved by Benny's intention, has released the landscape from barrenness and stasis into fertility and motion. In the final scene of this film it is the camera eye—read as the director's eye?—that embodies the film's unspecified "power," a power that is moved to benevolence by a child's intention to harm himself.

In *Caché* (2005), the return of the abused child takes its vengeance on the adult—another Georges involved in the culture industry. This child might have been his brother, had Georges not lied to prevent his adoption. Although *Caché* incorporates racial and political issues into its plot—the would-be adoptee is Algerian—the young Georges's motive for excluding the boy from his family is relentlessly Oedipal. This Haneke film glances back to the much earlier *71 Fragments,* set in Vienna, in which adoption is already the important political metaphor, and to *Benny's Video,* where both violence and love are enacted through videotapes.[21] While the failed adoption of the Algerian orphan in *Caché* reflects the political realities of France, it is grounded in the Freudian scenario operative in all of Haneke's films. The bourgeois family remains at the center of his filmmaking: *Caché* returns to its French origins, Denis Diderot's eighteenth-century insight that the wholeness of society is founded on the wholeness of the family. This seems a regressive position to take in the twenty-first century, but we should recall that metaphorical adoption allows for the possibility of a more liberal politics, as in Gotthold Ephraim Lessing's bourgeois drama *Nathan the Wise* (1779), inspired by Diderot.

In *Caché*, as in *Time of the Wolf,* the camera is all-powerful. From its static position opposite the protagonist's residence, a video camera produces tapes of slice-of-life realism—the occasional passing car, a lone cyclist, people coming and going. While the film seems to begin in a still image—in imitation of Hitchcock's *Rear Window,* master text of surveillance films—faint bird sounds indicate its status as film or video. When the camera holds on the scene for an unnaturally long period of time, it becomes clear that the recording function of the medium is at issue. Unlike *Code Unknown*—and Hitchcock's film—*Caché* relegates theatricality and performance to its periphery. As in *Benny's Video,* however, the spectators of *Caché* are repeatedly taken in as we are confronted with images we only retrospectively learn are being watched by diegetic viewers. Once again a Haneke film obscures the boundary between a diegetically "real" event and a performance when a dinner party guest narrates a "true" story that turns out to be a joke. And again a Haneke film has a fragmented narrative, with one small set of related fragments—the son Pierrot's participation on a swim team—proving to be a red herring, while an equally small set of narrative fragments is centrally significant. The latter begins with an insert shot of a boy standing at a window, bleeding at the mouth. We will see a shot of the boy again, ever so briefly—coughing blood—just before the dinner party sequence in which the guest tells his story. What is the nature of these images? Is the guest's story a key to these images, perhaps insofar as they too defy categorization as diegetic reality or illusion?

It is only much later in the film, when we are privy to a scene in which a chicken's head is being cut off and blood spurts into a boy's eye—images from a dream of Georges's—that we understand the link. Now coded as memory or daydream, these flashes of images relate to both of Georges's childhood lies: that Majid, the Algerian boy his parents wanted to adopt, was spitting blood (that is, that he had tuberculosis) and that Majid cut off a chicken's head as a random act of violence, rather than at Georges's instigation. Once again it is the child's relation to the family that is pivotal. Once again the family provides the key to a political scenario, to a different relation between the French and the Algerians that might have been. While the film is reticent about who is responsible for the surveillance tapes, it suggests that they are the collaborative effort of Majid's and Georges's sons.[22] But the surveillance tapes taken from the rue des Iris are technically continuous with the other images of the film, likewise shot in high-definition format, suggesting—as in *Time of the Wolf*—that the disembodied eye (Iris) of the camera is none other than the director's.

The surveillance tapes are linked to the insert shots of the bleeding boy by the drawings in which the tapes are wrapped. There are two childish black line drawings: the first, in crayon, of a boy with mouth open; the second, in marker, of a rooster with its head cut off. Both of these images are marked by a prominent stripe of painted blood. Toward the end of the film, a tape is wrapped in a photo of Georges clipped from a newspaper, also adorned with a stripe of red. The jarring presence of painted blood on the line drawings and on the photograph, with blood represented by the fluid, viscous medium of poster paint, produces a hybrid image of sorts. In some sense, it marks the blood on both the drawings—always denotative, according to Barthes—*and* the photograph (with its paradoxical message) both as "real" and as *the* Real.[23] Even *images* of blood serve as a reminder that, in an earlier time, blood was the substance that rendered visual representation authentic—even painted blood, for instance, served to authenticate the statues of Christian martyrs. Since the broad brushstrokes with which the blood is painted in *Caché* suggest that it was done by the hand of a child, the painted blood is figured as doubly authentic. But in what sense does it relate to the filmic images it resembles—to the bleeding boy in the insert shots or to Georges's dream images of the slaughtered rooster? Blood in or on the image, even if represented—indeed, even if represented by the video image, *Caché* suggests—brings the real into representation, introduces a "truth" into what is staged. Is the film's unexpected, bloody violence—the slitting of the chicken's throat, the suicide of Majid—designed to approximate the traumatic effect of the images of the dead for Georges the *photographer*? Are these images traumatic? It is their code that Georges the talk show host struggles to know, struggles to put into words.

## *Coda*

Sadomasochism is centrally present in most of Haneke's films—beginning with his first feature film, *The Seventh Continent*, moving through *Benny's Video*, *71 Fragments*, *The Castle*, *Funny Games*, *Time of the Wolf*, as well as *Caché*, and it is the center of attention in *The Piano Teacher*, a virtual case study of this emotional double bind. Sadomasochism, of course, is the mindset described in Powell's *Peeping Tom* as well. The adult Mark is the deadly filmmaker in whom his father—connected with the camera—and Mark himself as child are finally fused at the moment of his suicide. The camera is a deadly weapon in this film, complete with phallic spear. When Mark trains it upon himself and "shoots" himself, the sadistic aggression of the father (allied with the camera) and the sexual fulfillment of the child-victim (in the female position) collapse into one. There is a striking parallel between this collapse in Powell's film and a similar moment in Haneke's *Caché*. This moment occurs in the farmyard sequence we see after Georges has for the last time retreated to his bed; it is the final visualization of the childhood scenario produced when Georges's lies evict his rival Majid from Georges's parental home. Structurally, this is a signature shot of Haneke's—the shot from a dark space into a light space—and it reveals its human actors in long shot, across the expanse of the courtyard. Taken from a dark space—no doubt the barn—the location of the shot *suggests* that its point of view belongs to the six-year-old Georges, who is hiding in the shadows. However, since the sequence fails to establish who is the owner of this gaze, its point of view remains unclaimed, simply the look of the camera. This key sequence again brings *Benny's Video* to mind, where a similar camera setup is retrospectively shown to be from the point of view of Benny in his darkened room, videotaping his parents. In a stunning act of aggression, Benny will use the videotape that he shoots to implicate his parents in the murder that he himself has committed.

What I am suggesting is that the point of view of the farmyard sequence is deliberately double. As in Powell's film, child and father collapse into one: Georges's point of view as sequestered child and the eye of Haneke's camera—and, by implication, the surveillance camera—are aligned in this shot. In the diegesis of Haneke's film, of course, there are several couples across which sadomasochistic drives play themselves out. When Majid—Georges's victim—commits suicide, he forces the adult Georges to assume the role of spectator: by means of his masochistic act, he enacts sadistic revenge upon Georges. Further, with Benny in mind, we might read Georges's son, Pierrot, and Majid's son as wreaking vengeance upon their fathers—one need not see their collaboration, insofar as there is one, as a utopian allegory. But why are the videotapes—products of the paternal gaze of surveillance no matter who produces them—tightly wrapped in images that suggest the hand of a child, if not to represent their interconnectedness? My point here is that the relation of victim to aggressor—represented in this film by several pairs of fathers and sons—plays itself out multiply, in different constellations, as functions distributed across the text, hence no longer necessarily embodied in its characters. Note the way in which the shot from the barn into the farmyard articulates these relations almost abstractly. The abstractly rendered paternal/directorial function—familiar from *Peeping Tom*—suggests that the obscure source of human suffering in *Time of the Wolf,* ultimately given a cinematic context, as well as the disembodied director in the theatrical scene of *Code Unknown,* merely acousmatic, a voice, and, finally, the surveillance camera of *Caché* share a common provenance.

In recalling Haneke's metaphor of the puppet master, it should be noted that the masochistic scenario described by psychoanalysis is a theatrical one. "The actual scene [of masochism] corresponds to the staging of a drama," writes Theodor Reik, "and is related to the phantasies, as is the performance of the dramatist's conception."[24] Masochism involves control over time, and it is a performance. Entailing a ritual that plays itself out in the flesh, it is a game with reality intimately connected with representation. Just like games and plots—and just like masochists—filmmakers impose control over performance. "It's a game, is it?" Georges asks Majid in *Caché,* initially claiming that he does not want to play, only to agree later that "I'll play along." Like games, masochistic scenarios are governed by strict and complex rules, and by relentless repetition. Only in the case of the endgame is repetition no longer possible: when Majid invites Georges to visit, it is to ensure that Georges will be present as he slits his throat. The constant in *Caché*'s abbreviated history of repeated remediation, the image of the bloody throat in the childish drawings, migrates first to the newspaper photograph of Georges, then to the body of the film itself. Finally we are shown Majid's bloody performance on videotape, where it can be replayed repeatedly after all. The constant through multiple mediatic transformations, blood produces authenticity for representation by way of its strong influence on spectator affect. Perhaps it is for this reason that the "drawing" of blood—represented or metaphorical, imaged as well as elicited—seems the goal of Haneke's cinema.

## Notes

1. D. W. Winnicott, *Playing and Reality* (New York: Basic Books, 1971), 52.
2. Ibid., 3.
3. This narrative structure has become popular: Alejandro Gonzalez Innaritu uses the device of accidentally connected narratives in *Amores Perros* (2000) and in *Babel* (2006); Steven Soderbergh makes use of it, as director, in *Traffic* (2000) and, as producer, in *Syriana* (2005).
4. While critics such as D. I. Grossvogel distinguish Haneke's Austrian films from his French films, there is, in fact, a pronounced continuity of concern.
5. Fredric Jameson, "The Existence of Italy," in *Signatures of the Visible* (New York: Routledge, 1992), 169, 162.
6. Ibid., 162.
7. Ibid., 169.
8. My thanks to Ryan Cook for this suggestion.
9. Stanley Cavell's important work on the screen presence of the actor triggered these questions, as did Haneke's assertion that he needed to find just the right actors for the remake of his own film *Funny Games* and that he would not have made the film if Naomi Watts had not agreed to be in it.
10. Binoche gave birth to her daughter, Hannah, in December 1999.
11. Carol Clover famously distinguishes between the assaultive and the projective eye in *Men, Women, and Chainsaws: Gender in the Modern Horror Film* (Princeton: Princeton University Press, 1992), 99.
12. Michael Powell, *A Life in Movies: An Autobiography* (New York: Knopf, 1987), 24.
13. I have written elsewhere about the cruelty of Haneke's films. See Brigitte Peucker, "Violence and Affect: Haneke's Modernist Melodramas," in *The Material Image: Art and the Real in Film* (Palo Alto, CA: Stanford University Press, 2007), 129–58.
14. As characters, Peter and Paul would seem to derive from the two helpers in

Franz Kafka's *The Castle*. Indeed Frank Giering plays both Artur in Haneke's Kafka adaptation and Paul in *Funny Games*. Peter and Paul not only play sadistic games with the family they murder but have a sadomasochistic routine worked out between the two of them as well.

15. Roland Barthes, "The Photographic Message," in *Image-Music-Text,* ed. and trans. Stephen Heath (New York: Hill and Wang, 1977), 19.

16. Ibid., 18. Here I am referring—indeed, Barthes is referring—to the Real as that which cannot be adequately represented, as is the case with death. The term is taken from the writings of Jacques Lacan and famously deployed for film by Slavoj Žižek in *Looking Awry: An Introduction to Jacques Lacan through Popular Culture* (Cambridge: MIT Press, 1998).

17. Roland Barthes, "Rhetoric of the Image," in *Image-Music-Text,* 45.

18. Roland Barthes, *Camera Lucida: Reflections on Photography,* trans. Richard Howard (New York: Hill and Wang, 1981), 45.

19. *Peeping Tom* also links cruelty to performance spaces: two of Mark's murders occur in such spaces.

20. See Haneke's letter of March 2000 to his producer, Marin Karnitz, reproduced for the KinoVideo DVD of *Code Unknown*. Haneke's reference here is no doubt to Fritz Lang, who stylized both his character Dr. Mabuse and, by implication, himself as the great puppet master. As quoted by Lucy Fischer, Lang refers to Mabuse as the "great showman of the marionettes, the one who organizes the perfect crime." Fischer, "Dr. Mabuse and Mr. Lang," *Wide Angle* 3, no. 3 (1979): 26.

Some of the unanswered questions that linger in Georges's story—as well as in Anne's—are formulated in this letter, which presents itself as a supplement to, perhaps even as a means of deciphering, the film's unknowable code. In this letter, Haneke interrogates the boundaries of reality and illusion.

21. In the sequence set in Egypt, Benny and his mother interact by way of their mutual videotaping.

22. Here is another echo of *Benny's Video,* where the son's taping implicates his parents as accessories to his crime.

23. Barthes, "Rhetoric of the Image," 43.

24. Theodor Reik, *Masochism in Modern Man,* trans. Margaret H. Beigel and Gertrud M. Kurth (New York: Farrar, Straus, 1941).

*Funny Games* (1997): Torture and a light snack.

Brian Price

## Pain and the Limits of Representation

### *I*

In an interview in *Story Quarterly* in 1995, the contemporary American writer Brian Evenson was asked to address the violent character of his writing. This violence had already led to the writer's excommunication from both the Mormon Church and Brigham Young University (which asked him to stop writing novels altogether *or else*). Evenson responded:

To render a violent act in language is not at all the same as committing a violent act. The writing itself is not violent, but rather precise, measured, controlled, in the grip of certain arbitrary but self-consistent rules. Only rarely does real violence become endowed with aesthetic qualities. Like religion, language does violence to the immanent world by forcing the objects of that world to be understood in terms of generalities, by stripping them of their specificities and categorizing them. And this sort of violence is in everything. . . . If you've ever been involved in real acts of violence, you can see how profound the difference is.[1]

Here, Evenson conceives of violence as a process of categorization, as the gathering of the irreducibly particular into a homogenizing whole that founds, and is founded by, a larger generalization. And in so doing, I would like to propose, he offers us a crucial distinction for the consideration of violence in the work of Michael Haneke.

Above all else, Haneke's work is violent. It would be quite simple to describe Haneke as an immoral sadist who relishes in the desecration of the body as a form of entertainment. Of course, Haneke does not make a spectacle of violence; its appearance occurs in a phenomenological frame. It tends toward the blunt muteness of its actual occurrence in the world. And as Evenson implies, the occurrence of violence in the world is not banal; it is just not aestheticized. While an investigation of the phenomenologically motivated realism of Haneke's practice would not be without merit, it might direct us too simply toward the delineation of degrees of resemblance and how those levels relate to moral categories of consumer choice. In other words, it would suggest that the closer the representation of violence moves toward its occurrence in the world, the more we can learn from it; the farther the violence gets from the world, the more it contributes to our moral degeneration in a willfully self-commodifying culture. I would like to think of violence instead as a question concerning structuring. That is, it is a philosophical question concerning structure, and the ways in which structures produce different kinds of violence.

My question concerning structuring is especially germane to *Funny Games* (1997); the act and subject of torture, so thoroughly manifest there, is especially self-reflexive, pitched at questions of representation and containment, displeasure and relief. Despite the fact that my remarks here will be limited to *Funny Games,* the original as well as its remake, the question is nevertheless relevant to Haneke's oeuvre more generally.

The question raised by *Funny Games* is, then, it seems to me, what exactly do we long for as spectators of this film? And what are the implications of this longing?

*Funny Games* is an experience of a torture. The original version, much like its American remake, concerns two homicidal men, dressed in their Sunday whites, who move machinelike through a series of lakefront, weekend homes of the Austrian leisure class. The duration of the film is spent on the torture and eventual murder of one particular family. The act of torture begins almost immediately and will carry through until, as one of the murderers himself suggests, the film has reached the standard length of the feature film. As spectators, our experience is like the experience of this onscreen family, and yet not at all. Many of us would be inclined to describe our own viewing experience as torturous; once Haneke's camera is trained on this game of extreme violence, we are never provided with means of consolation. There is only a brief fantasy of it, when the wife manages to kill Peter, one of the murderers. However, Paul, the other murderer, quickly grabs a nearby VCR remote, rewinds the film that we ourselves are watching, and sets the film back on its nihilistic course. The torture of the family, and by extension the spectator, rolls on.

*Pain and the Limits of Representation*

However, to describe our experience watching the film *as* torture is to offer an analogy for pain, a sign that does not originate in the sentience of our own body. Our respective experiences of torture, family and spectator, are not the same. As Elaine Scarry has shown, physical pain is unrepresentable; thus we do not have the means necessary for genuine sympathy. In *The Body in Pain,* she writes: "Unlike any other state of consciousness, [pain] has no referential content. It is not *of* or *for* anything. It is precisely because it takes no object that it, more than any other phenomenon, resists objectification in language."[2] Scarry suggests that pain introduces a distinction between the subject who feels and the perceiver who searches for signs capable of expressing that feeling: "To have pain is to have certainty; to hear that another person has pain is to have doubt."[3] Doubt arises precisely because of the fact that pain has no object—hence, Scarry suggests, the all too common skepticism of doctors who distrust the signs we propose in an effort to locate the place and cause of our pain. The gulf between the sentient experience of pain and its representation is only furthered when its occurrence is caused by torture. As Scarry has noted, torture is a structure in at least three parts.[4] The first involves the infliction of pain itself. The second involves the "objectification of the subjective attributes of pain."[5] The infliction of pain then leads to the destruction of the subject's ability to perceive the objects of his or her consciousness; the torturer then appropriates those objects in an effort to produce power, to speak in the name of the other who has lost his/her ability to arrive at language.

For example, in *Funny Games,* the torturers do their work on the father of the family, Georg, with an object from his own home, a golf club. The golf club becomes a weapon, one that causes pain and an object that can be used to explain, however inexactly, what the pain feels like: that is, *my leg feels like it has been smashed with five iron.* Such an explanation might, if the prisoner could articulate it, provide us with a sense of the cause of pain, but not pain itself. More to the point, the objectification of that pain by way of the object that produced it leads to the externalization of pain from the body. The trouble with describing pain in relation to the instrument that caused it, Scarry tells us, lies in how easily those terms can be altered to erase the very trace of the pain.[6] If we were to call this act of torture "the golf club," as so often torture is renamed in light of a cultural product or value, we would lose the reference to a body altogether. Torture thus conjures up not pain but civilization. A golf club connotes both an object and a society. It is an elevated cultural value that betokens civilization, whiteness, not barbarity. And what is the goal of torture if not to reorient cultural values by way of the extermination of the other, a process that begins with the liquidation of the consciousness of the prisoner? Having effected the destruction of the prisoner's consciousness, language can then be put in the service of power. Violence becomes a force of categorization and thus generalization. That torture is so often predicated on religious ideology should not escape us. Our torturers in this film, remember, are named Peter and Paul.

Still, the notion of pain as unrepresentable, as the condition of the unmaking of consciousness, does more than merely clarify our role as spectators here. It *could* help us to distinguish the character of our emotional response in terms of sympathy, empathy, or some other form of identification. But these answers would only serve to offer a moral judgment of the work and its maker. Instead we need to know upon what the satisfaction of our longing for relief would be predicated. Torture not only liquidates consciousness but does so to erect a larger, generalizing structure of meaning—and the organization of signs that are made to overcome their nonidentity through an act of violence. To what extent, we need to know, is cinema motivated by these same principles? To what extent does it do "violence to the immanent world by forcing the objects of that world to be understood in terms of generalities, by stripping them of their specificities and categorizing them," to recite Evenson's idea about language and religion.

I am reminded here of Theodor Adorno's inquiry into the liberating potential of ugliness. In *Aesthetic Theory,* Adorno appears suspicious of what he had earlier in his career valued, namely, an abstract art that announces its autonomy by way of its total rejection of mimesis, by the free play of form. In his late work, however, Adorno was concerned with the ways in which an autonomous, abstract art still bore the traces of the cultural matrix that it seeks to reject; the harmonious play of abstract structures could be said to mirror the social totality out of which it arose in oppositional terms. The free play of structure in the autonomous, abstract work mirrors the play of structure—or at least the process of structuring—in culture. Such a harmonious ordering of aesthetic structures bears a resemblance to classicism and, of course, to Kant's purposive purposelessness, an aesthetic experience famously grounded in the conception of a transcendental subject—what Adorno will ultimately describe as Kant's "castrated hedonism, desire without desire."[7] The neoclassical impulse, Adorno tells us, is motivated by imperial politics and torture. "Hitler's empire put this theorem to the test," he writes, "as it put the whole of bourgeois society to the test: the more torture went on in the basement, the more insistently they made sure that the roof rested on columns."⁸ In this passage, then, Adorno suggests that our experience of beauty is not activated by the alignment of form, in classical and neoclassical structures, with the deep structure of the world; rather, the beautiful is a strategy of containment, and it is produced in an effort to create a harmonious structure that disguises the ugliness, and power, that resides at the foundation.

To return to the space of *Funny Games,* Haneke, too, seems interested in the relation between pain and its containment through the generalizing capacity of classical narration, and for reasons not unrelated to the conclusions arrived at by Adorno. That is, torture and pain are at the center of this film; however, their appearance effects a dismantling of a classical structure that would otherwise work to diminish or mask that foundation. What is unbearable here, unlike most American horror films, is the film's refusal to offer consolation through a strategy of generalization, to found meaning on a pile of corpses. This refusal to do more than dismantle leaves us in space without the means to make meaning and in so doing suggests a practice of cinema that is allied with the free reign of consciousness, not its extermination. But to get to an understanding of what this means, we need first to see two examples of the dismantling that takes place and how that dismantling is predicated on the unrepresentability of pain.

I refer you to two scenes. The first comes from the very opening of the film and announces straight away a relation between the classical and the ugly. *Funny Games* begins with a series of extreme long shots—sometimes overhead, sometimes from the side—of the family car as Georg, Anna, and their son make way toward their weekend home. On the way there, husband and wife play a game of naming. Each inserts a classical CD, and the other's job is to correctly identify the singer, to match voice to name. The satisfaction the couple takes in correctly matching name to sound, sign to signifier, is both an expression of cultural mastery and an expression of confidence in an essential bond between the word and sound, speech and an authentic self. This confidence is, of course, what will disappear through torture. And along such lines, John Zorn's terrifying, discordant music rages forth at the very moment in which Georg is unable to identify what he hears.

The ugly, chaotic sounds of the Zorn piece stand in sharp contrast to classical beauty of Handel and Mascagni. Curiously, in his interview with Christopher Sharrett, Haneke denied setting up an opposition here between classical and popular, claiming instead that "I have nothing against popular music and wouldn't think of playing popular against classical forms. I'm very skeptical of the false conflict that already exists between so-called serious music and music categorized strictly as entertainment."[9] Here, Haneke seems to be occupying the place of the recalcitrant, contrarian artist. But if we take his claim seriously we can also see that his dissatisfaction with the distinction between classical and popular might owe to the fact that popular culture is so often expressed in classical forms. The Zorn music, for instance, signals a popular form—death metal—but in an already deconstructed form. The game of nomination played by the couple with classical music, the securing of a relation between name and sound, is precisely what would fall apart in an attempt to name this deconstructed blast of metal, and thus announces an analogous dismantling that will occur at the level of cinema by the end of the film.

If we look at the visual style of this sequence, we can see that this dismantling is already taking place. This scene alternates between extreme long shots and close-ups. Haneke absents the medium shot, the middle term in the convention of classical narration, which serves to orient us in space as we move steadily closer from an establishing shot to a close-up. If the close-up is a kind of pointing, then we might say that the medium and long shots that precede that pointing provide us with a chain through which the particular should pass back out the general, to the world as it has been established thorough editing. Without the medium shot, the rhetorical quality of classical narration begins to break down. A close-up presents us with an object it identifies as meaningful and that must be understood in relation to other bodies, other objects. That rhetorical arrangement is then naturalized in the achievement of verisimilitude offered by the medium and long shot in that same system; even when it is absent, that structure is always implied.

It is worth noting here that the close-up in this sequence is of the car stereo, the source of this game of nomination, of pointing. It will be one of the last close-ups we will see in the film. It is also important to note that once Zorn's music appears, so do the credits. And it is not the usual hierarchy of star, director, producer. What Haneke shows instead are the full credits—the grips, assistant camera operators, sound people—the list normally reserved for after the film has ended, when the less curious are free to leave the theater. And this is also the moment at which the medium shot finally appears—last, out of order. At the very beginning, then, Haneke is making us aware of who made this film, of the numerous people who brought the work into being but who remain eclipsed by the very images they helped to produce. As such, Haneke is not constructing a sanctimonious memorial but making us aware of how a film is constructed so as to leave us in a space of reflection before this technology that would otherwise work to make us lose ourselves, as we so often and so positively proclaim in our collective, colloquial expression of the value of film as a form of entertainment. The alignment of entertainment and torture is, of course, a relation that the American remake, as we will see, more relentlessly pursues.

Having thus announced the breakdown of the structure of classical narration, what we subsequently get in *Funny Games* is a series of long takes, most often framed as medium-long shots, though it is important to note that Haneke's frames do vary in focal length; he is not simply trading one system for another. What he is rejecting is the interpolated close-up as a rhetorical device, as a means of seeing for another, and the promise of seeing all in an extended series of images. Think here of the notion of coverage in the parlance of production. Thus offscreen space becomes a necessary condition for reflection. For, as many have attested, *Funny Games* is agonizing precisely because the violence takes place offscreen. However, the absence of images of that violence is not due to questions of taste or morality, a refusal of the ugly. Rather, that which we do not see provides us with the necessary conditions for understanding that which we do. Consider, by way of a second example, the scene when Paul goes to the kitchen for a sandwich while Peter murders the son offscreen. Paul is seen, dressed head to knee in his well-bleached whites, in one continuous medium-long shot as he searches the refrigerator, removes butter and bread, and proceeds to make a sandwich. He pauses for a brief moment at the sound of the shotgun blast that will kill the son and spread his blood, skin, and organs throughout the room. The camera never looks away from Paul, who continues on with his sandwich making despite the guttural moans of a parent in the next room made witness to the horrific scene of his son's slaughter. On one level, this image embodies Adorno's notion that where there is torture in the basement, the roof must rest on columns. It is an overwhelming scene of whiteness; the whiteness of the bourgeois home echoes with both the white clothes of the murderer and the imperial whiteness of neoclassical architecture. And, of course, the sounds offscreen indicate a kind of torture in the basement. But more important, because Haneke does not cut at the first sound of strife in the next room, we are left to imagine what has happened. Moreover, the offscreen space sets up an important incongruity that editing, in the classical manner, would efface. That is, we are meant to entertain both a scene of extraordinary terror *and* of banal domesticity.

Accordingly, we are left to come to a reckoning about that overlay, one that continuity editing would reorient in a linear fashion. In the classical manner, we would hear sound, see Paul snacking, then cut back to the scene of violence, suggesting what could happen when Paul walks away. Instead we are left to think about the relation between bourgeois domesticity and violence, a late-night sandwich amid the sounds of someone else's agony. Sound here betokens the certainty of pain, but the image reveals doubt. And in the larger terms of my argument, doubt becomes the condition for generalization.

By contrast, Haneke's use of the long take in these scenes, and the offscreen space it opens, constructs a space for reflection rather than for pathos, which would lead to a structure of catharsis that ultimately works in the service of order, one that configures violence and someone else's pain in the service of an ideology, or, more plainly, entertainment. Instead, pain here mobilizes thought; but ironically, it does so by its refusal to find a word or image identical to it. Haneke, like Scarry before him, seems to recognize that to produce a word or image for pain is to speak for the person experiencing that pain. And the person speaking on behalf of the one who has lost consciousness is so often the one responsible for the pain itself. Such acts of nomination are integral to the realization, and further dispersal, of structures of power. And if we remember that the other close-up in this film is of the family television draped in the blood of the son, we might begin to sort out the ways in which Haneke identifies media as a structure of power predicated on the creation and subsequent quieting of someone else's pain. We see everything, and yet nothing at all; unless, of course, we are willing to contemplate in meaningful terms what lies beyond the edge of the frame.

## *II*

On March 14, 2008, Haneke's American remake opened in the United States to a reception of strange indifference, moral fury, and, worst of all—in the terms of the marketplace, in terms that deprive us of so much thought, much like torture itself—poor box office performance.[10] In that week's edition of *At the Movies with Ebert and Roeper,* a morally outraged and visibly shaken Richard Roeper asked with great incredulity: "Are we supposed to consider this some kind of performance art, some kind of comment on violence in the movies!?" Before one could assume that the question—however bitterly posed—was rhetorical, he sternly concluded: "It is ugly and pretentious." Roeper would go on by show's end to recommend instead the recently released DVD of Disney's *Enchanted,* a film about a cartoon princess who comes to life in the arms and world of a Manhattan divorce lawyer played by Patrick Dempsey. Dempsey, of course, is better known in American popular culture as McDreamy, a sexy young doctor on *Grey's Anatomy,* a television fantasy about the hospital as a site of romance and sexual intrigue for young, attractive MDs. *Grey's Anatomy* also articulates a relation to pain and representation: the ugly and the painful is but the necessary precondition for the beautiful and the aloof. In other words, it is just the sunnier side of the same understanding of representation offered in *Funny Games.*

I take Roeper's rather predictable dismissal of the film, not to mention the worried look on his face, as a primary aim of the remake. Haneke must surely have expected such a response to the film. The film offends two of the most conspicuous features of American culture: commodity fetishism and moral certainty. The remake—while not shot for shot, as was much rumored—is simply not different enough. As we know, one of the primary reasons for the American remake of a "foreign" film has to do with its economic promise. The rights to an obscure Japanese horror film can be cheaply purchased and remade, as if by mold, and refashioned in an American context. The story might remain the same, but the images are clearly different and thus marketable as new. The images are also whitened, morally recalibrated. The perceived failure of *Funny Games* on these grounds alone should indicate that moral feeling and capital now move in step.

That the remake of *Funny Games* could only be remade *as same* is a conceit built into the very plot of both renderings. The fantasy that what we see onscreen can be reversed and remade for a more positive, more desirable end is negated in the moment of Paul's rewinding of the scene in which Peter is murdered. And it is worth noting, again, that the reversal that takes place is authored by Paul; the scenario to be restored is the unrelenting brutality and the denial of catharsis, of any relief we might feel when Anna or Ann kills Peter. Haneke, like Paul, got to try again, and he did it mostly the same. In this sense, one can say that *Funny Games*—no matter which version one sees—is itself about the remake. It is about the recurrence of torture with only slight variation, as if variation were a meaningful distinction in the arbitrary logic that someone else's pain makes possible. Peter and Paul remake torture every day, from one family to the next. The game begins with eggs, an errand from a dead neighbor, and tales of unexpected houseguests. The result, as we know by the second time we see this scenario enacted, will be the same, no matter how often the names and houses change. But, of course, those changes, it should be said, are rather slight—and this, I suspect, is precisely what is so unnerving.

So, what difference, we have to ask, does difference actually make? To answer to this question we might turn, for a moment, to *Caché*, the film that precedes the remake of *Funny Games* and is itself about questions of torture and visibility. The event that goes missing in the images that flood the television in the bourgeois flat of Georges and Anne but haunts—albeit in very different ways—Georges and Majid is the massacre of October 17, 1961. On this day, an estimated two hundred Algerians protesting the ongoing French occupation of Algeria were brutally murdered by the French police, their bodies dumped in the Seine for all to see.[11] Of course, what Parisians were willing to see—what, in fact, they were able to see—is one of the major questions posed by *Caché*. While the bodies would have been visible to thousands, the circulation of images of those bodies in the popular press was forbidden. Despite Charles de Gaulle's professed desire to put an end to the Algerian war—a call, moreover, that made his seizure of power and its further consolidation with the establishment of the Fifth Republic possible—the "negative" images and reports of the war were increasingly subject to censorship, especially in 1961.[12] The reason for such thoroughgoing censorship—for this absence of images—is that France was using torture against suspected National Liberation Front members in an effort to combat the revolution. Any reference to torture in cinema, for example, would result in censorship. If France were shown to be using torture, then it would be in clear violation of the Nuremberg Principles established at the end of World War II, which expressly forbid the use of torture on political prisoners. It would also be to call forward the memory France's collaboration with the Nazi Party. The effects of censorship, moreover, long outlived their usefulness as a form of protection against the charge of war crimes. Patrick Crowley, for instance, reports that in 2001 *L'Humanité* published the results of an opinion poll in which it was revealed that most French citizens had never heard of the massacre.[13] This absence, at the level of the image, has been largely reproduced in the memory and history of France itself. This, one can quite easily conjecture, is what Haneke is getting at in *Caché:* the image is everywhere and reveals much less than it hides. Or, what the image shows is the obverse manifestation of what caused it. The image, we might say, is disinformatic. Such is the representational logic of pain.

*Funny Games* depicts torture quite directly. However, its reception in the United States strongly suggests something about the images that can be seen in the United States in 2008, as well as before. What the American *Funny Games* provokes most strongly are the moral forms of censorship that work—however unconsciously—to prevent us from considering what is occurring, at the moment of this writing, in Guantanamo Bay, where the U.S. army is torturing political prisoners in an effort to sustain a war on Iraq, an act of government-sponsored terrorism waged in the name of terror everywhere. The oblique relation (American torture taking place in Cuba) is what drives American foreign policy under the Bush administration. And it should be noted that the Nuremberg law against the use of torture still holds. In this respect, our sense of outrage at the unrelenting brutality of *Funny Games*—our refusal to watch and to think seriously about what the film is doing—is but an effort to silence an object that does precisely what the government would most like us to repress or, for that matter, understand in more positive and more obliquely representational terms. Ironically, *Funny Games* was projected in largely empty theaters. *Horton Hears a Who!* was everywhere and seen by millions. Consequently, *Funny Games* became—just as Richard Roeper feared—a piece of performance art, an installation: a film that plays but is not seen. Censorship, in other words, is now a synonym for entertainment in its most moralistic articulation. To repeat, to return to Adorno and without variation: "Hitler's empire put this theorem to the test as it put the whole of bourgeois society to the test: the more torture went on in the basement, the more insistently they made sure that the roof rested on columns."[14] *Funny Games* is ugly; *Enchanted* is beautiful.

What such moral prohibitions—all these judgments about entertainment—prevent us from understanding is a chain of equivalence Haneke establishes that links together Nazi Germany (which included Austria, absorbed Austria), Gaullist France, and the Bush administration. *Funny Games* (1997), *Caché*, and *Funny Games* (2007) are linked together by the names of the couples—the protagonists of each film—with only the slightest cultural variation: Georg and Anna (*Funny Games*, 1997), Georges and Anne (*Caché*), George and Ann (*Funny Games*, 2007). Through the repetitive naming of his main characters across three different films made in, and about, three different countries (Austria, France, and the United States), Haneke links them together as one, and can only do so because of the differences that prevail between them.[15]

In this way, Haneke comes very close to an enactment of the empty signifier and the concept of equivalence developed, across roughly the same period of time, by Ernesto Laclau. Laclau's conception of equivalence, which proceeds on the basis of an empty signifier—a signifier without a signified—is central to a positive conception of hegemony, one that can indicate the presence of evil in the very act of assembling a community on the basis of what each member will come to lack, collectively and individually: justice, power, freedom. As Laclau defines it, the empty signifier is made possible by the limits of language as Saussure conceived it, as a system of differences that constitutes meaning on the very basis of difference—a system that nevertheless depends in kind on a totality, on a finite set of all possible relations within that system. As Laclau sees it, the signifying totality is also the announcement of a limit and, thus, one that can be exceeded, interrupted, or remade as a series of alternatively formed, yet expansive, systems. It is the establishment of a difference beyond all difference. To exceed the limits of that system, which comes with any awareness of the totality itself, is to cancel difference in turn. Without a totality there is no difference, only a field of signifiers that have no definite signified. Or, as Laclau puts it:

Only if the beyond becomes the signifier of a pure threat, of pure negativity, of the simply excluded, can there be limits and system (that is, an objective order). But in order to be the signifiers of the excluded (or, simply of exclusion), the various excluded categories have to cancel their differences through the formation of a chain of equivalences to that which the system demonizes in order to signify itself. Again, we see here the possibility of an empty signifier announcing itself through this logic in which differences collapse into equivalential chains.[16]

The equivalential chain, then, is formed on the basis of the evacuation of pure difference and the establishment of what we might call, instead, a shared partiality: "The identity of each element is constitutively split: on the one hand, each difference expresses itself *as* difference; on the other hand, each of them *cancels* itself as such by entering into a relation of equivalence with all the other differences of the system."[17] One can imagine, for example, a collective of three people: an atheist, a willfully childless baseball fan who is a political radical opposed to the use of torture and the return of fascism; an Episcopalian and registered Democrat, a father of four, an opera-lover who is opposed to the use of torture and the return of fascism; and a registered Republican who hates sports, has a passion for the stock market, and opposes the use of torture and the rise of fascism. A chain of equivalences can be formed on the basis of what all three share, as well as what they collectively lack: a world without torture and fascism. The more this group expands on the basis of that shared and emphasized difference, the less the remaining differences will actually matter. Such is the work of the empty signifier and the chain of equivalence it provokes. Difference matters, but only insofar as it can define collectivity. What binds us—our collective protest against torture—is a meaningful lack, one that will point to the presence of evil by virtue of the collective presence of what we, as a group, do not have: justice, a world without torture. This lack is precisely what allows us to see, to mobilize, and to reverse the order of politics, to put an end to torture.

This, to return to Haneke, is what the chain of equivalence announced by Georg and Anna, Georges and Anne, and George and Ann most strongly suggests. The cultural and historical differences between Germany, France, and America do not matter here. What matters is what they all share: the recurrent presence of torture and a historical trajectory that clearly articulates the stakes of torture today; now, as then, the use of torture is a violation of international law, and its presence today links the Bush administration in a chain of equivalence that leads back to de Gaulle/Algeria and to Nazi Germany. Nothing less. This is also why the differences between the two versions of *Funny Games* matter so little. What good would it do us to tend, here, to matters of cultural specificity and difference? What we would notice is a difference of products. Ann buys organic products and shops at Whole Foods; Anna did not. George wears a gray shirt; Georg wears a white one. Likewise, this chain of equivalences points to a way of understanding visual style. And the questions of names, it should be noted, takes place within the film just as it does across this series of films. Paul, you will remember, occasionally refers to Peter as Tom (and to themselves as Tom and Jerry, the cartoon characters) and Beavis (and thus to themselves as Beavis and Butthead). What matters most, though, is Peter and Paul, the religious pair, who are themselves empty signifiers: "robbing Peter to pay Paul." That this particular name game would make reference to representation in the form of cartoon violence should cue us to understand equivalence as a way of understanding the minor, yet necessary, differences in terms of visual style. Most of the sequences are shot the same, but some are not, and there is always some difference at the level of mise-en-scène. The actors, in the end, *are* different, but their actions are the same, in art as in politics.

## Notes

1. Ben Marcus, "Brian Evenson," www.webdelsol.com/evenson/beven.htm (accessed May 15, 2006).

2. Elaine Scarry, *The Body in Pain: The Making and Unmaking of the World* (New York: Oxford University Press), 5.

3. Ibid., 7.

4. Ibid., 51.

5. Ibid.

6. Ibid., 51–53.

7. Theodor Adorno, *Aesthetic Theory*, trans. and ed. Robert Hullot-Kenner (Minneapolis: University of Minnesota Press, 1996), 11.

8. Ibid., 49.

9. Christopher Sharrett, "The World That Is Known: An Interview with Michael Haneke," *Kinoeye* 4, no. 1 (2004) www.kinoeye.org (accessed May 15, 2006).

10. In its opening weekend in the United States, *Funny Games* came in twenty-first place and grossed $544,833, which placed it right behind *Welcome Home, Roscoe Jenkins*. The highest grossing film that weekend was *Dr. Suess' Horton Hears a Who!* which took in $45,012,998. See www.boxofficemojo.com/weekend/chart/?view=&yr=2008&wknd=11&p=.htm (accessed March 25, 2008).

11. For a detailed account of the events and their influence on Haneke in particular, see Patrick Crowley's "When Forgetting Is Remembering: Haneke's *Caché* and the Events of October 17, 1961," in this volume.

12. For a thorough account of censorship in this period, see an early and important account by Martin Harrison, "Government and Press during the Algerian War," *The American Political Science Review* 2 (June 1964).

13. See Crowley, "When Forgetting Is Remembering."

14. Adorno, *Aesthetic Theory*, 11.

15. For a larger consideration of Haneke's use of names, see Michael Lawrence's "Haneke's Stable: The Death of an Animal and the Figuration of the Human," in this volume.

16. Ernesto Laclau, "Why Do Empty Signifiers Matter to Politics?" in *Emancipation(s)* (London: Verso, 1996), 38–39.

17. Ibid., 38.

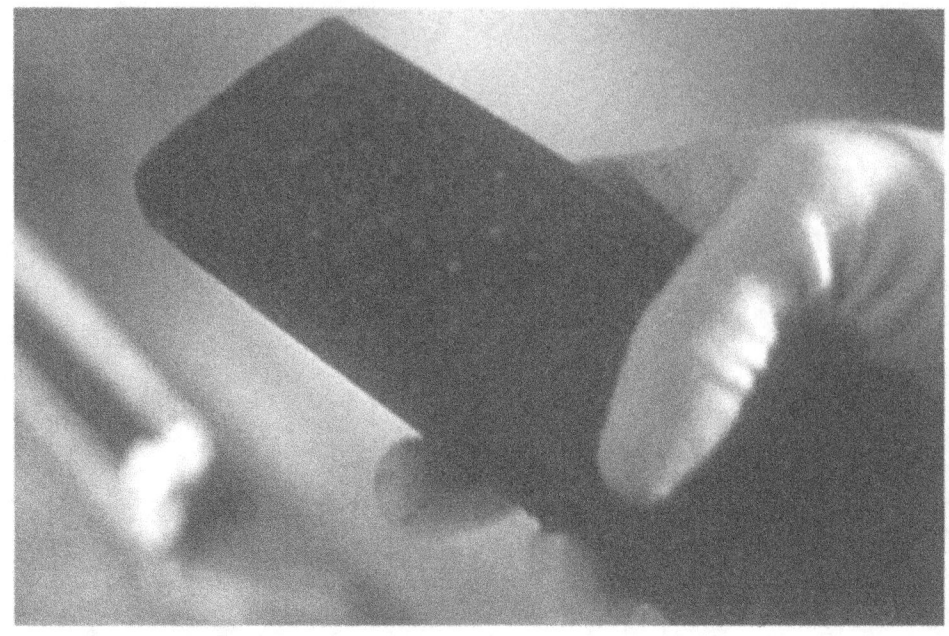

*Funny Games* (1997): Paul prepares to save Peter.

Tarja Laine

# Haneke's "Funny" Games with the Audience (Revisited)

It has often been established that, in the cinematic experience, the audience can realize certain emotions affectively without feeling them "concretely." In fact, the whole practice of cinema is built on the human capacity to be emotionally moved by what one knows does not "really" exist. Much academic discussion of the emotional response to cinema tends to capture these fictional emotions through the notion of willing suspension of disbelief, which guarantees safe involvement with the film. In the traditional feature film, emotions are placed at the service of the diegetic effect, experienced by the audience from a safe distance as privileged witnesses.[1] But in contemporary filmmaking the blurring of the boundaries between the diegesis (the film's story world) and the nondiegesis (the viewer's world) and the drawing of the audience's attention to the process of viewing itself almost seem to have become a rule rather than an exception. As a result, the traditional modes of seeing and experiencing no longer seem to be entirely appropriate for contemporary cinema. Films no longer simply "appear" before us from a safe distance; instead, they surround us, they expose us, and they confront us by any means possible. Films can look back at us, surprise us, and throw us into an objective apprehension of ourselves in the act of looking. Furthermore, we are not merely spectators in this way of experiencing: we participate, we are challenged, we are *forced* to respond, and we are often made very aware of our position of being "accomplices" (instead of witnesses) to the events depicted.

In Michael Haneke's controversial film *Funny Games* (1997), the audience is held to be an accomplice to brutalities committed by two film characters that are no "real" characters at all, precisely because they emerge out of that cinematic space where the diegesis and the nondiegesis cancel each other out. The film is affective in a very "primal" way; critics frequently define it as offensive, provocative, and shocking. Furthermore, the film is often seen as particularly emblematic for Haneke, a filmmaker who wishes unambiguously to confront the audience within the paradigms of affective intelligence, beyond the emotionally distanced Brechtian anti-illusionism. In the film, two decent-looking, polite, and seemingly well-educated young men who call themselves Paul (Arno Frisch) and Peter (Frank Giering)—but at times also Beavis and Butthead or Tom and Jerry—force their way into the holiday residence of Anna (Susanne Lothar) and Georg Schober (Ulrich Mühe) and their little son, Schorschi (Stefan Olapczynski), and start to torture the family systematically. First, Paul kills the family dog with a golf club. Then, Peter strikes Georg with the same club, shattering his kneecap, after which Anna is forced to undress to stop the young men from torturing her son. With a friendly smile on his face, Paul suggests a "funny" game: "I'll wager a bet that in twelve hours you three will be kaput?" The game of physical torture and psychological humiliation now begins in earnest.

*Funny Games* is a shocking film experience by any measure. According to some critics, it is also a shockingly contradictory film experience. This may be the case because the film is not meant to be "merely" a thriller (even though it clearly is) but simultaneously a critique of thrillers, violent mass media, and mainstream cinema in general. *Funny Games* is purposefully shocking rather than enchanting, and it is meant to question the use of violence, rather than to actually use violence itself, as a major narrative element. Instead, we are forced to experience the effects of violence afterward, particularly as they are reflected in the close-ups of Georg's and Anna's faces. As a result, Georg's and Anna's faces become the sites of pain and shame for being tortured and humiliated up to the point where both move beyond humiliation, dwelling in a trancelike state. As Jürgen Felix and Marcus Stiglegger write: "In *Funny Games,* it is Anna's ravaged face especially that we must stare at again and again: a face that gradually loses—torture by torture—all traces of human dignity, destroyed by escalating acts of humiliation forced upon her by her tormentors."[2]

Traditionally, one of the central ways in which a film is made emotionally significant for the audience is in the use of the human face in the scene of "emotional contagion."[3] Yet, even though Haneke does indeed use the human face to promote emotional contagion between the victims and the audience, even more important to the emotional effect of *Funny Games* is the fact that the terrible situation the victims are facing is simultaneously both very real and very absurd. The victims' pain refers to the reality of physical necessity that nevertheless is isolated from any psychological motivation or rational explanation, and this is established from the very beginning of the film through the use of sound. The film opens with a series of eerie aerial shots of the Schobers' car driving toward their beach house. Elevated classical music is playing on the soundtrack (Handel and Mascagni). This appears to be diegetic sound played on the car stereo as a subject for Georg and Anna's music quiz, which is revealed to us by the offscreen dialogue between them, while the camera maintains its "God's eye" perspective.

However, there are several, apparently deliberate, continuity mistakes in this opening sequence: "elliptical jumps" indicate that some time has gone by while the music and the dialogue continues undisturbed. The idyllic playfulness of the family heading out for the holidays is then interrupted abruptly with John Zorn's screaming and chaotic avant-garde speed metal jazz that drowns out every other sound.[4] With its heavy font and aggressive red color, the title of the film that dashes against the medium close-up image of the unsuspecting family stands in harsh contrast with the saturated stativity of the filmic image on the background. The music continues as the opening credits roll, and it is clear that whatever is going to happen to this sympathetic family will in all likelihood not end well. Haneke's play with diegetic and nondiegetic sound involves us from early on in his game, which, however, is not "playable" at all due to its senseless set of rules. The opening sequence, therefore, establishes the correspondence between the diegesis and the nondiegesis, expanding the diegetic world to include the audience and, by so doing, to hold the audience to be an accomplice for the brutalities yet to come, since we now know that a terrible crime will soon be committed.

After the opening sequence, the film starts off in a normal and relaxed domestic atmosphere, even though the audience is made to notice how strangely Anna and Georg's neighbors behave upon their first meeting. The family settles in for the weekend. Georg unpacks their luggage while Anna fills the fridge; then Georg and Schorschi put the boat in the water, and Anna prepares for dinner. But the normalcy quickly turns into a senseless, homicidal situation brought upon by Paul and Peter. Anna's first reaction to this senselessness is irritation—in the film she grows increasingly frustrated with Peter's deliberately clumsy behavior. First, Peter drops Anna's eggs on the ground; then he throws her cell phone in the dishwater, a calculated sabotage given that the Schobers now can neither receive any phone calls nor call for help themselves when they are later left alone in the house. In the distance, the family dog barks ominously, like a warning sound for the sadistic invasion that will follow closely. However, Anna's annoyance is soon replaced by horror as the situation skids out of control with the first violent outburst. This moment makes our worst fears come true, but unlike in a traditional horror film, the moment is not followed by a sense of relief for the audience for no longer having to carry the awareness of the threat alone.[5] The moment when the Schobers are finally aware of the threat is not a relief for the audience for the simple reason that the Schobers are unable to act to save themselves. Therefore, the audience cannot release their emotional stress by identifying with the action on the screen.

But even more important, the audience is not granted any relief, as neither the Schobers nor the audience have any rational access to the world of senseless violence with which they are confronted within/by the film. The audience shares Anna and Georg's helplessness caused by their inability to protect either their son or themselves from this nightmarish situation. Yet what is even more unbearable in the film is its refusal to offer its audience the means to find meaning in the escalating acts of violence and humiliation.[6] In the beginning, Anna cannot explain her irritation toward Paul and Peter to Georg or even to herself even though she (unlike Georg) can sense that something is terribly wrong. In the next moment her frightful expectations are raised to the power of infinity when Peter shatters Georg's kneecap. The hostage situation that then follows keeps both the Schobers and the audience captive. The Schobers are on their toes because they know that any wrong move will escalate the violence, while we are on our toes because we are concerned both about the Schobers' fate *and* about our own involuntary role in assisting or encouraging the psychopaths in an unexplainable way.

Needless to say, the Schobers' situation is unlike any other hostage situation because it is utterly beyond comprehension. Throughout the film, both the Schobers and the audience ask the killers the same question: "Why are you doing this?" only to receive banal "psychobabble" in response. Paul, for instance, justifies Peter's actions by citing dysfunctional family circumstances in which Peter's mother "wanted to have her little teddy all to herself and since then, he's been a queer and a crook," while

Peter himself cries inconsolably and begs Paul to stop his recitation. Later Paul refers to Peter as "a spoiled child tormented by ennui and world weariness—weighed down by the void of existence," at the same time winking directly at the camera. The killing of Schorschi and the scenes that follow differ radically in style from the rest of the film. As is the case throughout almost the entire film, the audience is not shown the violent event itself. As a result, the audience is not provided with a source for catharsis, a conventional relief of suffering when the scene of the victim's suffering comes to an end.[7] Since the audience's horror and agony cannot find an outlet through a moment of catharsis, they become enduring, bespeaking the traumatic reality of violence.

In the scene discussed earlier, the camera stays with Paul, who is nonchalantly making sandwiches in the kitchen while the fatal shooting takes place in the living room. This is a scene intended to shift the responsibility of the events in the film to the audience, for even though the audience are "spared" an otherwise ruinous emotional investment in the sadistic events observed, they are nevertheless forced to listen to and imagine the violence, the blast of the shotgun, the engine sounds of the race cars on television, and the terrified, desperate cries of Anna and Georg screaming in unison in the background. On the visual level, then, the film refuses to aestheticize the violence, but its soundtrack expands the diegesis to involve the audience in a way that literally hurts in order to reassign the accountability of the violence to them. The next shot shows a close-up of a television screen with the car race still on, streaks of blood all over the monitor, while Paul and Peter argue offscreen about which family member should have been shot first instead of Schorschi. This is followed by a static long shot of the Schobers' living room where the killing took place, with no movement whatsoever within the frame for more than a minute, again allowing the diegesis to expand and to swallow the nondiegesis with its devastating stillness. Anna's paralysis finally ends, and she frees herself from the binds and attempts to escape together with Georg. All this time, the camera hardly moves, and the next change of camera angle does not take place for another thirteen minutes. Instead of having to watch the pain reflected on Anna's and Georg's faces, we now have to listen to it in Georg's desperate and heart-wrenching wounded animal cries that enter into us without distance, and it is with the most inward part of ourselves that we establish their affective meaning.

## *Audience Responsibility*

By expanding the diegesis to involve the audience in a most immersive way, *Funny Games* unsettles and dislocates the audience to the point of devastation. Haneke's game with the audience is to invite us to share Anna and Georg's helplessness, while compelling us to be accomplices in the violent actions that determine the Schobers' fate. With regard to *Funny Games*, Haneke himself states, "Anyone who leaves the cinema doesn't need the film, and anybody who stays does."[8] I am inclined to disagree with this statement, since it seems to me that we stay in the cinema because we hope (against hope) that things would eventually go well for the Schobers. Haneke, in fact, does give us (torments us with?) crumbs of hope: when first Schorschi and then Anna manage to escape, only to be caught again quickly afterward; when the damaged cell phone suddenly gets a signal; or when, toward the end of the film, Anna manages to snatch the shotgun from Peter and shoot him at close range.

Elsewhere I have argued that it is precisely the empathic sharing of fear and helplessness that is the key to understanding the violence depicted in *Funny Games* not as an innate part of life but as inconsolable. It might even be said that we have no choice but to stay with the Schobers and the killers without the "luxury" of occupying a position of safe distance, and being very aware of this entrapment all the time. David Sorfa calls this entrapment "the double bind of the engaged" that in Haneke's films characteristically becomes a matter of being a partner in crime without the means to resist: "In [Haneke's] films the spectator is put in the same position of powerlessness that many of his characters experience. Just as they cannot alter the course of their lives or their predicaments, so we cannot alter the concrete and pre-recorded inevitability of the films (however much we may wish to do so)."[9] This means that the Schobers cannot escape because their fate is overdetermined, always already happened. Their fate is overdetermined due to the way in which they have attempted to maintain their domestic boundaries and to insulate themselves from the world with their wealth, dumping the unfamiliar on the other side of the fence. What is more, the Schobers' fate is overdetermined because the film collaborates with the killers, who already know the outcome of the sadistic film-game. Therefore, even when things in the film take an unfavorable turn for the two killers, Paul can simply grab the remote control, "rewind" the scene in question, and reverse the episode to maintain the predestined course of events. But our fate in the audience is also overdetermined because of the way we have anaesthetized ourselves to emotions in everyday life (Haneke would say that we have sunk into emotional "glaciation") and sought our affective thrills in the cinema instead.

By expanding the diegesis to include the audience, *Funny Games* holds the audience accountable for their "perverse" desire to seek pleasure in violent cinema. In this connection, many critics have argued (regardless of Haneke's conscious intentions to demand responsibility and active participation from his audience) that Haneke in fact manipulates and subjugates the audiences into emotional states and intellectual conclusions that are not of their own choosing, unless it is the choice of leaving the cinema altogether or the "masochist thrill" of being made aware of the shallowness of one's spectatorial desires.[10] Haneke can also be criticized for shifting all the responsibility back to the audience without taking his own role as a filmmaker into consideration in the cruelties that the Schobers have to face. Yet the way in which Haneke muddles the distinction between the diegesis and the nondiegesis holds the audience responsible for what the Schobers experience and, in doing so, confronts the audience with their own attitudes and challenges them to either accept or change those attitudes.

It is popularly believed that, faced with the horrific scenes like those depicted in *Funny Games,* the audience tends to identify with the victims automatically. Yet by having the killers constantly looking into the camera, winking, and addressing the audience directly (with sentences like "Do you think they will have a chance? You're on their side, so who will you bet with?") Haneke denies the audience this kind of easy solution. As a result, the audience realizes that they are the observers, not the victims. Haneke's game with the audience is to make them share the Schobers' agony, while permitting them to move between the diegesis and the nondiegesis together with the psychopathic killers. This suggests that the audience functions as an accomplice to the torture of the Schobers, who cannot move between the diegesis and the nondiegesis in the ways the torturers can.[11] So even though our compassion and concern is clearly with the Schobers, we are "playing the game" on the wrong side, together with the killers, whether we like it or not. This is why the first time Paul directs his gaze to the camera and winks at us comes at the point when he makes Anna play hot and cold to find the body of the Schobers' German shepherd, as if we were part of his sadistic intrigue.

Paul's continuous acknowledgment and addressing of us in the audience is unsettling because it extends the accountability of his violent game to us. Needless to say, we do not want to have any part of what happens to the Schobers, but we are forced to, against our will. In this way, Haneke confronts the audience with their own attitudes toward violence in the media, which then becomes a question of negative emotions, such as the spectator's repulsion, shame, and guilt for being unable to stop watching what he or she no longer wants to see. Rather than the tactics of detachment or irony that made films like *A Clockwork Orange* (1971) or *Natural Born Killers* (1994) too clever for their own good, too self-reflective to be truly critical, it is precisely the "thinking through affect" that lies at the core of the ethical pursuit in Haneke's film.[12] The negative emotions that *Funny Games* evokes remind the audience of their own possibilities for suffering and pain, as well as their capacity to cause suffering and pain for others, including the act of looking at (media) violence for one's own pleasure. In Haneke's own words, "I give back to violence that which it is: pain, a violation of others."[13]

Susan Sontag wrote in *Regarding the Pain of Others* that "our failure is one of imagination, of empathy"; we have failed to hold the reality of violence in mind because of the steady flow of acceptable ("entertaining") violence in films and mass media in general.[14] However, it is not the quantity of violence that anaesthetizes us to it but the passivity with which violence is consumed. Haneke himself sees his film as a polemical statement against the "taking-by-surprise-before-one-can-think" cinema and the way in which it renders the audience passive.[15] But if one asks which audience reaction would then be desirable, it would seem too easy a solution to answer with empathy after all, since "so far as we feel [empathy], we feel we are not accomplices to what caused the pain."[16] As has been stated throughout this essay, in *Funny Games* we are held to be accomplices to what causes the Schobers' suffering: in response to Anna and Georg's pleading with Peter and Paul to put an end to the torture of the whole family by killing them, Paul states that losing control over the game would spoil the pleasure for everyone, since "we are still under feature length." Addressing the audience directly, he continues: "Is it enough already? You want a proper ending with plausible development, don't you?" The Schobers' suffering does not stop as long as there is an audience willing to keep watching. This is why there are negative emotions involved in watching *Funny Games:* we really are responsible for the Schobers' torment whether or not we intend to be. Or better, the Schobers' torment is a game that is played out for our "entertainment" only, a statement that is made even more explicit in Haneke's own 2007 U.S. remake of the film.

In this sense, Haneke's film is a cinematic version of the philosophical riddle of a tree falling in a forest, leading not only to a heightened sense of being an accomplice on the part of the audience but also to asking questions regarding the audience's responsibility, the obligation to think about what it means to look at violent imagery and the pain of others and the capacity to understand the absurdity, randomness, and brutality that the violent images actually show. *Funny Games* is meant to lead to reflection, to catch the audience looking in order to make them conscious of their own look. By establishing an interconnection between the diegesis and the nondiegesis, the film creates an "ethical space" (a term coined by Roger Poole in *Towards Deep Subjectivity*) where the audience is held as an accomplice to a representation of violence that they do not even want to see. This includes a consciousness of the (unseen) conditions of apprehending the film in general and of the (problematic) pleasure involved in the process of looking at violent images. The audience position in *Funny Games,* then, is of necessity ethically charged, since this consciousness cannot arise without simultaneously revealing moral values with regard to (media) violence.[17]

## *Notes*

1. Ed S. Tan, *Emotion and the Structure of Narrative Film: Film as an Emotion Machine* (Mahwah, NJ: Lawrence Erlbaum Associates, 1996), 55.

2. Jürgen Felix and Marcus Stiglegger, "Austrian Psycho Killers and Home Invaders: The Horror-Thrillers *Angst* and *Funny Games,*" in *Fear without Frontiers: Horror Cinema across the Globe,* ed. Steven Jay Schneider (Surrey: FAB Press, 2003), 175.

3. Carl Plantinga, "The Scene of Empathy and the Human Face on Film," in *Passionate Views: Film, Cognition, and Emotion,* ed. Carl Plantinga and Greg M. Smith (Baltimore: Johns Hopkins University Press, 1999), 239.

4. The tracks are titled "Bonehead" and "Hellraiser" from the album *Torture Garden,* released by Zorn's band Naked City in 1989.

5. Tarja Laine, "Empathy, Sympathy, and the Philosophy of Horror in Kubrick's *The Shining," Film and Philosophy,* special edition on Horror (2001): 84.

6. Brian Price, "Pain and the Limits of Representation," *Framework* 47, no. 2 (2006): 25.

7. Yet, as Brian Price points out, this kind of catharsis "ultimately works in the service of order; one that configures violence and someone else's pain in the service of . . . entertainment." Ibid., 28.

8. Quoted in Richard Falcon, "The Discreet Harm of the Bourgeoisie," *Sight and Sound* 8, no. 5 (1998): 10–12.

9. David Sorfa, "Uneasy Domesticity in the Films of Michael Haneke," *Studies in European Cinema* 3, no. 2 (2006): 94.

10. Amos Vogel, "Of Nonexisting Continents: The Cinema of Michael Haneke," *Film Comment* 32, no. 4 (1996): 75; Sorfa, "Uneasy Domesticity," 96.

11. Ibid., 98.

12. For Haneke, the goal in *Funny Games* was indeed a kind of "counter-program" to *Natural Born Killers:*

> In my view, Oliver Stone's film, and I use it only as example, is the attempt to use a fascist aesthetic to achieve an anti-fascist goal, and this doesn't work. What is accomplished is something the opposite, since what is produced is something like a cult film where the montage style complements the violence represented and presents it largely in a positive light. It might be argued that *Natural Born Killers* makes the violent image alluring while allowing no space for the viewer. I feel this would be very difficult to argue about *Funny Games. Benny's Video* and *Funny Games* are different kinds of obscenity, in the sense that I intended a slap in the face and a provocation.

Haneke quoted in Christopher Sharrett, "The World That Is Known: An Interview with Michael Haneke," *Kinoeye* 4, no. 1 (2004), www.kinoeye.org/04/01/interview01.php (accessed August 21, 2007).

13. Haneke quoted in Adam Minns, "*Funny Games,*" www.filmfestivals.com/cannes97/cfilmd17.htm (accessed August 18, 2007).

14. Susan Sontag, *Regarding the Pain of Others* (New York: Farrar, Straus, and Giroux, 2003), 8.

15. Haneke quoted in Vogel, "Of Nonexisting Continents," 73.

16. Sontag, "Pain of Others," 102.

17. Many thanks to Wim Staat and Dan Hassler-Forest.

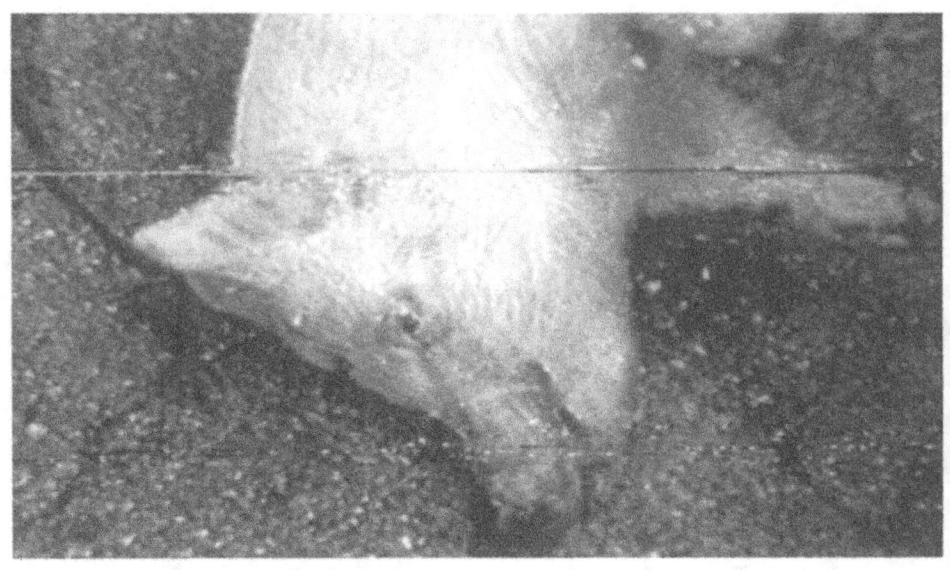
*Benny's Video* (1992): The death of a pig.

Michael Lawrence

# Haneke's Stable
## The Death of an Animal and the Figuration of the Human

> I never said all actors are cattle; what I said was all actors should be *treated* like cattle.
> —Alfred Hitchcock

Michael Haneke has often described his films as a "protest" against mainstream Hollywood cinema.[1] One of the ways his work differs from Hollywood cinema is in its approach to violence. Haneke says: "The society we live in is drenched in violence. I represent it on the screen because I am afraid of it, and I think it is important that we should reflect on it."[2] The representation of violence in Haneke's cinema, however, largely takes place *off*, rather than *on,* the screen: consider, for example, the killing of the teenage girl in *Benny's Video* or the shooting of the son in *Funny Games*. Mattias Frey has suggested that a central aspect of Haneke's work is "the denial of visual access to acts of violence."[3] Similarly, Brigitte Peucker notes how "Haneke's famously ascetic cinema refuses the choreography of violence, the special effects and other aestheticizing means than render extreme violence cinematically pleasurable."[4] Haneke says: "The question isn't 'how do I show violence?' but rather 'how do I show the spectator his position vis-à-vis violence and its representation?'"[5] The difference or distance *between* "violence and its representation," however, is frequently collapsed in Haneke's cinema, when animals are shown being killed. His most widely seen films present scenes in which animals are killed, often (though not always) onscreen, and usually involving real animal death events. Regina Berecca has suggested that death provides a "structural principle" that separates experience from the representation of experience.[6] I wish here to examine how the real deaths of animals in Haneke's cinema function as "representations" of the deaths of animals in his films' fictional worlds.

Haneke's representation of animal death is an index of his cinema's difference from Hollywood. It is predominantly in films produced outside the United States that we watch real animals being killed.[7] The American Humane Association has, since 1940, sought to ensure that "no animals were harmed" during the making of feature films.[8] This famous disclaimer, Akira Mizuta Lippit has suggested, "reveals a totemic anxiety, one that surpasses the humanitarian concern for animals as living creatures and exposes a unique unease with the death of the animal as spectacle and as such."[9] Whereas Hollywood generally avoids showing violence to animals, it does however frequently show violence done to human bodies. In comparing Haneke to mainstream cinema, the presentation of human violence and animal death is reversed. It would seem that one of the ways Haneke wishes to "show the spectator his position vis-à-vis violence and its representation" is by denying access to the aestheticized spectacle of human violence, and by instead showing images of real animal death. Haneke writes:

The boundary between the real existence and its representation has been hard for the viewer to discern from the outset, and it is precisely this which has given film its fascination. The oscillation between the disconcerting feeling of being involved in something genuinely happening now, and the emotional security of seeing the depiction of an artificially created reality, was indeed what first encouraged development of cinema.[10]

Real animal death events in Haneke's films are disconcerting precisely because they show "something genuinely happening" (despite their position within carefully and "artificially created [realities]") and thus obliterate the boundary between "real existence" and "representation."

In this essay I consider scenes depicting real animal death in several of Haneke's films in relation to these films' representation of, their figuration of, the human. By focusing on the presence of real animals and real actors in the presentation of Haneke's fictional worlds, we confront the difference in representing diegetic animal and human subjects in films. Animals are killed *in* (though not always *for*) these films, which present themselves as serious examinations of alienation, violence, and death characterized by a humanist perspective. Haneke says: "I always try in all my films to be humanist, shall we say, because I think if you are truly and seriously interested in art, you can't be otherwise. It's a necessary condition."[11] How, then, does the presentation of real animal death events contribute to the films' humanist project?

Violent animal death in Haneke's films often functions in an overdetermined relation with the deaths of fictional human characters. While the animals in Haneke's films are often killed "for real," however, the humans in these films are not presented in a conventional realist mode. The figuration of the human in Haneke's cinema thus stands in a strangely inverse relationship to the representation of animals. Whereas mainstream cinema avoids showing violence to animals (even simulations of this) and is typically dedicated to realist human characterization, Haneke's cinema repeatedly shows real violence to animals (as well as simulations of this) and is on the whole disinterested in realist human characterization. Here, I concentrate on two strategies that have determined Haneke's figuration of the human across his films: the repeated use of the same name for his fictional characters and the repeated use of the same actors in his films. As is well known, Haneke prefers to give the protagonists of his films the same names: Ann (or Anna), Georg (or George), Eva (or Evi), Benny. Their surnames are also the same: Schober (in several of the German-language films) and Laurent (in the French-language films). In *Time of the Wolf* eight of the cast members (the majority of the speaking parts) had appeared in either *Code Unknown*, *The Piano Teacher,* or his earlier German-language films. I am interested in how these films, through their use of animals and humans, challenge a set of assumptions about the filmic representation of both the animal *and* the human. How might the presentation of real animal death events in these films make problematic our "position vis-à-vis violence and its representation"? What, if anything, might connect the use of "disposable" animal subjects to depict animal death in fictional narratives and the reusing of names and actors to depict allegorical human characters?[12]

The word "stable" originally referred to a barnlike building for farm animals such as cattle and goats, then to a building in which horses were kept. The word later referred to the group of horses belonging to a particular stable (specifically racehorses), then to groups (of persons) associated with establishments such as boxing clubs. It is in this way that the word is used to refer to a group of actors associated either with a studio or a particular director. This essay seeks to reflect on Haneke's recourse to both real stables (by which I mean his use of real animals, particularly farm animals and livestock) and his metaphorical stable (by which I mean the actors who he repeatedly reuses in his films). I shall first consider some theoretical responses to the filmic representation of the animal death event, then address Haneke's presentation of animal death before reflecting on his figuration of the human.

## *The Death of an Animal*

In "Death Every Afternoon" André Bazin suggests that the spectacle of death (in this case, the death of a bull in Pierre Braunberger's 1951 documentary *The Bullfight*) provides a way to understand "cinematic specificity."[13] Cinema has the "exorbitant privilege" of being able to repeat time, including the time of death, "the unique moment par excellence," "the absolute negation of objective time, the qualitative instant in its purest form."[14] Because death only takes place once, the cinematic representation of real death is, according to Bazin, a metaphysical obscenity. Cinema can re-present the "elusive passage" from one state (life) to another (death); its "exorbitant privilege," then, is this power to manipulate reality itself as material, including death's absolute, irrevocable negation of material being.

Of the animal death events presented in nondocumentary cinema, the killing of a large number of wild rabbits during the hunting sequence in Jean Renoir's *Rules of the Game* (1939) is perhaps the most famous. Raymond Durgnat has called this sequence "the massacre of the rabbits."[15] The death of André Jurieu, the pilot at the center of the plot, is, according to Durgnat, "prefigured" by the rabbits' death.[16] The film utilizes the real deaths of animals before presenting the death of a fictional human character. Vivian Sobchack has suggested that since "it is a real rabbit that we see die in the service of the narrative and *for* the fiction," the rabbit, unlike Jurieu, "is not perceived by us solely as a character in the narrative."[17] The rabbits' death "violently, abruptly, punctuates fictional space with documentary space," it "momentarily fractures the classical coherence of the film's narrative representation, introducing the off-screen and unrepresented space in which the viewer lives, acts, and makes distinctions as an ethical social being."[18] The representation of the rabbits' death is a presentation of real (documentary) death, whereas the representation of Jurieu's death remains just that, a (fictional) representation.[19]

Jonathan Burt, however, has argued that the animal image in film is *always* "a form of rupture in the field of representation."[20] Watching the animal, Burt suggests, our attention "is constantly drawn beyond the image and, in that sense, beyond the aesthetic and semiotic framework of the film."[21] The animal image "[points] beyond its significance on screen to questions about its general treatment or fate in terms of welfare."[22] The film animal is, for Burt, always a doubled animal, diegetic and documentary, fictional and real. Burt suggests that "ethical questions arise most severely at the point at which the line between the fictitious and the *real* animal is most difficult to draw."[23] The nonsimulated death of a film animal only intensifies the original rupturing that its presence invariably produces. The death of the animal is the point at which the difference or distance between the fictitious animal and the real animal disappears, along with the animal itself. Lippit has suggested that "documentary moments of animal death in narrative films" present animals that are "parergonal, never fully inside nor outside the diegesis but against, beside, and in addition to it."[24]

The death of the animal is, then, the end of figurative representation. It is the point at which the fictional figuration is ruptured by documentary space (and time). The film's "aesthetic and semiotic framework" is, if only momentarily, rent. Representation becomes presentation. The death of the animal is the ultimate film animal event. An animal cannot understand that it represents a fictional animal, and its death in and for the film paradoxically reminds us of the animal's singular and material being at the very moment of the being's demise. It furthermore presents a degree of documentary actuality that threatens the efficacy of the animal's (and its death's) metaphorical or rhetorical function in the narrative figuration of reality. In its death, the film animal paradoxically figures the destruction of the difference (the distance) between reality and the representation of reality. Bazin says: "I cannot repeat a single moment of my life, but cinema can repeat any one of these moments indefinitely before my eyes. If it is true that for consciousness no moment is equal to any other, there is one on which the fundamental difference converges, and that is the moment of death. For every creature, death is the unique moment par excellence."[25] If a film animal always points toward its own life and welfare outside the framework of the film in which it appears, then the death of a film animal instantiates the ending of the animal's life *outside* the film, its relation to the "'elsewhere' where it lived its . . . life," *inside* the film's fictional framework.[26]

Animal death events in films need not be as clearly situated in diegetic space as the massacre of the rabbits in Renoir's film. *Strike* (Sergei Eisenstein, Soviet Union, 1925) uses images of real animal death as part of its experiment with intellectual montage. Documentary footage of bulls being killed in an abattoir punctuates the closing sequence, which depicts the massacre of hundreds of workers. Eisenstein wrote: "I wanted to take the terror of the finale to a high point. The most horrible thing in the representation of blood is blood itself. In the representation of death—death itself."[27] Anne Nesbet suggests that as "the real blood of the slaughterhouse is brought in to supplement the inadequate realness of the acted massacre, . . . tenor and vehicle seem turned almost inside out."[28] David Bordwell calls this "a literal slaughter in an abstract time and space, a figurative slaughter in the story world."[29] However, Eisenstein later considered this sequence a "hilarious failure": the slaughter imagery demonstrated for him the "inevitably class-based effectiveness" of montage, how "a particular stimulant is capable of provoking a particular reaction (effect) only from an audience of a particular class character." For example, "On a peasant, used to slaughtering his own cattle," Eisenstein reflected, "there will be no effect at all."[30] Eisenstein's comments demonstrate that the presentation of "death itself" within the "representation of death," through the presentation of scenes showing animal death within a sequence depicting human death, depends upon the human audience's "class character," their familiarity with the spectacle of animal death. Nesbet suggests that the inclusion of real animal death in *Strike* removes the potential power of the simulation of human death by emphasizing that it is mere simulation. Eisenstein notes that such images have no figural capacity if they do not shock the intended audience; familiarity with animal violence reduces its potential power. As we shall see, the efficacy of images showing real animal death is dependent upon the audiences' ordinary, everyday experience. Haneke has called the audience (and, indeed, the focus) of his films "die Überflussgesellschaft" (the abundance society); he does not present this audience with reconstructions of contemporary historical catastrophes, but he nevertheless deploys the spectacle of real animal death throughout his work.[31]

Bourgeois alienation from animal death is the basis for Georges Bataille's interest in the abattoir. When he included in the sixth issue of his journal *Documents* a series of photographs taken by Eli Lotar at the La Villette slaughterhouse, he was deliberately provoking a particular class that was completely alienated from industrialized animal slaughter. In the accompanying dictionary entry "Abattoir," Bataille wrote: "Nowadays the slaughterhouse is cursed and quarantined like a boat with cholera aboard. . . . The victims of this curse are neither the butchers nor the animals, but those fine folk who have reached the point of not being able to stand their own unseemliness, an unseemliness corresponding in fact to a pathological need for cleanliness."[32] For Bataille, these photographs' shock value depends upon bourgeois alienation from industrialized animal slaughter but also upon their disavowal of the fact of death in their everyday experience as consumers.

Discussing *The Blood of the Beasts*, a documentary filmed at the La Villette abattoir in Paris by Georges Franju in 1949, Siegfried Kracauer compared shots of calves' heads in the film to the "litter of tortured human bodies" in films about Nazi concentration camps: "It would be preposterous to assume that these unbearably lurid pictures were intended to preach the gospel of vegetarianism; nor can they possibly be branded as an attempt to satisfy the dark desire for scenes of destruction."[33] These images "beckon the spectator to take them in and thus incorporate into his memory the real face of things too dreadful to be beheld in reality"; in "experiencing" these images (of slaughterhouses or concentration camps), "we redeem horror from its invisibility behind the veils of panic and imagination."[34] For Kracauer, then, the "redemptive" power of such images is due to their analogous relationship with historical trauma too dreadful to behold.[35] While Eisenstein introduced images from abattoirs to augment his film's reconstruction of historical events, Kracauer's response establishes the association with events outside those presented by the film imaginatively, an interior "intellectual montage."

Ted Benton has described how animals slaughtered for food are "subjected to an intensified reification" in industrial and postindustrial societies: "As meat-eaters, we purchase meat as a commodity, processed, cut up, packaged, and re-named in ways which set us as consumers at a safe distance from any recognition of our purchase as the carcase of a once-sentient being."[36] The slaughter of an animal for food is, in other words, a particular kind of death event, an event the materiality of which is disavowed in the reification of animals as food. As Kenneth Clark, in his study of representations of animals in Western art, has noted: "The only aspect of animal killing that is almost entirely unillustrated is that against which there are the fewest objections, killing for food."[37] Images of animal slaughter, such as the spectacle of abattoir death deployed by Eisenstein and Bataille, provide, then, a particularly complex kind of rupturing, of both an aesthetic tradition and slaughter's physical and psychical sequestration. The image of an animal being slaughtered for food, the presentation of "the qualitative instant in its purest form" (Bazin), individualizes this particular animal at the moment of its death, despite industrialization's deindividualizing of animals as livestock. The violence of its death is thus matched by the violence whereby we are reminded that the production of meat consists of discrete death events, rather than a reified transformation of animals into food.[38]

When a fiction film, aimed at a bourgeois Western audience, includes sequences showing real animals being killed for food (in abattoirs, for example, or on farms), then a number of rupturing processes take place simultaneously. Fictional representation is ruptured by documentary presentation, and the reification of the animal within industrialized meat production is ruptured by the documentary presentation of an individual animal death event. The presentation of real animal death—"death itself"—in films that attempt to examine seriously and responsibly violence and death in contemporary society (and the consumption of images of violence and death) is, as we shall see, a particularly problematic strategy.

Violence to animals is presented in Haneke's films in close-up, while violence to humans usually takes place offscreen. Real animal slaughter in Haneke's cinema is, furthermore, usually functioning in overdetermined figural relationships with simulated violence done to humans, and particularly to "paranoid-hygienic" bourgeois subjects. As will be suggested, Haneke's repeated presentation of real animal death is interesting precisely because of the relationship it produces between the documentary presentation of the animal at the moment of its death (at which point it is made individual, particular) and the allegorical representation of the bourgeois subject, in which human characters are deindividualized (and thus made "general"). At this point, however, I wish to consider three real animal death events from Haneke's cinema.

## *Haneke's Animals*

*Benny's Video* begins with a video image showing a pig being led out into a yard. The handheld image insists on the presence of a living body operating the camera: this is Benny's video. The video image also denotes a certain "live-ness"; this is happening "now." A man (Benny's father) looks into the camera and gestures toward the momentarily offscreen pig, as if to direct the filmmaker to focus on the event about to take place. A few seconds after the pig has been stunned with a bolt pistol, the image freezes. This event, this death, is not taking place (being recorded) in a diegetic present after all. This event has already taken place, and it is the video recording of this event that is being watched in the present. When the image of the pig pauses, freezes, it is as if the film itself had been suddenly stunned; the live-ness of this image is destroyed along with the pig. At the precise moment this pig is killed, it is revealed to be an image of a pig, produced by a fictional character, in the past. At the same time, it is an image produced by a real director in which his fictional characters are shown observing (and recording) the death of this pig. The video is being made, as a souvenir perhaps, of this particular weekend spent away from the city in the countryside, but it also provides Benny with a more authentic representation of violence than he is able to find in the action cinema he habitually watches on video, which he knows is simulated with "plastic and ketchup." The documentary reality of the pig's death is immediately contained (within the film) within the video recording belonging to Benny. It is impossible, however, to tell whether Arno Frisch, who plays Benny, actually recorded the video himself. While the pig's death functions to efface the distance between an event and its representation, the freezing (and subsequent rewinding and replaying) of the video image reasserts this difference. The replaying emphasizes the video recording's capacity to reanimate an image of the pig after the pig's death, to reverse and repeat the moment of its death, and to re-present the spectacle in slow motion.

We might consider Benny's (Haneke's) morbid manipulation of the video footage showing the pig's death as an allusion to a celebrated sequence in Dziga Vertov's *Kino-Eye* (Soviet Union, 1924). A woman ("Kopuchiska's mother") is shopping for beef at a cooperative. A title informs us that "Kino-Eye" will "move time backwards," and we watch the stunning and slaughter of a cow in reverse. Nesbet has suggested that Vertov's slaughterhouse "turns time into a game—into 'child's play.'"[39] Benny's manipulation of the video, his rewinding and replaying of the pig's death, functions, *fort-da* fashion, to give him a sense of control over the image or the representation, if not (not yet) the actual event, of death.

The pig's death recorded on Benny's video prefigures, as Durgnat might say, Benny's killing of the teenage girl. Benny plays the girl the video of the pig before killing her, and he also replays for her the last section of the tape, again in slow motion. The death of the girl is also recorded by Benny's video camera, and the recording is played to Benny's parents upon their return from their weekend away. The repeated playing and replaying of, first, the video of the pig's death and, second, the video of the girl's death invites the spectator to equate the two events. While the first video shows the pig's face in close-up, the second video offers only the sounds of the girl's offscreen death. What is missing from the video recording of the pig's death, the completion of the creature's disposal—its being stuck, drained, and eviscerated and transformed into meat—is emphasized during the sequences that follow Benny's killing of the girl: he must mop up the blood that leaks from her body, and his father, we eventually learn, must cut her body into pieces to more easily dispose of her, as if she were a slaughtered animal being divided into "cuts" to eradicate any trace of the once-living creature.

The death of the pig in Haneke's film forces upon us the conflation of representation and the real. The dual status of the pig (as a pig in the fictional world and a pig in the real world) that its death forces upon us is mirrored in the film by the pig's dual status as a pig killed in the past and an image of that same pig being watched in the present. The death of the girl, however, we know to be a simulation. By prefiguring the killing of the girl with the killing of the pig, Haneke's film brings the real (the death of the pig) into an overdetermined narrative relationship with a simulation of reality (the death of the girl). *Benny's Video* wishes us to consider the relationship between the two deaths within its fictional narrative, and to contemplate the possible connections between Benny's fascination with his video and his killing of the girl. However, the inclusion of documentary footage showing real animal death ruptures the coherence of the fictional narrative representation.[40]

Toward the end of *Time of the Wolf*, a hypothetical science-fiction narrative concerned with the possibility of hospitality in postcatastrophic circumstances, a horse is shot to provide food for the group of survivors camping at the station.[41] At the beginning of the film, Georges Laurent (Daniel Duval) is shot by the father of a family who have occupied the Laurents' chalet. The film cuts abruptly to Anne Laurent's face, on which Georges's blood has splashed; Georges's body is not shown. In contrast, after the horse is shot and collapses to the ground, the film cuts to a close-up of the horse's head, and a knife is plunged into its throat. (Two horses were used to create this sequence; the first horse was trained to fall to the ground in response to the gunfire; the second horse was an abattoir horse, whose death was recorded for inclusion in Haneke's film.) The documentary truthfulness of the second shot/horse reaches back and envelops the first shot/horse. This scene takes place immediately after Anne has unsuccessfully sought justice for her husband's death and informed the leaders that she has recognized her husband's killer among the group. The death of the horse, then, takes place at the precise moment the death of a fictional character is being discussed. The violent death of the horse, the sight of which appears to exacerbate Anne's frustration and grief, is a spectacle of documentary violence within Haneke's most allegorical work and functions as an instance of death in a narrative in which it remains unclear how many humans have died as a result of the unspecified catastrophe. The death of the horse, however, by momentarily puncturing the fiction with documentary time, rends the allegorical texture of the film by cutting out of the film's hypothetical world and into the real world of the horse's life and death.

*Caché* includes a sequence representing a nightmare. Georges Laurent (Daniel Auteuil) dreams of the farmhouse where he grew up. In the dream, Majid, the son of Georges's parents' Algerian worker, decapitates a rooster. We later learn that Georges tricked Majid into killing the bird so that his parents would send him away. If the dual (documentary-fictional) status of the pig in *Benny's Video* was mirrored by its appearing as a video image within the fiction of the film, the dual status of the rooster in *Caché* is mirrored by its appearing as a dream image based on a character's memory of the past within the narrative. The dream builds upon this memory, however: while the headless rooster flaps about the yard, Majid, his face covered in the bird's blood, approaches Georges, who backs away. In the unfolding logic of this dream, then, the death of the rooster putatively prefigures the violence Majid would inflict upon Georges, as if the dream of Haneke's protagonist operates according to the earlier narrative balancing of animal death and human death that we saw in *Benny's Video*. The dream sequence presents a series of point-of-view shots, the first shot of Majid being from the rooster's perspective on the chopping block, the second being from Georges's perspective several feet away. Georges is further connected to the dream rooster by the overlapping of the sound of the rooster flapping by the breathing of the dreaming Georges. However, as *Caché* continues, it is the adult Majid's violent death—staged, like the dream rooster's, as a spectacle before Georges—that balances the real death of the film bird with a simulated death of a fictional human. And the power of the scene in which Majid cuts his throat is partly due to its breaking with Haneke's conventional representation of human death. The blood that sprays across the walls of Majid's flat evokes the blood that spurts from the rooster's neck in Georges's dream. The death of the rooster in the dream sequence functions to provide the spectator with a false sense of security concerning the film's representation of violence, particularly for those spectators familiar with Haneke's earlier films (and perhaps *Benny's Video* most of all).

The relationship between the dream and its source (events in Georges's childhood) is reproduced in the film's relationship to real historical events that took place in Paris in October 1961.[42] While Georges admits he tricked Majid into killing the rooster when they were children, his dream builds on that event and presents Majid attacking Georges with the axe. *Caché* makes explicit reference to the deaths of Algerians at the hands of the police and builds its allegorical investigation of denial and responsibility around that historically specific event. The dream of the protagonist, then, which presents the spectator with the real death of a rooster, encloses this death event within two distinct allegorical frameworks, Georges's dream and Haneke's film. The death of the rooster presents a spectacle of real death in the place of any simulation or reconstruction of the events of October 1961. Eisenstein, we recall, used scenes of animal slaughter to confront the spectator with "real death" during his (composite) simulation or reconstruction of real historical events. Haneke's presentation of the rooster's death, as a documentary moment in an allegorical film, links the events of the narrative (including Majid's suicide, which is graphically linked to the rooster's death) to the real deaths of Algerians in October 1961; the death of the rooster in the film dream anchors *Caché* in the real world in which it was made, and to which it refers at an allegorical level.

In these three films, Haneke presents the death of an animal not as part of an investigation of the lives of animals nor as part of a realist project but as part of an allegorical representation of bourgeois alienation from, and responsibility for, *human* others. The deaths of the animals in these film fictions, however, because of the presentation of real animal death to figure these events, exceed their metaphorical function as a result of the spectacle of their incontrovertible and material deaths. The relationship between the world in which these films circulate and the fictional worlds these films present is made more complicated by such moments, in which the spectator is confronted with the violence of the fictions' sudden shift into the real violence of an animal's death. However, as I shall suggest, the presentation of animal death in Haneke's films is even more significant given his particular figuration of the human.

## *Haneke's Figuration of the Human*

As I have already noted, it is widely known that Haneke repeatedly gives his characters the same names. In *The Seventh Continent, Benny's Video,* and *Funny Games,* the central couple are called Anna and Georg, and in both *The Seventh Continent* and *Benny's Video* the daughter is named Evi.[43] In *The Seventh Continent* and *Funny Games,* the surname is Schober.[44] These

*The Death of an Animal and the Figuration of the Human*

first names also return in Haneke's French-language films: the characters played by Juliette Binoche in *Code Unknown* and *Caché* and by Isabelle Huppert in *Time of the Wolf* are all named Anne Laurent, and Anne's partner in all three films is named Georges (played by Thierry Neuvic in *Code Unknown,* Daniel Auteuil in *Caché,* and Daniel Duval in *Time of the Wolf*). Children's names are also the same as those used before (Eva and Benny). The bourgeois family groups at the center of six of Haneke's films, then, are given German or French versions of the same names. This naming strategy works against the individualization that the naming of fictional characters conventionally aspires to and instead invites spectators to conceive of these characters as related to one another in important ways, as representing multiple versions of a particular type, not particular individuals at all. The naming of these characters paradoxically removes their individuality and threatens their particularity, their individual singularity. Anna/Anne and Georg/Georges signify allegorically: these names suggest incarnations or reincarnations rather than distinct fictional human individuals realistically represented in consecutive films. Haneke has suggested that the killers in *Funny Games,* who refer to one another by a variety of names, "really don't have names" and "in a way . . . aren't characters at all."[45] I would suggest that the numerous Schobers and Laurents, and other "characters" in Haneke's cinema, are similarly not characters at all.

The naming of the bourgeois subjects in Haneke's films presents a deliberate nondifferentiation of individuals of a particular class character. "Anne Laurent" names separate and potentially multiple instances of a particular species (or subspecies) only, and it is the similarities rather than the difference between these separate instances that this name, and this kind of naming, emphasizes. In both *Code Unknown* and *Caché,* Anne Laurent's blonde friend is played by Nathalie Richard and is named Mathilde. It is as if the "second" Mathilde were simply a clone, another version or incarnation of, the "first" Mathilde. Then again, neither of the two Mathildes could properly be said to be an (or the) "original" Mathilde; each one is only an allegorical representation, a type, and with Haneke's figuration of the human the historically and culturally specific class or group that is the original or base subject is variously incarnated (but never realistically presented) by actors and actresses. The effect of Haneke's naming strategy is compounded further by his repeated use of the same actors.

Haneke has reused actors in a deliberate fashion throughout his career: Ulriche Mühe, Benny's father in *Benny's Video,* also plays the father in *Funny Games* and K. in Haneke's adaptation of Kafka's *The Castle;* Arno

Frisch, Benny in *Benny's Video*, also plays one of the killers in *Funny Games;* Susanne Lothar, the mother in *Funny Games,* is also in *The Castle, The Piano Teacher,* and *The White Ribbon;* and Frank Giering appears in both *Funny Games* and *The Castle.* Actors also feature repeatedly in minor roles throughout Haneke's cinema: Udo Samel is in *Variation, The Rebellion, The Seventh Continent, 71 Fragments,* and *The Piano Teacher* (he is also the narrator of *The Castle*); Branko Samarowsky is in *The Rebellion, 71 Fragments, The Castle,* and *Time of the Wolf;* and Georg Friedrich is in *71 Fragments, The Piano Teacher, The Seventh Continent,* and *Time of the Wolf.* In addition to Isabelle Huppert, Juliette Binoche, and Nathalie Richard, many actors have acted repeatedly in Haneke's French-language films: Maurice Bénichou in *Code Unknown, Time of the Wolf,* and *Caché;* Annie Girardot in *The Piano Teacher* and *Caché;* Luminata Ghiorghiu in *Code Unknown* and *Time of the Wolf;* Florence Loiret-Caille in *Code Unknown* and *Time of the Wolf;* Costel Cascavel in *Code Unknown* and *Time of the Wolf;* Daniel Duval in *Time of the Wolf* and *Caché;* Walid Akfir in *Code Unknown* and *Caché;* Aïssa Maïga in *Code Unknown* and *Caché;* and Laurent Suire briefly as a policeman in both *Code Unknown* and *Caché.*

While directors often work with the same actors or group of actors, Haneke's strategy seems a particularly deliberate and self-conscious use of actors to represent fictional human characters in his films, particularly when this is considered alongside his naming strategy. Given he is an admirer of Robert Bresson, who was resolutely opposed to using his "models" more than once, Haneke's use of the same lead actors in successive films, and of the same actors to play minor roles, is striking.[46] The reappearance of the same actors emphasizes the films' collective identity as an oeuvre but also complicates the singular identity of the various human subjects in these films. And while Haneke's use of recognizable art cinema faces in his French-language films is related to the funding of his projects, there are important aspects to his casting practice that exceed the effects produced by the participation in his films of particular stars such as Huppert, Binoche, Béatrice Dalle, or Daniel Auteuil. In fact, the presence of certain stars in his films paradoxically works to emphasize his films' general and deliberate deindividualization of the human; that both Huppert and Binoche, or both Duval and Auteuil, can play "Anne Laurent" or "Georges Laurent," or that Binoche can play "Anne Laurent" *twice,* suggests that the character exceeds any particular performance, that the character cannot be identified with a single actor (or a single performance by an actor), and that the actor is simply standing in for, providing the human form necessary to produce, an image of a particular kind of a human type (rather than a particularized fictional human character). The recognizable actor simply emphasizes the strange lack of particularity that constitutes these characters. The repeated use of less well known actors in Haneke's cinema also contributes to the films' unique figuration of the human. The repeated use of Ulrich Mühe and Arno Frisch in *Benny's Video* and *Funny Games,* or Maurice Bénichou and Walid Akfir in *Code Unknown* and *Caché*, like the use of Nathalie Richard mentioned earlier, threatens the singularity produced by a particular screen performance and ruptures the hermetic diegetic identity of the individual films. This strategy insists on each film's dependence upon—and documentation of—the bodily labor of particular actors. But the results of Haneke's naming and casting strategies, I suggest, work in the opposite direction to the effects produced by his presentation of animals' bodily deaths, even though both direct the spectator toward the real living bodies used in the production of the film. Where scenes of real animal death emphasize the material particularity of the individual animal, Haneke's allegorical figuration of the human, through the use of real human actors, emphasizes the generality of the characters. In other words, Haneke's cinema presents the human as an animal. Haneke presents the human subject, both the white bourgeois subject and its various others, in specific environmental contexts, specifically (but not always) the modern metropolis, in a way that might be compared with the wildlife documentary's presentation of animal subjects in their environments. In wildlife films, sequences showing different animals of the same species are carefully edited together to represent one "narrative" subject, one that is often given a name by the film and one that functions as an embodiment of the behavior and experience of the animal *as a species* rather than of any real individual and historical animal.[47] Haneke's cinema repeatedly presents studies of various human types, gives them the same names (in stark violation of the convention of naming characters in nonserial cinema), and, by preventing us from seeing them as realistic fictional individuals, instead encourages us to attend to their behavior as embodying, allegorizing, particular socially distinct and discrete groups or classes.

## *The Death of an Animal and the Figuration of the Human*

Lippit refers to "the singularity ascribed to humanity and the multiplicity that is said to determine animality"; to violate the singularity of a human subject is to force it to become multiple, like an animal. The killing of an animal, on the other hand, grants it singularity, "allowing it to become unique, to become-human."[48] The reusing of names and actors in Haneke's cinema, I would suggest, constitutes a deliberate violation of conventional fictional figurations of human singularity or individuality. Allegorical figuration presents individuals as general types. The repeated use of the same names and the same actors gives Haneke's fictional characters a strangely inhuman status; these subjects are not exactly singular and therefore not quite human. Haneke's humanist project, then, proceeds by deliberately representing allegorical incarnations of human types rather than individualized human characters.[49]

The presentation of real animal death in Haneke's cinema can be usefully contrasted with the presentation of human life. It is through death that the animal ruptures the fiction with documentary actuality. In its death, the animal moves from the general to the particular, from "the animal" to "an" or "this" animal or rather "the animal that was killed, once." With Haneke's actors it is the other way around: from the particular to the general. While the disposing of an animal can only take place once, the figuration of the human in this cinema insists on the reusable: the reusable name, the reusable actor, and the repetition of this reuse itself as an aesthetic technique. The actors move *from* particularity and actuality *to* (first) fictionality and (second) generality in ways that the animals (who cannot act) cannot. The tension between the general and the particular is central in Haneke's allegorical cinema. The use of animal death, on the other hand, anchors these nonrealist and allegorical cinematic representations in the real world to which they are singularly (self-consciously) stylized responses.

The animals that die in Haneke's films have (usually) also died in the real world. The real human losses presented by the news images of Bosnians in Sarajevo (incorporated in *Benny's Video*) or Iraqis (*Caché*) function as traces of an historical and material reality within their explicitly allegorical frameworks. Haneke says: "I am most concerned with television as the key symbol primarily of the media representation of violence, and more generally of a greater crisis, which I see as our collective loss of reality and social disorientation. Alienation is a very complex problem, but television is certainly implicated in it."[50] The death events that are shown (but rarely watched) on the television screens in Haneke's films, like the animal death events presented (on the whole) in close-up, provide a disconcerting connection between the fictions being presented *by* the film and the violence that is "genuinely happening" (or has really happened) *in* the world in which these films circulate.

Haneke has called the "censorious reaction" to scenes showing real animal death in his films "hypocritical," "especially from carnivores."[51] It is perhaps due to our alienation from the spectacle and reality of animal slaughter, which is in sharp contrast to the diet of images of human violence provided by twenty-four-hour news media (to which we have become habituated), that the instances of real animal death in Haneke's films function so disconcertingly. By violently puncturing their aestheticized and hypothetical representation of humans living in the world with the documentary presentation of real animals leaving the world, Haneke's films strategically avoid replicating or reproducing the alienation with which they are concerned, and indeed rupture the reification and sequestration of animal death in postindustrial society. Documentary animal death in Haneke's films thus functions as a conduit that connects his allegorical figuration of the human to an historical, and material, violent real.

## Notes

1. See, for example, Richard Porton, "Collective Guilt and Individual Responsibility: An Interview with Michael Haneke," *Cineaste* 31, no. 1 (2005): 50–51.

2. Haneke quoted in Karen Badt, "Family Is Hell and So Is the World: Talking to Michael Haneke at Cannes 2005," *Bright Lights Film Journal* 50 (November 2005), www.brightlightsfilm.com/50/hanekeiv.htm (accessed May 28, 2008).

3. Mattias Frey, "Michael Haneke," *Senses of Cinema* (August 2003), www.sensesofcinema.com/contents/directors/03/haneke.html (accessed May 28, 2008).

4. Brigitte Peucker, *The Material Image: Art and the Real in Film* (Palo Alto, CA: Stanford University Press, 2007), 132.

5. Frey, "Michael Haneke."

6. Regina Berecca, "Writing as Voodoo: Sorcery, Hysteria, and Art," in *Death and Representation,* ed. Sarah Webster Godwin and Elisabeth Bronfen (Baltimore: Johns Hopkins University Press, 1993), 174. Elisabeth Bronfen has called death "the one privileged moment of the absolutely real, of true, non-semiotic materiality as de-materialising or de-materialised body; it is a failure of the tropic." Bronfen, *Over Her Dead Body: Death, Femininity, and the Aesthetic* (London: Routledge, 1992), 54.

7. Notable examples of postwar fiction films that include scenes of real animal death include *Weekend* (Jean-Luc Godard, France, 1967), *Mouchette* (Robert Bresson, France, 1967), *Viva la Muerte* (Fernando Arrabal, France, 1971), *Touki Bouki* (Djibril Diop Mambéty, Senegal, 1973), *Moses and Aron* (Jean-Marie Straub and Danièle Huillet, West Germany, 1975), *The Tree of Wooden Clogs* (Ermanno Olmi, Italy, 1976), *Maîtresse* (Barbet Schroeder, France, 1976), *Insiang* (Lino Brocca, Phil-

ippines, 1976), *Padre Padrone* (Paolo and Vittorio Taviani, Italy, 1977), *In a Year of Thirteen Moons* (R. W. Fassbinder, West Germany, 1978), *Cannibal Holocaust* (Ruggero Deodato, 1980), *Japón* (Carlos Reygadas, Mexico, 2002), and *Los Muertos* (Lisandro Alonso, Argentina, 2004); documentaries include *The Blood of the Beasts* (Georges Franju, France, 1949), *Le Cochon* (Jean Eustache, France, 1970), *Our Daily Bread* (Nikoalus Geyrhalter, Germany, 2005), and *Return to Normandy* (Nicolas Philibert, France, 2007).

    8. See www.americanhumane.org/site/PageServer?pagename=pa_film (accessed May 28, 2008).

    9. Akira Mizuta Lippit, "The Death of an Animal," *Film Quarterly* 56, no. 1 (2002): 11. See also Lippit's *Electric Animal: Toward a Rhetoric of Wildlife* (Minneapolis: University of Minnesota Press, 2000), 162–97. A recent interest in "animality" is evidenced by, for example, H. Peter Steeves and Tom Regan, eds., *Animal Others: On Ethics, Ontology, and Animal Life* (New York: State University of New York Press, 1999); Steve Baker, *The Postmodern Animal* (London: Reaktion, 2000); Steve Baker, *Picturing the Beast: Animals, Identity, and Representation* (Urbana: University of Illinois Press, 2001); Nigel Rothfalls, ed., *Representing Animals* (Minneapolis: University of Minnesota Press, 2002); Cary Wolfe, ed., *Zoontologies: The Question of the Animal* (Minneapolis: University of Minnesota Press, 2003); and Giorgio Agamben, *The Open: Man and Animal,* trans. Kevin Attell (Palo Alto, CA: Stanford University Press, 2004).

    10. Michael Haneke, "Believing Not Seeing," *Sight and Sound* 7, no. 11 (1997): London Film Festival Supplement, 22.

    11. Michael Haneke, "Retour sur un Tournage," extra on *Time of the Wolf* DVD, Artificial Eye, 2003.

    12. Derek Bousé has considered the killing of animals in and for films in relation to the conception of them as "disposable subjects." See Bousé, *Wildlife Films* (Philadelphia: University of Pennsylvania Press, 2000), 42. Perhaps the most famous "disposable subject" was Topsy, New York's Coney Island's performing elephant, who was killed by electrocution before a paying audience at Luna Park in 1903 and filmed by Thomas Edison. The lemming sequence in Walt Disney's Oscar-winning "true life adventure" documentary *White Wilderness* (James Elgar, 1958) is a notorious example of filmmakers treating animals as disposable. See Richard Kilborn, *Staging the Real: Factual TV Programming in the Age of Big Brother* (Manchester: Manchester University Press, 2003), 147.

    13. André Bazin, "Death Every Afternoon," trans. Mark A. Cohen, in *Rites of Realism: Essays on Corporeal Cinema,* ed. Ivone Marguiles (Durham: Duke University Press, 2003), 29.

    14. Ibid., 30.

    15. Raymond Durgnat, *Jean Renoir (*Berkeley: University of California Press, 1974), 201. There was, Durgnat adds, "a very detailed shooting script" that took several men two months to finish: "The sequence proved astonishingly expensive, since rabbits shot in mid-course and dying are not the most obliging of extras. An enormous number of rabbits, which had first to be collected and loosed, ran the

wrong way, or were missed by the marksman, or died in a visually or dramatically unsuitable manner" (186).

16. Ibid., 206.

17. Vivian Sobchack, *Carnal Thoughts: Embodiment and Moving Image Culture* (Berkeley: University of California Press, 2004), 245.

18. Ibid., 246.

19. Seung-Hoon Jeung and Dudley Andrew describe the violent effects caused by the sudden switch between fictional and documentary space when they suggest that such images "throw the spectator outside the diegesis of a film into . . . the actual conditions of filmmaking and the problem of real rather than represented death" and "pull us across the border between language and fact, figure and event, between the inside and the outside of cinema." See Jeung and Andrew, "Grizzly Ghost: Herzog, Bazin, and the Cinematic Animal," *Screen* 49, no. 1 (2008): 6. In his consideration of violence in the cinema, William Rothman refers to the deaths of the rabbits in *The Rules of the Game* to demonstrate how "in the medium of film the distinction between fiction and nonfictions can be difficult, or impossible to draw." See Rothman, "Violence and Film," in *Violence and American Cinema,* ed. J. David Slocum, 37–46 (New York: Routledge, 2001), 41. The distinction between real and simulated violence (or death) in cinema is often organized, as is the case with Rothman's examples, around the distinction between animal and human subjects and their use in film.

20. Jonathan Burt, *Animals in Film* (London: Reaktion, 2002), 11.

21. Ibid., 12.

22. Ibid., 11.

23. Ibid., 12.

24. Lippit, "Death of an Animal," 14.

25. Bazin, "Death Every Afternoon," 29.

26. Vivian Sobchack, "Towards a Phenomenology of Nonfictional Film Experience," in *Collecting Visible Evidence,* ed. Jane M. Gaines and Michael Renov (Minneapolis: University of Minnesota Press, 1999), 246.

27. Sergei Eisenstein quoted in Anne Nesbet, *Savage Junctures: Eisenstein and the Shape of Thinking* (New York: I. B. Tauris, 2003), 24. Eisenstein's original outline for the final sequence of *Strike* had nine separate shots or shot sequences showing the bull being killed, decapitated, and skinned spliced into the massacre of the workers, finishing with these four images: "35. 1,500 bodies at the foot of the cliff. 36. Two skinned bulls' heads. 37. A hand lying in a pool of blood. 38. (*c.u.*) Filling the entire screen: the eye of the dead bull." Sergei Eisenstein, *The Film Sense,* trans. Jay Leyda (London: Faber and Faber, 1986), 184–85.

28. Nesbet, *Savage Junctures,* 24.

29. David Bordwell, *The Cinema of Eisenstein* (Cambridge: Harvard University Press, 1993), 58–59.

30. Sergei Eisenstein, "The Method of Making a Workers' Film," in *Selected Works Vol. 1: Writings, 1922–34,* ed. and trans. Richard Taylor (London: BFI; Bloomington: Indiana University Press, 1988), 65. Gilberto Perez, discussing *Strike,* has suggested that the "massacre is equated with the slaughterhouse both in its bloodiness

and in its impersonal matter-of-factness: this sort of violence, the juxtaposition implies, is done every day." Perez, *The Material Ghost: Films and Their Medium* (Baltimore: Johns Hopkins University Press, 1998), 152. The juxtaposition is ambiguous precisely because it uses an image presenting the bloodiness of the everyday.

31. Stefan Grissemann, "Interview mit Michael Haneke," www.wolfzeit.at/web/interview_grissemann.htm (accessed February 25, 2008).

32. Georges Bataille, "Abattoir," quoted in Denis Hollier, *Against Architecture: The Writings of Georges Bataille,* trans. Betsy Wing (Cambridge: MIT Press, 1989), xiii. Dawn Ades and Simon Baker suggest that "the mere admission of these images into the pages of the journal constituted an avant-garde shock tactic designed to expose the paranoid-hygienic bourgeoisie to the abattoir, whose accursed nature Bataille interprets as a symptom of the sclerosis of polite society." See Ades and Baker, *Undercover Surrealism: Georges Bataille and Documents* (London: Hayward Gallery; Cambridge: MIT Press, 2006), 112. See also Ian Walker, *City Gorged with Dreams: Surrealism and Documentary Photography in Interwar Paris* (Manchester: Manchester University Press, 2002), 126–36.

33. Siegfried Kracauer, *Nature of Film: The Redemption of Physical Reality* (London: Dennis Dobson, 1961), 306. Comparisons between the extermination of European Jews during the Second World War and the intensive farming and killing of animals by the meat industry continue to cause controversy. Representative are the comments made by Elisabeth Costello and Abraham Stern, two characters in J. M. Coetzee's *The Lives of Animals,* ed. Amy Gutmann (Princeton: Princeton University Press, 1999), 19–22, 49–50.

34. Kracauer, *Nature of Film,* 306.

35. Adam Lowenstein suggests Franju uses "graphic, visceral shock to access the historical substrate of traumatic experience." See Lowenstein, "Films without a Face: Shock Horror in the Cinema of Georges Franju," *Cinema Journal* 37, no. 4 (1998): 37.

36. Ted Benton, *Natural Relations: Ecology, Animal Rights, and Social Justice* (London: Verso, 1993), 72. Similarly, Robert McKary has suggested that the meat-eating public seeks to sustain "a quasi-pastoral ideal in which meat is produced without the visible reality of death by farmers whose intimate relationship with their living herd counteracts the meat consumer's alienation from the animal that is slaughtered." See McKary, "BSE, Hysteria, and the Representation of Animal Death: Deborah Levy's *Diary of a Steak,*" in the Animal Studies Group, *Killing Animals* (Urbana: University of Illinois Press, 2006), 146.

37. Kenneth Clark, *Animals and Men: Their Relationship as Reflected in Western Art from Prehistory to the Present Day* (London: Thames and Hudson, 1977), 196. A notable exception is Jean-François Millet's *The Death of the Pig* (1868), which shows the moment preceding a pig's slaughter. See Clark, *Animals and Men,* 222. Less well known is *The Butcher's Shop* (c. 1890–1900) by the Belgian Jan Stobbaerts, which shows a cow that has just been stuck. See Louise Lippincott and Andreas Blühm, *Fierce Friends: Artists and Animals, 1750–1900* (London: Merrell, 2005), 118. André Masson, who visited La Villette abattoir with Eli Lotar, produced several works inspired by the abattoir, for example *The Horse Butcher* (1928), *Bull with Throat*

*Cut* (1930), and *Abattoir* (1930). Significantly, Masson was to paint or draw almost nothing but human massacres between 1930 and 1934, in response to the offensive at Chemin des Dames (April–May 1917) in which he fought and during which ninety-six thousand French troops were killed. See Laurie J. Monahan, "Violence in Paradise: André Masson's *Massacres*," *Art History* 24, no. 5 (2001): 707–24.

38. Lippit suggests: "Cinema . . . can be seen as the simultaneous culmination and beginning of an evolutionary cycle: the narrative of the disappearance of animals and that of the rise of the technical media intersect in the cinema. The advent of cinema is thus haunted by the animal figure, driven, as it were, by the wildlife after death of the animal." See Akira Mizuta Lippit, "From Wild Technology to Electric Animal," in *Representing Animals,* ed. Nigel Rothfels (Bloomington: Indiana University Press, 2002), 131. The reification of the animal in industrial and postindustrial meat production is central to the "disappearance of animals" in modernity. See also John Berger, "Why Look at Animals?" in *About Looking* (London: Writers and Readers Publishing Cooperative, 1980), 1–26.

39. Nesbet, *Savage Junctures,* 34. Annette Michelson considers Vertov's experiments with "temporal digressions" in her "The Kinetic Icon in the Work of Mourning: Prolegomena to the Analysis of a Textual System," *October* 52 (Spring 1990): 16–39.

40. Significantly, *Benny's Video* is the only film in Haneke's "glaciation trilogy" that is not based on a real historical event: *The Seventh Continent* (1989) was inspired by a news story about a family opting for collective suicide (and, incidentally, contains several shots of tropical fish flapping about on the floor after their aquarium is smashed, which prefigure the family's own demise), and *71 Fragments of a Chronology of Chance* (1994) concerns a mass-shooting in a bank in Vienna on December 23, 1993.

41. France legalized the eating of horses in 1866. See Kari Weil, "They Eat Horses, Don't They? Hippophagy and Frenchness," *Gastronomica* 7, no. 2 (2007): 44–51. In *Time of the Wolf* Haneke uses images of destroyed and dead livestock to suggest the scale and nature of the unspecified disaster that has taken place. Anne Laurent and her children pass by several skips in which piles of dead cattle are burning. The next morning, following the railway tracks, they walk past several dead sheep. For audiences in Europe, these images inevitably evoke the destruction of 6 million animals (including nearly 5 million sheep) in the United Kingdom during the "foot-and-mouth" crisis of 2001 and the 4.4 million cattle killed during the BSE ("mad cow disease") crisis in 1991.

42. See Patrick Crowley, "When Forgetting Is Remembering: Haneke's *Caché* and the Events of October 17, 1961," this volume.

43. In the American remake of *Funny Games,* the couple are Ann and George. As with the original, the son is named after his father.

44. The surname of the family in *Benny's Video* is not given; Benny's computer studies teacher, however, is called Dr. Schober. A Mrs. Schober also features in *The Piano Teacher.* The word *Schober* is a Middle High German word meaning "barn" or "haystack." The surname is a German and Austrian topographic name for someone who lived near or worked in a barn. "Schober" evokes a preindustrial period, when

one's very name referred to a distinct (in this case rural) lifestyle. The fact that the bourgeois subjects in these films that allegorize contemporary alienation in postindustrial society are named Schober is bleakly ironic.

45. Michael Haneke quoted in Christopher Sharrett, "The World That Is Known: An Interview with Michael Haneke," *Cineaste* 28, no. 3 (2003): 29.

46. Julien Murphet has argued that Haneke's films are influenced by what he refers to as the gradual "animalization of man" that characterizes Bresson's cinema, specifically its "defacialized approach to the human form." See Murphet, "Pitiable or Political Animals," *SubStance* 37, no. 3 (2008): 109. Much of Murphet's argument resonates with my own. For example, he notes that since its beginning, cinema's "gigantic two-dimensional images of human faces, gaits, gestures, seemed always already to have drifted into the territory of the 'non-man,' the automated machine-proxy or animal domain of deathless doubles, since every aspect of this uncanny movement was perfectly repeatable and invariable, embalmed in a timeless mechanical continuum out of all synch with the stochastic durations of 'real' social bodies" (101).

47. See Jan-Christopher Horak, "Wildlife Documentaries: From Classical Forms to Reality TV," *Film History: An International Journal* 18, no. 4 (2006): 462.

48. Lippit, "Death of an Animal," 11. See also Jacques Derrida: "Among nonhumans and separate from nonhumans there is an immense multiplicity of other living things that cannot in any way be homogenized, except by means of violence and willful ignorance, within the category of what is called the animal or animality in general." Derrida, "The Animal That Therefore I Am (More to Follow)," *Critical Inquiry* 28 (Winter 2002): 416.

49. For example, in a discussion of *Caché*, Guy Austin argues that Georges "incarnates postcolonial France" and "is an allegorical figure whose personal demons represent the cultural phenomenon of *la fracture coloniale*." See Austin, "Drawing Trauma: Visual Testimony in *Cache* and *J'ai 8 ans*," *Screen* 48, no. 4 (2007): 531.

50. Haneke quoted in Sharrett, "World That Is Known," 30.

51. Haneke quoted in Nick James, "Darkness Falls," *Sight and Sound* 13, no. 10 (2003): 18.

# Part 2

## STYLE AND MEDIUM

*71 Fragments of a Chronology of Chance* (1994): Long-take ambiguity.

John David Rhodes

# The Spectacle of Skepticism
## Haneke's Long Takes

Witness two statements by two filmmakers:

While the cinema used to make one situation produce another situation, and another, and another, again and again, and each scene was thought out and immediately related to the next (the natural result of a mistrust of reality), today, when we have thought out a scene, we feel the need to "remain" in it, because the single scene itself can contain so many echoes and reverberations, can even contain all the situations we may need. Today, in fact, we can quietly say: give us whatever "fact" you like, and we will disembowel it, make it something worth watching.

How can I restore to my representation the value of reality which has been lost?
Or in other words, How do I give viewers the possibility of perceiving this loss of reality and their own involvement in the process, so that they can thereby free themselves from being victims of the medium and become its potential partners? The question is not, What may I show? Rather it is, What opportunity do I give the viewer to recognize what is shown for what it is?

An emphasis on fact, on duration ("remain[ing] in it"), on reality and the loss thereof and the restoration thereof and the restoration thereof through vision, through looking, through cinema—neorealism, that Esperanto of political filmmaking—is being spoken here.

The first quotation is from neorealism "proper," from Cesare Zavattini, the warm and loveable humanist from the Po River Valley. The second is from Michael Haneke, the "bearded prophet" of "glaciation" from Vienna.[1] How can two filmmakers working at such a historical remove from each other speak the same language? Zavattini, a serious filmmaker and thinker, found it possible, in his collaborations with Vittorio De Sica, to conclude his films with a working-class boy silently slipping his hand into that of his father (*Bicycle Thieves*, 1948) or with the great unwashed and underhoused of Milan flying into the future on broomsticks (*Miracolo a Milano*, 1951). Both endings might be understood to offer self-consciously feeble or ironically impossible diegetic "conclusions" to problems that would find no such solutions in the real world of Rome in 1948 or Milan in 1951. Can we not, however, at some level, regret, or least note, that both films evaporate from our view leaving behind a slightly sticky residue of either sentimentality or fantasy? Among Haneke's films' many memorable endings, on the other hand, we might count a long shot of Isabelle Huppert staggering out of the Vienna Konzerthaus and into the Austrian night, having just plunged a kitchen knife into her breast (*The Piano Teacher*, 2001), or the ending-and-beginning-again of two tennis-clad murdering teenagers begging breakfast from a family that we know will be their next victims (*Funny Games*, 1997 and 2007). Surely these are at least different cinematic dialects, if not different languages altogether?

Yet, although the contents of a Haneke film may seem ever so far away from those of Italian neorealism, the rhetoric of neorealism persists, and not only in Haneke's writing and published statements, interviews, and the like; the films themselves participate in the formal rhetoric of neorealism. The use of the long take, that formal gesture most privileged in connection with the neorealist aspiration to capture the space-time of reality as it bodies forth, is one of Haneke's most persistent traits.[2] Haneke's frequent and paradigmatic deployment of the long take will be the subject of this essay. The long take and its vicissitudes allow for an evaluation of the ethical and epistemological imperatives in Haneke's filmmaking, imperatives felt most keenly in the formal features of the long take itself.

## *Bazin, the Enforcer*

A consideration of the long take, of course, means a return to André Bazin, the theorist most responsible for installing it as a kind of summa, not only of filmmaking, but also of moral behavior. Bazin's investment in long-take/depth-of-focus cinematography is as well known as it is worth rehearsing. For Bazin the virtues of this form of cinematography are, first, these two:

1. That depth of focus brings the spectator into a relation with the image closer to that which he enjoys with reality. Therefore it is correct to say that, independently of the contents of the image, its structure is more realistic;
2. That it implies, consequently, both a more active mental attitude on the part of the spectator and a more positive contribution to the action in progress . . . he is called upon to exercise at least a minimum of personal choice. It is from his attention and his will that the meaning of the image in part derives.[3]

This form of cinematography is more like being in the world, which is to say, closer to a mode of being in which one acts as an agent and not an object. The invitation to activity, "personal choice," and "attention" are all bound up with the third of this form of cinematography's virtues, which is its reintroduction of "ambiguity": "The uncertainty in which we find ourselves as to the spiritual key or the interpretation we should put on the film is built into the very design of the image."[4] If we were to work backward through Bazin's propositions, we might gain a clearer sense of their priority: depth of focus produces an ambiguous image in response to which we must play a more active role in understanding, and in playing a more active role in coming to understand the image, our behavior in the cinema more closely resembles our behavior (or at least our best behavior) outside the cinema. Long-take/depth-of-focus cinematography is a medium for the production of agency, or at least the practice of a kind of virtual agency. It is good for us because it makes us exercise our freedom. However, strangely enough, the experience of the long take/depth of focus ends up being the experience of a coercive sort of freedom, or a coercive invitation to experience freedom: "It is no longer the editing that selects what we see, thus giving it a sort of *a priori* significance, it is the mind of the spectator which is *forced to discern* [*qui se trouve contraint à discerner*] . . . the dramatic spectrum proper to the scene."[5]

For Bazin, the cinema can be ethical and can be properly aesthetic (which is to say, mature, evolved) only insofar as it is able to produce this complex of epistemological and moral effects. The exemplarity of the neorealist filmmakers consists in their "never forget[ting] that the world *is,* quite simply, before it is something to be condemned."[6] I am interested here in the experiences of condemnation and discernment—how realist cinema, in other words, solicits and then delays our interpretation. The ambiguity of long-take/depth-of-focus cinematography triggers a relay from film to spectator and back that is initiated by the duration of the shot but seems to put into motion an experience of time-based discernment that is almost in competition with the film image that has triggered the experience. This is a cinematography that produces a luxury of effects, a surplus of facts, a sensual excess, all of which, however, are produced only insofar as they demand of the spectator the performance of his or her best judgment.

In an interview with Christopher Sharrett, Haneke has spoken of his practice in terms that are uncannily Bazinian. In response to a question about his use of the long take, Haneke makes the following answer, with particular reference to *Code Unknown:*

Perhaps I can connect this to the issue of television. Television accelerates our habits of seeing. Look, for example, at advertising in that medium. The faster something is shown, the less able you are to perceive it as an object occupying a space in physical reality, and the more it becomes something seductive. And the less real the image seems to be, the quicker you buy the commodity it seems to depict. Of course, this type of aesthetic has gained the upper hand in commercial cinema. Television accelerates experience, but one needs time to understand what one sees, which the current media disallows. Not just understand on an intellectual level, but emotionally. The cinema can offer very little that is new; everything that is said has been said a thousand times, but cinema still has the capacity, I think, to let us experience the world anew. The long take is an esthetic means to accomplish this by its particular emphasis.

*Code Unknown* consists very much of static sequences, with each shot from only one perspective, precisely because I don't want to patronize or manipulate the viewer, or at least to the smallest degree possible. Of course, film is always manipulation, but if each scene is only one shot, then, I think, there is at least less of a sense of *time* being manipulated when one tries to stay close to a "real time" framework. The reduction of montage to a minimum also tends to shift responsibility back to the viewer in that more contemplation is required, in my view.[7]

While long-take cinema can "*let us* experience the world anew," we must be clear (for Haneke certainly is) that this is an allowance, something granted us by the film and to which we are now responsible. What begins as liberty ends as obligation. The tension between these possibilities of agency and constraint, as well as the matter of agency as a modality of constraint, are the issues that I want to explore in several of Haneke's long takes.

## Endurance Tests

*Code Unknown*'s credits are interrupted by a prologue: in a static long take a young girl cowers against a blank white wall, then shrinks to the floor, seemingly in fear. She then stands back up, and the film cuts to a series of shots of children who, we realize almost immediately, have been watching what we now understand to have been a performance staged for them. The third child to whom the film cuts asks, in sign language, "Alone?" The film cuts back to the first girl, the performer, who must shake her head "No," just as she must do to each of the following five children who venture (in sign language) similar interpretations. The last child (seemingly of north African descent) that we see offering a response, ventures (by crossing his upraised wrists) "Imprisoned?"; the camera cuts to a shot of the girl, again, shaking her head in contradiction. The prologue ends, and the film's credits resume, granting us for the first time the film's title and its director's name.

To translate into different, more general terms, an image is presented in a single long take. It is presented to an audience that does not understand it but that must try, or feels itself obliged, to interpret it. The audience must fail in this activity, or at least this hermeneutic inquiry is cut short and thereby suspended. Code unknown. This sequence is the film *in nuce*. We, the spectators of *Code Unknown*, should recognize the deaf children as our onscreen doubles. The prologue's gesture is an obvious one. Leonard Quart finds it a "literal, heavy-handed embodiment of Haneke's vision."[8] But given the fact that this prologue actually constitutes a part of the credit sequence, its literalness would seem apposite—no more literal, in other words, than the title itself or the information regarding the name of actors, directors, and production companies. The prologue may be as "literal" as all that: its long-take aesthetics (and its resultant ambiguity) are as much a mere fact of the film's mode of production as its many actors' names and its transnational funding.[9]

The formal predecessor for *Code Unknown*'s loosely, at times inconsequentially, intertwined narrative construction is Haneke's *71 Fragments of a Chronology of Chance* (1993). The long take features prominently here, although not exclusively. The longest of the film's long takes features an elderly pensioner in his kitchen speaking on the phone to someone we assume (because of what we hear of his side of the conversation as well as information granted us earlier in the film) is his daughter. It is an unhappy sequence and lasts seven and a half minutes, during which the camera does not move. The film forces us to attend to the meandering plaintiveness of the man's conversation with an intensity that we would rarely give our own loved ones. This shot constitutes the second time in *71 Fragments* that we visit this man's kitchen; the first visit is granted via a long take (some three to four minutes in length) in which a panning camera records the man's preparation of a simple meal that he eats before a television. Neorealism, we know, generated kitchen stories in abundance: the metabolically decelerated spectacle of Clara Calamai nodding off amid piles of dirty crockery in *Ossessione* (Luchino Visconti, 1943) figured, perhaps, an instance of neorealism *avant la lettre*. And in *Umberto D.* (1952) Zavattini's and De Sica's portrait of a mistreated pensioner has its apotheosis in the kitchen scene in which the young maid makes coffee, a scene that for Bazin epitomized neorealism's aspirations. It was this scene that led him to declare that in De Sican and Zavattinian neorealism, "the narrative unit is not the episode, the event, the sudden turn of events, or the character of its protagonists; it is the succession of concrete instants of life, no one of which can be said to be more important than another, for their ontological equality destroys drama at its very basis."[10]

For Bazin, the destruction of drama is a sacrificial rite that, like most sacrifices, is meant to generate life, vitality: "De Sica and Zavattini are concerned to make cinema the asymptote of reality—but in order that it should ultimately be life itself that becomes spectacle."[11] By life becoming spectacle, Bazin intends something like a process by which life itself is reinvested with a plenitude that it already possesses but that human beings have been dulled into missing. Cinema can perform a vital reeducation of the senses, and, in fact, it does so only through its ability to make its spectator aware that cinema is not, in the end, to be confused with life itself. However, *Umberto D.*'s kitchen scene offers a wealth of editing, of close-ups of metonymic details that endear the maid to us: "We see how the grinding of the coffee is divided in turn into a series of independent moments; for example, when she shuts the door with the tip of her outstretched foot. As it goes in on her the camera follows the movement of her leg so that the image finally concentrates on her toes feeling the surface of the door."[12] Bazin's complex account of the cinema is rather more acute than his grasp of poverty: the phenomenology of this moment surely means more to the art cinema spectator than any struggle with kitchen appliances has ever meant to any historical teenaged girl, pregnant, jilted, and employed in domestic service.

Something else is served to us in Haneke's kitchen. In a documentary interview about *71 Fragments*, Haneke is asked about his use of the long take in the film. He responds by describing the stages of the spectator's responses to one of his long-take sequences: "I get it, next scene. . . . Then, it amuses me. Then, it infuriates me. Then, it tires me. Then, I say, 'Let's see where this goes.' And at one point, I begin to watch." In other words: "Because the scene lasts as long as it does you come to another understanding."[13] The long take slows down the film's and the spectator's metabolic processes such that drama eventually dies from starvation; once drama dies, vision begins. But if neorealist cinema is the asymptote of reality, then Haneke's cinema is the asymptote of neorealism. Despite the apparent congruency with the rhetoric of neorealism (extinction of drama/ birth of vision), Haneke's version of realist kitchen aesthetics does not have the sublimatory end of life becoming spectacle. In Bazin's account, one is already watching, always: his spectator's attention is already as fastened onto the cinematic image as is the camera that "goes in" for the maid's foot. (What more fitting metonymic figure than this working-class foot to serve as material support for Bazin's somewhat fetishistic account of neorealist spectatorship?) In Haneke's version, the duration of the long take is the space required for watching itself to die as consumption ("I get it, next scene") and be reborn as actual watching. However, watching is not (re)born so that we may then turn to life itself as "visible poetry." Haneke says, in the long passage quoted earlier, that his long take is the "aesthetic means" of performing a deceleration of our consumption of images. Although Haneke uses strong Bazinian language (the long take "let[s] us experience the world anew"), the real emphasis is not on the production of an ontological encounter with reality but rather on an obtuse distension of the mediated image of reality.

## *Formal Responsibility*

In another long-take scenario that is overdetermined by a neorealist iconography of the domestic quotidian, we witness Anne Laurent (Juliette Binoche), an actress, doing the ironing in her living room (*Code Unknown*). Her attention is divided between the precision of her ironing and a television that we cannot see, apart from the reflection of its images in the glass-paned door to Anne's left. The direction of Anne's gaze is toward the camera, which would mean that there is a triple coincidence of the positions of the television, Haneke's camera, and the implied (or real) spectator. As this long take extends itself, the audible (if not exactly apparent) insipidity of the television program (what seems to be a documentary about modernist art), as well as the drudgery of Anne's ironing (that least-pressing of household tasks most often postponed for lack of time), accumulate into an image of fascinating tedium. It would seem at first as if we are being asked to witness the process by which everyday life is reborn as "spectacle." Yet, however much we might feel ourselves tempted by the possibility of becoming absorbed in the spectacle of Binoche at the ironing board, the television's drone of information and its reflection in the glass of the door undermine this ontologically rich experience. The stubborn presence of the television provides just enough mediatic dispersal to prevent an experience of this scene as evidence of the often-overlooked plenitude of the everyday (*pace* Bazin and neorealism). Our identification of the television's location in space also works to undermine such an experience. Its location is the (unseen) camera's, whose spatial positioning also anchors our (the spectators') own purchase on what is seen. Binoche's distracted spectatorship is chiasmically returned by our own rather more absorbed spectatorship of her. These gazes do not meet, for hers, when not looking down at the ironing board, is directed at the unseeing screen of the television. The neorealist gambit (domestic drudgery, long take) is weakened and frayed by the television's antiontological ubiquity.

Then something else happens, something we cannot see but, with Anne, only hear. Above the din of the television, Anne hears (as do we) the cries of a child and an adult's voice shouting. After a long and piercing cry from the child's voice, Anne mutes (but does not turn off) the television with the remote control. Her brief glance upward suggests that the cries and shouts that sound very much like a scene of child abuse are coming from an apartment upstairs. Eventually the cries seem to stop, Anne pauses, resumes ironing, takes a gulp from her glass of wine, recalls the television (whose flickering image on the door's glass has been present throughout), and turns the sound back on with the remote. The scene (shot) ends.

Already worried by the television, the performance and spectacle of neorealist domestic labor is interrupted completely by the impingement of another "realist" scenario that we and Anne cannot see. The long take's duration makes us sense the effect of the frame as a making-blind, a regime of occlusion. In this shot, the frame's limits are very similar to the architecture of Anne's apartment. The stubborn arbitrariness of its immutable boundaries work to exhaust whatever plenitude might be promised by the generosity of the shot's temporal duration. Television, we might remember, has classically been considered a weak visual medium, as much heard as seen.[14] Anne can "watch" the television while ironing, even though she only infrequently directs her gaze in its direction. Sound, dialogue, and audio information tell us almost everything we need to know about what is on the television screen. Sound also tells us pretty much all we need to know about what is going on upstairs. Whereas it is inconceivable that we could intervene in the events we hear/see reported on television news, we might imagine proposing some intervention when we hear a child being beaten upstairs.

It seems to me that this shot has three activities, and they do not merely happen in sequence: (1) The shot proposes the neorealist spectacle of a subject engrossed in quotidian labor—a spectacle in which we might become equally engrossed. (2) The shot undermines such spectatorial absorption in the ontological status of the action it records by way of the television's aural and (faintly) visual presence. (3) The shot's superaddition of the offscreen child's beating layers another strata of "realism" to the already-weakened neorealist spectacle of housework. This superaddition of sound enlarges, in turn, the ethical dimensions of the scene. Into this weakened scene of neo-neorealism, into this living room of a small apartment, the film's sound design introduces new ethical contents that refasten us to the image in a mode of absorption, similar to the way in which Anne is fastened to what she hears.

It is as if the long take's observation of the scene first renders that scene in Anne's apartment as a kind of solid whole. Slowly, however, the television's spatially uncanny position and its audiovisual drone seem to gnaw away at this solid whole, hollowing it out. The shot promises at its outset to perform an absorbing reinvention of the everyday as low-metabolism Bazinian "spectacle." It becomes, over time, a shot of an actress playing an actress who is doing her ironing. By holding the shot but adding the child's cries through the artifice of sound design, the film pours the new set of ethical contents into this hollow, this cavity, and in so doing summons anew our absorption in the spectacle. However, now the film presents a melodramatically charged spectacle, brimming with imperatives of right and wrong. Before our very eyes, Binoche becomes Anne Laurent again, and we are transformed from skeptical art cinema spectators into spectators of any genre film; we judge her diegetic (in)action with the self-satisfaction of morally superior moviegoers everywhere. Because of its fundamental properties of temporal duration and spatial integrity, the form of the long take becomes the necessary medium in which this deconstruction and reconstruction of neorealist, spectacular cinema can take place. The realism of the long take is not something that is merely de-ontologized, debunked, deconstructed. Rather, its fluctuating, asymptotic empty plenitude is the medium for the emergence of an urgent ethics of media, *in media.*

Anne's resort to the remote control in this scene of realist plausibility recalls the most implausible scene in all of Haneke's cinema: the scene in *Funny Games* (1997) in which "Paul" (Arno Frisch; we never learn the character's "real" name) uses the remote control to rewind the murder of his accomplice "Peter" (Frank Giering).[15] The controversial Brechtian hyperbole of this trick in *Funny Games* is forever vulnerable to the charge of obviousness or crudeness. However, the power of this moment, this trick, is the way in which it echoes forward in the moment at which Anne manipulates her television by remote. Paul's manipulation of the rewind button destroys the diegetic world and our belief in it, whereas Anne's manipulation of the mute button restores the diegesis and its fictional hold on us. Paul can rewind or reverse Peter's murder and in so doing can startle us into an awareness of our generically moral (and morally generic) desire for revenge and narrative closure. Anne, on the other hand, can mute the television to startle us into a highly mediated moral absorption in the diegesis, even though the film had already performed a weakening of the film's diegetic hold on us through its demonstration of its mediated nature (the television's drone; our awareness of Binoche as Binoche). In both cases, what is diagnosed or exemplified is not so much the control or vitiation of our ethical and imaginative agencies by media but rather the way in which media itself functions as the medium of a kind of audiovisual ethical performance rather than as medium in which events that pose ethical questions are represented.

The offscreen violence that Anne (and I am tempted to write "Anne" in the same way I have written "Paul"[16]) hears being done to the child upstairs also returns us to the scene in which Schorschi, the young boy, is killed in *Funny Games*. In the earlier film, we remain in the kitchen with Paul as he makes a sandwich, a boring task observed in Zavattinian detail and Bazinian duration, while offscreen we hear Schorschi executed by rifle shot. The correspondence between Paul's situation and Anne's is striking. In both cases we as spectators are pinioned in place by the unbudging camera, which will continue to produce its document of the profilmic's temporal duration but, in a gesture of cruel mercy, will refuse to show us the scene of violence itself. This scene of child murder is something we are relieved *not* to witness, but this relief is also appalling, as it seems to exempt us from the spectacle of violence that we had hitherto followed uncomfortably but intently nonetheless. Anne does, of course, flinch and pause in sympathy. She even agonizes over her indecision about how to respond to this abuse in two more scenes that occur later in the film. In the end, however, she chooses to exercise her metropolitan right to ignore the cries of the suffering child. We might identify with what we, as spectators of this unusual but nonetheless realist fiction, imagine is Anne's skepticism: What if what she hears is not actually abuse? What if there is a story that would explain those cries? Can we discredit her entirely for not wanting to police her neighbors upstairs? From inside a scene to which we have been invited to respond skeptically ("That is Juliette Binoche, not Anne Laurent"), a representation of the ethical (and perhaps political) failure of skepticism is enacted: Anne cannot be certain about what she hears, and this uncertainty, the product of which is her failure to intervene, contributes, surely, to the death of the child, whose funeral Anne will attend later in the film. We are implicated unbearably in the film's dilemmas. Wrong media cannot be watched rightly. Thus, we are wrong for watching and wrong for not watching and wrong in every way that we watch.

## *Attention/Deficit*

In the long take with which *Caché* (2005) ends (but does not conclude), we are presented with another immobile frame. The camera sits at some considerable distance from the majority of the human figures trapped in or merely passing through its rectangle of profilmic reality. What it observes is the entrance of the school apparently attended by Pierrot (Lester Makedonsky), the son of George and Anne Laurent (Daniel Auteuil and Juliette Binoche). Students loiter on the school steps, hailed by friends, teachers, and parents there to collect them. The camera is rigorously centered in regards to the school's entrance; the two major doorways of the entrance are in symmetrical harmony with the edges of the right and left sides of the frame. Yet, despite this rigor, close to the camera the hood of a black car occupies, almost aleatorily, the better part of the bottom third of the frame. This image is shot at the intersection of precision and the (seemingly) haphazard.

Of course, anyone who has seen documentary footage of Haneke at work shooting a film knows that whatever appears contingent or arbitrary (for example, the car's hood blocking the lower register of the frame) is, in fact, the result of careful planning. Every pedestrian who seems to saunter casually across the horizontal axis of the frame testifies to Bazin's assertion that "realism in art can only be achieved in one way—through artifice";

these passers-by have been rigorously stage-managed by Haneke and his crew.[17] However, as in the past, the shot's duration absorbs us as such, and we relinquish our awareness of the shot's contrivance to contemplative expectation. We know from *Code Unknown* that some new force—a sound, a person, an action—might enter this image and render this innocuous scene more sinister. We might also scour the image for meaning, a clue, something already present in it that would offer a motivation for its duration. If we are attentive (or if we have been tipped off by word of mouth), we notice that Majid's son (Walid Afkir) enters the frame from the right and walks up the steps of the school toward the left of the frame. At this same moment, a group of boys, among them Pierrot, emerge from the doorway on screen left. Majid's son (the film gives him no name) approaches Pierrot with what looks like serious intent; their meeting seems exquisitely timed, even choreographed. Majid's son draws Pierrot away from his friends, and the two descend the stairs to speak on the sidewalk. We do not have the impression that the two speak for the first time, but that, like so much else in this film, is only a conjecture. Their conversation finished, Majid's son exits the frame from the direction he entered, while Pierrot rejoins his friends on the steps before descending, in their company, to the sidewalk and exiting screen left. As soon as Pierrot has left the image, the credits slowly move up the screen from the bottom of the frame. The film is over, yet the shot remains, endures beneath the ascending credits. All this time, the only sound is the ambient noise of voices and automobile traffic, the sounds of urban human busyness.

Does it matter that the first time I saw *Caché* I missed the colloquy of Pierrot and Majid's unnamed son? I think I remember being too caught up with trying to decide if one of the adults waiting on the sidewalk was Anne or Georges. I assumed that Haneke decided to let the film end on a note of radical inconclusiveness, and I approved of this ending. I caught Pierrot and Majid's son on my second viewing, and by chance. What difference does this difference make? The film, perhaps, is more inconclusive once we recognize the presence of the older boy and the younger boy than it was before, except that now it is generically, mysteriously inconclusive: what is this image telling me? The effect is something like that of the scene of Anne ironing in *Code Unknown*: what at first feels like ontological preoccupation with cinematic duration suddenly shifts into the hermeneutics of criminal melodrama.[18] Are the boys in collusion? Is Majid's son manipulating Pierrot? Are we meant even to entertain such questions? Given that we do not even know when this image might be assigned in the order of the film's fabula, entertaining them as the credits expire onscreen seems rather pointless. Maurice Merleau-Ponty might have been offering a reading of this shot when he wrote that "inattentive perception contains nothing more and indeed nothing other than the attentive kind . . . the additional clearness brought by the act of attention does not herald any new relationship."[19]

I might have been said to have perceived Majid's son and Pierrot on the screen even before my attention had singled them out, both as objects of vision and as objects of knowledge. However, my new knowledge—my attentive perception—that they are in the frame offers me as little to go on as my previous, less spatially and dramatically cathected perception of the shot as merely one in which a broad perceptual array (children, adults, a school, the busy streets and sidewalks of Paris) was being offered to my vision. Rather than seeing more when I see Majid's son and Pierrot, perhaps I see less: it will forever be harder to force my eyes from the area of the image occupied by their bodies. In a sense, everything else in the frame might as well be banished to offscreen space. Whatever my broader engagement with the whole of this image might be or might have been is now foreclosed to me, unless by perverse intention to ignore the bodies of Majid's son and Pierrot I force myself to pay attention, for instance, to the man in a khaki jacket wearing a black shoulder bag who, for almost the entire duration of the shot, waits at the bottom center of the image until he is met by a boy in jeans and a green t-shirt (the man's son?) and the two walk out of the shot, screen left. And if I pay attention to this man and this boy, what then have I perceived, and what do I know? Perhaps knowledge is not the issue. Perhaps, instead, this shot tells us something about thinking: "This passage from the indeterminate to the determinate, this recasting at every moment of its own history in the unity of a new meaning, is thought itself."[20]

The shot that precedes this long take of the school's steps is another, more haunting but less mysterious long take. This is the shot in which the boy Majid is taken by the authorities from Georges's family after Georges has deceived his parents into believing Majid is wicked and into giving him up for adoption by the state. The shot is seemingly taken inside the shadowy interior of the barn that faces the farmhouse. The events of the shot (the entry of the car, the handing over of Majid, Majid's attempt at his escape, his capture and imprisonment in the car, the car's exit) are rendered impassively by the long take. In the foreground chickens wander the farmyard; on the soundtrack, birdsong.[21] In the scene that precedes this one, we see Georges, wracked, we suppose, by guilt, take what we assume are sleeping pills, draw the curtains of his and Anne's bedroom, and crawl into bed. We might assume the long take of the farmyard and Majid's spiriting away to be the rendering of Georges's dream.[22] Though the camera is positioned in shadow, its immobility does not feel like any dream, even if we wanted to entertain a reading so intent on character subjectivity.

More important than possibly giving us the contents of Georges's dream, this long take gives us the fact of Majid's removal from Georges's family's life, from provincial, agrarian bourgeois comfort; the shot tells us one way in which this scene might look or might have looked. We know, in any case, what it means, and, given Majid's suicide (rendered, of course, in an immobile long take), we hardly have to think about how we feel about the actions played out across its duration. In this sense, its function is very different from the film's last shot, a shot about which we do not know how to feel, or if it is meant to occasion feeling at all. I doubt that this last shot's setting at a school is anything other than a typically obvious clue. The film ends on a pedagogical and hortatory note. We are warned, I think, to be cautious of our easy association of seeing with knowing and of knowing with feeling.

What is "worth watching" (Zavattini), and what is "the value of reality" (Haneke)? Haneke's long takes do not, in and of themselves, provide answers for these questions. They do seem, however, to provide the necessary conditions for a critical apprehension of how questions of worth and value have dominated the production and consumption of images. In a way, Haneke's long takes give us sensuous, but also theoretical, evidence of the way in which value seeks constantly to insert itself into the image or to adhere itself to the image's surface. The colonization of the image by value happens in an instant and all too easily; witness the work of a child's voice crying in offscreen space. Haneke's filmmaking should not be understood as telling us that concern for others should be no concern of ours, or of the cinema's. However, his durational audiovisual aesthetics gives us the means toward, and the experience of, a skeptical engagement with value's infatuation with the image, and our infatuation with assigning value to images. If the world is indeed worth watching, it is not so because we have already found it worth contemplating but because we will have already found it worth changing. Haneke's spectacles of skepticism constitute an unnerving series of ethical and epistemological durations in which we can sensually think our way toward an historical experience in which the thrilling prospect of cinema as the asymptote of reality will need to enthrall us less than it has done.

## Notes

1. Cesare Zavattini, "Some Ideas on the Cinema," in *Film: A Montage of Theories,* ed. Richard Dyer MacCann (New York: E. P. Dutton, 1966), 218–19; Michael Haneke, "Believing Not Seeing," *Sight and Sound* 7, no. 11 (1997): London Film Festival Supplement, 22. The epithet "bearded prophet" was used by Scott Foundas in his interview with Haneke: "Interview: Michael Haneke: The Bearded Prophet of *Code Inconnu* and *The Piano Teacher,*" *IndieWire* (originally published December 4, 2001), www.indiewire.com/people/int_Haneke_Michael_020329.html (accessed May 27, 2008). Haneke's first three feature-length films are generally referred to as the director's "glaciation trilogy."

2. Haneke shares this interest in long-take cinematography with others of his contemporaries, particularly East Asian directors like Tsai Ming Lang, Hou Hsiao-Hsien, Jia Zhang-ke, and Apichatpong Weerasethakul, as well as North American directors such as Gus Van Sant.

3. André Bazin, "The Evolution of the Language of Cinema," in *What Is Cinema?* vol. 1, ed. and trans. Hugh Gray (Berkeley: University of California Press, 1967), 35–36.

4. Ibid., 36.

5. André Bazin, "An Aesthetic of Reality: Neorealism (Cinematic Realism and the Italian School of the Liberation)," in *What Is Cinema?* vol. 2, ed. and trans. Hugh Gray (Berkeley: University of California Press, 1971), 28; Bazin, "La réalisme cinématographique et l'école italienne de la libération," in *Qu'est-ce que le cinéma?* (Paris: Les Éditions du Cerf, 2002), 271 (my emphasis).

6. Ibid., 21.

7. Christopher Sharrett, "The World That Is Known: An Interview with Michael Haneke," *Cineaste* 28, no. 3 (2003): 31.

8. Leonard Quart, "*Code Unknown,*" *Cineaste* 27, no. 2 (2002): 36.

9. The film received production funding from the following: Bavaria Film, Canal+, Filmex Romania, France 2 Cinéma, Les Films Alain Sarde, MK2 Productions, the Romanian Culture Ministry, ZDF, and Art France Cinéma. See the film's credits and www.imdb.com/title/tt0216625/companycredits (accessed May 27, 2008). Regarding the film's title, Brigitte Peucker asks, "Need we add that the words of the film's title are overdetermined?" Peucker, "Games Haneke Plays: Reality and Performance," in this volume.

10. André Bazin, "*Umberto D.;* A Great Work," in *What Is Cinema?* 2:81.

11. Ibid., 2:82.

12. Ibid.

13. *71 Fragments d'une Chronologie du Hasard: Entretien avec Michael Haneke par Serge Toubiana,* available on *Michael Haneke Trilogy* (*The Seventh Continent, Benny's Video, 71 Fragments of a Chronology of Chance),* Tartan Video, 2006.

14. "For TV, sound has a more centrally defining role. Sound carries the fiction or the documentary; the image has a more illustrative function. The TV image tends to be simple and straightforward, stripped of details and excess meanings. Sound tends to carry the details." John Ellis, *Visible Fictions: Cinema, Television, Video* (London:

Routledge, 1982), 129.

15. In the first version of *Funny Games* the rewind function is registered as the rewinding of videotape, as if the film we were watching had suddenly become a home viewing of VHS. In the 2007 version of the film this effect is registered as the fast search function on a DVD. In both instances, the remote control is connected to acts of violence and questions of the audience's and characters' absorptive attention to or alienation from acts of violence and, significantly, violence directed at children. At this moment in *Funny Games* the television has already been seen to be dripping with the blood of Schorschi (Stefan Clapczynski), the son of Anna and Georg, whose murder by gunshot earlier the film is heard (but not seen).

16. On the serially repetitive naming of characters in Haneke's filmmaking, see Michael Lawrence's essay, "Haneke's Stable: The Death of an Animal and the Figuration of the Human," in this volume.

17. Bazin, "An Aesthetic of Reality," 26.

18. In a sense, the shot is the peaceable kingdom version of the mobile long take that begins *Code Unknown* in which Amadou (Onu Lu Yenke), a young black man, confronts Jean (Alexandre Hamidi), a younger white adolescent, for having thrown a piece of rubbish in the lap of the Romanian beggar Maria (Luminita Gheorgiu).

19. Maurice Merleau-Ponty, *The Phenomenology of Perception,* trans. Colin Smith (London: Routledge, 2002), 32.

20. Ibid., 36.

21. Elizabeth Ezra and Jane Sillars point out the fact that in this scene "we see chickens but we hear sparrows." Ezra and Sillars, "Hidden in Plain Sight: Bringing Terror Home," *Screen* 48, no. 2 (2007): 220.

22. In fact, the other time the camera occupies this position is the scene in which the young Majid (Malik Nait Djoudi) kills the cockerel. It is explicitly marked as a dream, since it precedes Georges's suddenly waking up.

*Caché* (2005): Georges looks into the rue des Iris and finds no one looking back.

Hugh S. Manon

## "Comment ça, rien?"
### Screening the Gaze in *Caché*

> L'écran n'est pas un cadre comme celui du tableau, mais un *cache* qui ne laisse percevoir qu'une partie de l'événement.
> —André Bazin, *Qu'est-ce que le cinéma*

> The gaze looks at me, but I can never catch sight of it there where it looks; for there is no "there," no determinate location, no place whence it looks.
> —Joan Copjec, *Imagine There's No Woman: Ethics and Sublimation*

Film theorists sometimes introduce their work as reading a certain cultural artifact "through a psychoanalytic lens." This essay reads the opening long take of Michael Haneke's *Caché* (2005) *as* a psychoanalytic lens, one that both magnifies the desire of protagonist Georges Laurent (Daniel Auteuil) and exposes his actions as a catastrophic performance for the desire of the Other. As such, the opening shot (and others like it later in the film) can be understood as an invitation to look at, indeed to scrutinize, what Jacques Lacan calls *le regard*—"the gaze"—a crucial psychoanalytic concept that has suffered decades of misinterpretation by theorists of various stripes. Whether or not Haneke is familiar with Lacanian theory—and I make no such claims here—it is to the writer-director's great credit that *Caché* represents the gaze with all the complexity Lacan intended.

*Caché* screens the gaze on two levels. First, for Georges Laurent, the gaze appears as an impossible black hole that must remain foreclosed for everyday reality to retain its consistency. Second, for the film's audience, the gaze becomes evident at those gaps in representation where the film self-reflexively "looks back" at the viewer—acknowledging, among other things, how cinematic desire is constructed. By conflating these two gazes at crucial points in the narrative, especially through the trope of the video camcorder, Haneke makes clear that Georges's problem with the gaze belongs to all of us. In such moments, form and content become indistinguishable, and it is here that Haneke's film most pointedly functions as a work of theory, rendering a final verdict on the positivistic oversights of 1970s apparatus theory, especially its tendency to position the gaze on the order of the imaginary (that is, in the content of the image or its framing) rather than on the order of the real (that is, where the image fails, decomposes, becomes nonsensical) as Lacan would have it. As I go on to argue, the opening shot of *Caché* is an example of the gaze *par excellence*, provided we understand the gaze, *contra* the primary tenet of apparatus theory, as "mark[ing] a disturbance in the function of ideology rather than its expression."[1]

As a point of entrance into this discussion, it may be useful to consider a nuance in the film's title that is glossed over in its English-language translation as "Hidden." In French, the word *cache* (without the *accent aigu*) has direct implications regarding film style and can refer to the cardboard "mask" that cinematographers, especially during the silent era, employed to block out one portion of an image and lend emphasis to another. The term also appears in one of the most repeated aphorisms of film theory: André Bazin's famous claim that the cinematic screen must be understood not as "a frame like that of a picture but a mask [*cache*] which allows only a part of the action to be seen."[2] In both of these cases, the word *cache* is less indicative of a material object than a psychic tendency, present in all human subjects; the "mask" of cinema is not a disguise or cover but an act of part-concealment that, in its partialness, reorients our relation to what remains visible.[3]

The keystone concept in Lacanian theory is the *objet petit a*, of which the gaze is one "paramount embodiment."[4] Although the term resists easy definition, if asked to sum up the structure of the gaze in a single word, we would be hard pressed to find a better approximation than "masked-off-ness." When Todd McGowan rightly states that the gaze "promises the subject the secret of the Other, but this secret exists only insofar as it remains hidden," we can be sure that his use of the word "hidden" does not mean "unnoticed" but rather "masked off," partially obscured, *caché*.[5] Accordingly, it will be useful to analyze *Caché*'s quiescent opening shot in terms of its three remarkable formal lacks—lack of editing, lack of sound, and lack of movement—each of which functions as a *cache,* or mask. This extended long take—a film-within-a-film we might call "Plastic Bag Video #1"—is surely one of the most acute representations of the gaze in all of contemporary cinema. As I go on to explain, it is owing in large part to Haneke's structuring of his opening shot around a series of formalistic masks that *Caché* can deliver such a trenchant theorization of what the gaze is, and what it is not: the look.

## *Masking Tape*

In 1990s Hollywood, bravura long takes became a conventional way for well-established high-profile directors, as well as younger would-be auteurs, to begin their films with a bang. In the opening shots of films such as *The Player* (Robert Altman, 1992), *Strange Days* (Kathryn Bigelow, 1995), *Boogie Nights* (Paul Thomas Anderson, 1997), and *Snake Eyes* (Brian De Palma, 1998), the camera bobs and weaves to follow complex onscreen action in an unstated directorial competition to see who can keep it going the longest. In this context, the entirely static three-minute shot of the Laurent residence that begins *Caché* can be understood not only as a subversion of the long take but as a *perversion* of it, risking disinvestment and boredom to show the audience nothing—or, more precisely, to show us what nothing looks like.

Over the course of his career, Haneke has consistently paired the long take not with variation but with dronelike repetition. I am thinking specifically of the half-minute shot of female gymnasts vaulting over a horse in *The Seventh Continent* (1989), the three-minute shot of Max (Lukas Miko) practicing table tennis returns in *71 Fragments of a Chronology of Chance* (1994), and the forty-five-second shot of a drum performance by hearing impaired students at the end of *Code Unknown* (2000). Initially, these dialogueless long takes are hypnotic, drawing the viewer into their autistic rhythms. Beyond a certain point, however, we cannot help but wonder when the shot is going to cut away, the director having violated our expectations about how long an "actionless" take should be allowed to persist. Not all of Haneke's long takes frame such banal scenes, though, and we could say that Haneke evinces a kind of calculated indifference in deploying the long take, treating mundane events and life-shattering traumas with cold equanimity, observing them all with the same unflinching stare. Consider the videotaped killing of the young girl in *Benny's Video* (1992) or the infamous ten-minute shot following the son's murder in *Funny Games* (1997). Far from banal in terms of content, it is nonetheless the obdurate inertia of the camera at these moments of high drama—an aggressively passive refusal to deliver us beyond the present scene, or to indicate how we should feel about it—that is most disturbing of all.

When *Caché* begins, the viewer must endure two and a half minutes of mundane street activity, accompanied only by the sound of chirping birds and mild traffic noise, before anything like a narrative commences. "Well?" asks a voice that we later learn belongs to Georges. "Nothing," responds Georges's wife, Anne (Juliette Binoche). The exchange will resound throughout the film. Indeed, I want to argue that the entire point of the tape, misunderstood by the protagonists at every opportunity, is to show Georges that no one is looking at him—not only in this instance, but all of the time. Quite significantly, Anne reveals that the duration of the video she found on the doorstep is about two hours—the length of a standard VHS or Hi-8 cassette tape. In an interesting counterpoint to Alfred Hitchcock's *Rope* (1948), which employs various techniques to camouflage the periodic need to change film magazines on-set, the camcorder footage comes to an end precisely when the recording medium itself "times out." By indicating that an arbitrary technological limitation caused the camera to shut itself down, Haneke implies another, perhaps more ideal, scenario in which the camera would *always be running*, a perpetual robotic witness.[6] What Lacan calls "the split between the eye and the gaze" is thus literalized in the trope of a video camera that is "rolling" but is doing so automatically, with no apparent director, no subject to look through the eyepiece and call "Cut!"[7]

In addition to functioning as a perverse long take, the duration of "Plastic Bag Video #1" may also be construed as a mockery of the conventional Hollywood establishing shot—usually a stock image of a building, house, or other recognizable setting that lasts only for a few seconds, time enough for the viewer to register a sense of location. By contrast, the three minutes of immobility at the beginning of *Caché* does not launch us into the scene that follows but instead captures us in the process of establishing. Establishing what? We do not know, because the duration of the shot masks it off. The resounding question for the viewer is, Why this? or more pointedly, What does this camera want? Michel Chion explains the use of extended duration in cinema as follows: "If a camera remains fixed on a setting once the actors have left the frame . . . it is impossible for us not to see an intention, even as we sense that this empty setting does not care in the least. The opaqueness of the setting is redoubled by a second opaqueness that we might put this way: what is happening right now *in the head of the camera?*[8] Chion is, of course, being ironic here, since the basic apparatus of the camera—by which I mean the optics, imaging sensor, recording system, and so on—once it is running, has no "head," no built-in consciousness (or unconsciousness), to direct what we see. At the level of the machine, then, it would be a mistake to read the image in terms of the "male gaze" or "the postcolonial gaze" because the camera-machine does not look. This is not to say that such a mechanism could not be mobilized for ideological purposes, only that on some level—for Lacan, the order of the real—we are always by definition outside ideology. Yet if there is no subject "in" the machine, only the physical processes of image capture, the cinematic audience is rarely reminded of this. The camera appears naturally to know what it is doing, except when it becomes distracted, lethargic, or obstinately static. It is this deathly static gaze—which is to say the gaze in its purest form—that Haneke delivers for our extended consideration in his opening shot.

*Caché* underscores the nonempirical, essentially vacant locus of the gaze by staging duration in the form of a mise-en-abyme in which we are not only shown ad nauseum the street-level view of a city residence but also, without initially realizing it, the video itself as an object. Whereas common sense dictates that the plastic bag videos are designed to show the Laurents their own gated, bourgeois existence from an outsider's perspective, this is not their real function. Rather, the videos work in a more primal way to call attention to the field of vision itself by establishing a point from which one might look—an angle on reality that *would look like this* if there were anyone there to do the looking. This is not a negligible theoretical distinction but instead the very crux of the film: an insistence, reemphasized through the subsequent arrival of a series of similar-looking videos, that while one can reckon with an unexpected onlooker, no one occupies the place of the gaze.

## Chè vuoi?

By depicting his protagonists' responses to an unseen (and ostensibly unseeable) video camera, Haneke repeatedly reminds us that the gaze is not the look, which is to say that the gaze is not on the side of the subject but on the side of the object. Two crucial implications follow from this. First, whereas the look can be manipulated for gain—for instance, to impel someone to desire in a certain way—the gaze, understood as a site of failure in a perceptual field, is less obviously deployable. It resists being manipulated or imposed, because there can be never be any guarantee as to how or to what extent or whether at all a given subject will respond to its appearance. This is a fundamental point that 1970s apparatus theory, along with Laura Mulvey's feminist account of classical Hollywood style, largely misses, having incorrectly assigned the Lacanian term "gaze" to what is actually a "look."[9] To borrow Bazin's terminology, theories such as Mulvey's seek to account for the way cinema frames its objects at the expense of any theorization of how it masks them. Whereas a given look—a particular desire-inflected view of an object—can itself be represented and seen, the gaze lacks this ontologically positive status. This is not to say that looks are unimportant. There can be little question, for instance, that the camera of classical Hollywood functions exactly as Mulvey contends, as a kind of shill for patriarchy—seeking, through the sheer repetition of its gendered way of seeing, to coerce the audience into adopting a masculine desire for imaginary mastery. However, such a dynamic has nothing to do with the way Lacan conceives of the gaze. When the subject encounters the gaze in a truly Lacanian sense—either as a black hole that both disrupts and sustains one's desire in a field of vision or as a point at which a representation impossibly "looks back" at the viewer—the potential for ideological interpellation (or "hailing") of the subject is at once more potent and less predictable. The obtrusive nonsensicality of the gaze can hardly fail to usurp the viewer's attention, yet all bets are off as to how the viewer—always and already a subject of unconscious desire—will behave in response to this call. A shocking eruption of the real within one's symbolic network may lead to a radical break, but it may also lead to deeper ideological retrenchment, as *Caché* so pointedly demonstrates.

Secondly, for Haneke as for Lacan, the gaze is not the look because the gaze is nonconfirmative in its very structure. One senses that one is being looked at precisely because one cannot verify that anyone is watching. If, in Georges's case, the face or voice of the mysterious videographer (or indeed any trace of his/her identity) were to appear, either on tape or in person, the gaze would necessarily disappear. The videocassettes Georges receives are thus much more (or much less) than anonymous—the term often used to describe so-called poison pen letters, which by definition spell out their intent. Instead, they are a message whose message is that there is no message. To attempt to attach a name—be it "Majid," "Majid's son," or even "Pierrot"—to the tapes does nothing to alleviate the disturbance they cause, because the gaze cannot be pinned down in this way; its dim unresponsiveness confounds any effort to make sense. When Georges confesses his predicament to his editor-in-chief at the television station (Bernard Le Coq), he says that the police will not act on the case so long as it remains "n'a rien de dramatique." This is a useful way to describe the gaze: nothing too dramatic.

The plot of the 1999 film *The Blair Witch Project* (Daniel Myrick and Eduardo Sánchez) develops similarly around a series of remarkably undramatic objects, points of encounter at which the film wisely does not mistake the gaze for the look. The real horror of the film's pseudodocumentary approach derives not from any face-to-face encounter between the filmmakers and the elusive witch (who never actually materializes on screen) but instead from the occasional discovery of a nondescript pile of rocks on the ground or a knot of twigs hanging from a branch, each of which implies (but never confirms) a cryptic author hovering patiently just beyond the horizon of the protagonists' campsite. In this sense, *Blair Witch* "never reduces the gaze to the field of the visible," to borrow Todd McGowan's formulation.[10] Moreover, the film's makeshift witch objects—oddly captivating in their dearth of signifying elements—help to clarify that the subject's relation to the gaze is in no way hermeneutic; the gaze does not bear the structure of a question mark, which implies the possibility of a solution. Rather, the gaze is a lacuna, a structural dead end, the significance of which can neither be intellectually probed nor triangulated. Any response to the gaze must thus come wholly from the unconscious of the subject, since there can be no "answer" from the side of the object.

As I have hopefully made clear, such desubjectified inertness typifies the gaze as object/cause of desire in Lacanian theory—in other words, the gaze as it appears to the subject on the order of the imaginary. At the same time, the uncanny objects at the center of *Caché* and *Blair Witch*—objects that do not see but nonetheless seem to be watching—can also illuminate Lacan's conception of the gaze on the order of the real, for instance his assertion that the "gaze as such" is designated by its "pulsatile, dazzling, and spread out function."[11] As you read this essay, you presumably have no sense that you are being watched; nor are you aware of any gap or blind spot in your field of vision. Now imagine how the room you occupy might look from a nondescript spot in the corner, any one of the millions of points in space with a clear view of your body. Where in this arrangement does the gaze reside? Inasmuch as your body forms a seeable part of the room, the gaze cannot belong *to* you because it also includes a multitude of perspectives *of* you. Likewise, the gaze cannot belong to any other (small "o") that you can see peering back at you from the corner—betrayed perhaps by a pair of eyes or a camera lens—since this look cannot include itself as part of what it sees. Instead, the gaze must be understood as encompassing both of these looks simultaneously, along with every other available line of sight in the room. In this sense, the gaze is perhaps best conceptualized as the potential inhabitability of the corner of your room, despite the obvious absence of any identifiable looker to receive the rays of light that nonetheless continue to reflect off your body in all directions.

Because it amounts to the sum total of all possible looks, the gaze is wildly undiscriminating, blindly indifferent to all that appears. As human subjects operating on the order of the symbolic, we most often apprehend the gaze as a disruptive failure of completeness; for instance, we suddenly become transfixed by a spatial recess in which we cannot see if anyone sees us. However, the "gaze as such" (that is, in the objective, material real) is different; it is neither a point of specular convergence nor does it momentarily emerge or dissipate. Instead, in its pure form, the gaze is the ceaselessly throbbing, "spread out" multiplicity of the field itself—the set of all possible points from which one may be viewed, provided we acknowledge that the vast majority of these points are not occupied by onlookers, and need not be occupied in order for us to sense that they regard us.

The fact that we rarely become aware of such nonlooks is precisely the point. Indeed, our best gauge of the quiet omnipresence of the gaze is that our sudden awareness of it is always unsettling—an uncommon shock. Haneke produces just such a disruption in the prolonged duration of the first image of *Caché*; what the tape records is a gaze because the viewpoint refuses to confirm that anyone is looking, refuses to humanize itself. At the same time, working to underscore this refusal of the look, an aural version of the gaze is at play in the relative silence, or more pointedly the muteness, of "Plastic Bag Video #1." As the tape plays, no voice on the audio track says, "My camera has captured you, Georges Laurent, and here is what you look like to me," although this is exactly the sort of confirmative judgment Georges seeks. Imagine how a Hollywood director might handle the same video (again De Palma comes to mind). In this imaginary remake—perhaps titled *The Watchers*—the opening proceeds just as in Haneke's original. After a series of red herrings—random cyclists and pedestrians passing through the frame—Georges exits the house and walks toward his car. Suddenly, the camera frame springs to life, detaching from its perch and following Georges as he walks. Like clockwork, a strangely disembodied voice emerges on the soundtrack: "So there you are, the man by the name of Georges Laurent." What this not-so-absurd hypothetical stalker scenario makes clear is that for Haneke, silence itself can be made to speak. The ambient sounds of the street are like the lone cricket chirping at the end of an overblown stage performance in a cartoon; they permit the hush to become legible as "remarkable quietude." Moreover, in the intent-driven set of assumptions surrounding the video, the stark absence of voice can be understood as the message of the Other spoken loud and clear: *I do not tell you what I want.*

It is no coincidence that the most repeated question in *Caché*—its most distinctive line—is both deceptively simple and seemingly impossible for the film and everyone in it to answer: *What do you want?* This is the question Lacan invokes when he proclaims that "man's desire is the Other's desire" or, translated differently, "that it is *qua* Other that man desires": "This is why the Other's question [*la question de l'Autre*]—that comes back to the subject from the place from which he expects an oracular reply—which takes some such form as '*Chè vuoi?*' 'What do you want?' is the question that best leads the subject to the path of his own desire."[12] What Georges wants has everything to do with the answers he posits to the unfathomable question of the Other's desire. The videos he receives can in this way be understood as pure allegory—a highly literal representation of the Lacanian thesis that, for the neurotic human subject (which is to say all of us), the gaze is "not a seen gaze" (in other words, not a set of eyes that look) "but a gaze imagined by me in the field of the Other."[13] This imaginary gaze is exactly what Georges encounters later in the film when an unexpected ring of the doorbell interrupts the Laurents' dinner party. Georges goes down to answer the door, but no one is there. Visibly frustrated, he steps out past the gate and, facing the aptly named rue des Iris, shouts his question to no one: "What's this all about? Show yourself, you coward! Show yourself and say what you want!" In return, the silent, empty maw of the street offers no more of an answer than does the endlessly immobile, unspeaking video that inaugurates the narrative.

## *Dead Eye*

When Georges asks, "Well?" and Anne returns, "Nothing," her response is a perfect summation of the acute indifference that typifies the video's form—its lack of editing, its lack of voice, and a crucial third component I will now introduce: its lack of motility. By refusing to budge, the shot forces us to look "objectively" at the pacing of real life, which, as it turns out, is not very exciting. If, as I indicated earlier, the video is remarkable because its ostensible creator does *not* give Anne and Georges the sniper treatment, it is also notable for Haneke's rejection of a whole series of other audacious camera movements—techniques that, had they been employed, would have added another layer of commentary to the image. After a couple of minutes of intense looking, and once attuned to the shot's minimalism, the viewer almost expects to discover that the camera has (very slowly and imperceptibly) zoomed in a bit—as in the opening shot of Francis Ford Coppola's *The Conversation* (1974) or perhaps Michael Snow's *Wavelength* (1967). Again, this is not the case.

Haneke's great insight here is that far from rendering a neutral or truthful/vérité view of things, an excess of stasis paradoxically distorts the image by *refusing* to alter it (through editing, zooming, and so on). In other words, there is no need to resort to subtle extradiegetic techniques because the prolonged fixity of the frame itself has the potential to "move" viewers to desire—most commonly, one imagines, to seek an answer to the question, Why this? The sporadic movement through the frame of various pedestrians only enhances this effect, reminding us that this is not a still photograph or painting but rather a perversely recalcitrant "motion" picture—a cinema sans attractions. At the same time, the stasis of the shot helps to demarcate its source as punctiform—a statuelike, singular coordinate in space that stubbornly resists subjectification. In this sense, the locked-down long take displaces its own most logical countershot, a shopworn convention that has come to be associated with the thriller genre, especially in its Gothic and noir variants: the fleeting appearance in the protagonist's field of vision of a shadowy figure in a window across the way. Indeed, the conspicuous absence of any such apparition is part of what makes the rue des Iris so disturbing, both for the viewer and for Georges. We do not get any sense of a subjective being that is doing the looking but rather the dead-eye perspective of a windowpane itself: an iris whose view of things is untainted by desire, markedly neutral. The video eye belongs not to any human onlooker but to the unmanned, zombielike mechanism of the camera lens—an opening in space that does not lead, follow, or judge what it sees.[14]

The dead stillness of the video can usefully be compared to a much-imitated shot from Carl Theodor Dreyer's 1932 film *Vampyr—Der Traum des Allan Grey*.[15] In the film, protagonist Allan Grey (Julian West) spends the night at a remote castle and has a hallucinatory dream in which his dead body is placed into a coffin with a small glass window in the lid, just above his face. Intercut with shots of Allan's glassy open eyes, Dreyer and cinematographer Rudolph Maté provide what can only be described as a corpse's-eye view as the coffin travels on a horse cart toward the burial site. Like the austere opening of *Caché*, the shots are at once audacious and crude. The traveling camera points directly up at the sky, revealing the undersides of trees, the spires and buttresses of a passing cathedral, and at one point an elderly female vampire who rests the base of a candle on the glass, underscoring its perverse status as a window on the world for a passenger who cannot look. "Plastic Bag Video #1" recapitulates this technique but without benefit of any passing objects to bring the deadness of the gaze into high relief. Nonetheless, both of these unusual shots invite us to behold the gaze from "its own" viewpoint, as it were—an alienating perspective, to be sure, and one that seems designed to polarize viewers of *Caché* from the outset.

If the shot from *Vampyr* is instantaneously unsettling, owing to both its inertia and its representation of a grave-bound angle that no one ever sees, the *unheimliche*, "living dead" quality of *Caché*'s opening shot becomes apparent more gradually, eventually benefiting from the series of contextual clues that come to overlay it: the image-distorting "scan lines" that appear when the video rewinds, as well as the characters' running commentary on what they see. "It's dumb," Georges says to Anne, finally stopping the video player. "I don't know what to say." Joan Copjec describes the gaze in exactly these terms—as a confrontation in which one expects to find a living, responding look back and instead encounters the abject stupidity of an unmotivated blank stare:

When you encounter the gaze of the Other, you meet not a seeing eye but a blind one. The gaze is not clear or penetrating, not filled with knowledge or recognition; it is clouded and turned back on itself, absorbed in its own enjoyment. The horrible truth . . . is that *the gaze does not see you*. So, if you are looking for confirmation of the truth of your being or the clarity of your vision, you are on your own; the gaze of the Other is not confirming; it will not validate you.[16]

As Copjec implies, the human subject, virtually by definition, seeks confirmation and recognition of various sorts. Yet even when our status is affirmed, we cannot help but seek further validation. To be clear, in Copjec's reading of Lacan, the Other (capital "O") is not any individual person or group of persons but a desire-motivating, judgmental function that cannot be satisfied because it has no objective status; it is a pure projection by the subject, albeit a necessary one for the subject to continue as a social being. Likewise, Georges's problem is one of nonconfirmation, nonvalidation. He cannot determine whether or not he is being watched, or by whom. If he could, *Caché* would be a very different movie, and ultimately much simpler. More to the point, Georges cannot discern *in what way* he is being watched. In other words, he cannot determine the attitude of the watcher, that is, what the watcher wants.

"Plastic Bag Video #1" can in this sense be understood as the material embodiment of the old cliché "Did you ever have the feeling you were being watched?" reified and given narrative weight in the form of a reviewable strand of tape. Yet, when Georges investigates the rue des Iris, anticipating the discovery of a look, he instead encounters the truth about the gaze: that it is a pure semblance. There is no sign of a camera, and although he can recall walking by the spot from which the footage appears to have been shot, he does not remember seeing anything out of the ordinary on that day. How do we account for this apparent contradiction? The answer is that Georges cannot locate the camera that produced the gaze on the tape because his desire has distorted his view of the world such that it cannot appear. In a strong sense, any subject's vision cannot exist except insofar as it is polarized by desire, mobilized for desire. As such, our field of vision must contain a point of failure—an inscrutable blot that sets the chain of desire moving. As Slavoj Žižek notes: "I can never see properly, can never include in the totality of my field of vision, the point in the other from which it gazes back at me."[17] The location of the gaze is a scotoma, or blind spot, and it is surely no accident that Georges's investigative desire to ascertain what this spot masks off leads him in the direction of his boyhood rival Majid (Maurice Bénichou).

## *The Psychodynamics of Escalation*

In the previous sections, I have argued that the set of formal features that distinguish "Plastic Bag Video #1"—its lack of editing, voice, and movement—are united by paradox; they are all instances in which nullity takes on a profound and positive weight. The video is structured around a series of masklike blockages: inert zones capable of energizing desire in unexpected ways, aberrations that "[appear] to offer access to the unseen, to the reverse side of the visible."[18] What remains unaccounted for, however, is the escalation of tensions that are touched off by the video, resulting in the jarring and unforgettable image of Majid's suicide—a slash of blood that, for startled first-time viewers, pierces through the screen to reveal the audience's own complicity in Georges's illusion of mastery. Despite his visibility in the public eye, the fact is that no one is looking at Georges, and his inability to fathom the Other's nonexistence is what transforms the film from a mystery thriller into a tragedy. If someone *were* looking at Georges, the solution would be easy enough for a relatively wealthy and respected man. Instead, as I have indicated, the film's primary conflict is not that Georges is being attacked but that he cannot divine an answer as to what the Other wants. The videos are, after all, utterly neutral in what they portray—the motivation behind them does not appear in them—and the result is escalation, a kind of "road rage" of intersubjective presupposition regarding the Other's malicious intent.

This theme is not uncommon in Haneke's films. Both in *Caché* and in *Code Unknown*, we see street-level confrontations develop between men of different races. In *Caché*, Georges and Anne are exiting the police station when a young black cyclist (Diouc Koma) nearly runs into them. When Georges accosts the man and a fistfight seems imminent, it becomes clear that no offense was intended by the cyclist (did he stop to complain or to apologize?) and that Georges's insular, self-righteous attitude is the real problem. In *Code Unknown*, the complex opening street scene culminates when Amadou (Ona Lu Yenke), a young, first-generation African immigrant, is arrested by Parisian police. He is not guilty of anything but says that he will nonetheless come along to the station of his own free will to clarify the matter. He does not need to be touched since he has done nothing wrong and will peacefully comply. The police take this passive gesture as an active affront and begin violently grappling with Amadou. Although it is no great leap to read both of these scenes in terms of prevailing Western attitudes about racial otherness, their overriding logic has more to do with the function of inertia in a dynamic of escalation. In other words, they raise the question, What happens when one subject is confronted by another's obstinately neutral signification? For Haneke, the answer seems to be that *violence* inevitably happens, the result of an ever-intensifying feedback loop fueled by the foreclosure of the Other's desire.

In terms of its primary generic convention—a domestic terrorist who will not reveal himself—*Caché* bears a surprising resemblance to Steven Spielberg's 1971 made-for-television movie *Duel*.[19] The connection is especially salient given the tenuous, strangely inscrutable sources of the films' respective conflicts and the rapidity with which they escalate. If a first-time viewer were shown a short sequence from the middle of either *Caché* or *Duel*, it would be abundantly clear who the antagonist is. However, when we watch either film from beginning to end and then reflect back upon its inciting incident, we realize that we cannot say with any certainty which of the two warring parties initiated the conflict to begin with. What if Georges had simply ignored the appearance of the first tape? Would the problem have just gone away, precluding Majid's suicide? What if *Duel*'s protagonist, David Mann (Dennis Weaver), had been more patient when the smoke-spewing tanker truck passed him on a downhill grade, instead of becoming aggravated when his progress was slowed? Although in both films it initially seems clear who we are supposed to side with, at a certain point we become less sure. To quote the cyclist in *Caché*, perhaps it does not ultimately matter "which moron stepped out without looking."

Despite their similarities in theme, however, *Caché* and *Duel* diverge quite radically at the level of form. Whereas *Duel* represents the gaze objectively, in the protagonist's impossible relation to the shadowy cab of the "killer" truck (photographed in various ways so as to obscure the driver's face and eyes), the videos in *Caché* insist on a more reflexive relation to the gaze. In permitting the Laurents' television screen to fill the cinematic frame entirely, Haneke constructs a subjective point of view that is not unlike the many point-of-view shots out of the windows of David Mann's speeding car. Yet our experience of the videos is never comfortably or "purely" diegetic because we do not perceive anything beyond their edges. Moreover, at no point do we see any room light reflections on the screen. Consequently, our own act of watching is oddly decontextualized, calling into question whether what we are seeing is a look or the gaze—whether this is Georges's perspective or solely the camera's.

Too, unlike *Duel*, the gaze is not universally faceless in *Caché*, and the nonconfirmative countenance of the Other is nowhere better illustrated than in Georges's initial face-to-face visit with Majid at his low-rent flat. In terms of performance, it is crucial that Maurice Bénichou, the actor who so sensitively portrays Majid, for the most part looks directly at Georges with his head up and his face fully available to the camera. In Georges's symbolic context—which the viewer is led to share—this rather ambiguous, pedestrian expression of attentiveness uncannily emblematizes Majid's defiance and suggests that he is smugly withholding some secret motive. Georges cannot view the inhabitant of the room as anything but hostile—anything but the video terrorist—and the film's audience by this point has so thoroughly identified with Georges's mindset regarding the contents of apartment number 047 that it takes a second viewing to recognize that Majid's expressions may be something other than disingenuous. Only on a second pass can we appreciate that what we formerly interpreted as a kind of mocking sarcasm on Majid's face is, in actuality, an indicator of real confusion about Georges's sudden appearance at his door.

In his essay on Haneke's use of the long take, John David Rhodes likens *Code Unknown* to a mystery film in which "we realize too late that we have misread clues." The difference, however, lies in Haneke's seemingly all-too-objective "matter-of-fact unspooling" of plot information: "Here there is no mystery, there are only facts. These facts become mysteries retrospectively only because we realize that we did not know that we did not know, or that we did not know that our not knowing was at all an issue."[20] This assessment speaks equally well to *Caché*. At the point in the film when Georges first encounters Majid, the viewer is firmly ensconced in just such a syntax, rather than its opposite. In other words, we fail absolutely to see that this is *the point in the film when Majid first encounters Georges*. In a very real sense, it is impossible to fathom that *Caché* is (and always has been) Majid's story; indeed, the story is Majid's to the precise extent that Georges's very being (including his occupation, his class status, his role as a husband and father, and so on) is founded on the repression of everything Majid signifies for him. Beyond Haneke's efforts to create the experience we expect from a thriller, and beyond any attempt at ideological consciousness-raising, the director's larger effort, both here and in other films, is to make us see the way our own desire creates a distorted field of engagement from the outset—in *Caché*, our all-too-easily-held assumption that Georges's explicit threats against Majid have been entirely justified. The real horror of Majid's suicide, and what makes first-time viewers inevitably gasp and jerk to attention in their seats, is not only Haneke's uncharacteristically graphic depiction of violence but also the fact that we instantaneously become aware of the extent to which we have been aligned with Georges's subjectivity, his particular worldview. Suddenly, "we realize that we did not know that we did not know."

Oddly distanced from the action and a bit overexposed, the camera in the suicide scene never moves, and it seems clear that the style of the shot is meant to recall the hidden-camera video of Majid crying in the apartment midway though the film. In the context of this clinical, excessively objective view, the bold streak of red that appears on the wall behind Majid is, for the viewer, the film's ultimate eruption of the gaze. Preceded by Majid's statement to Georges, "I called you because I wanted you to be present," the arterial spray from Majid's neck is so preposterous in the context of our sympathy for the (apparently) persecuted Georges that it is as if our look itself has ruptured, revealing the heretofore invisible obverse of the filmic world we have shared with him.

In its cold framing, Georges's final visit to Majid can be understood as a suicidal inversion of the climax of Hitchcock's *Rear Window* (1954), when "Jeff" Jeffries (James Stewart) receives an ominously silent phone call from Lars Thorwald (Raymond Burr), signaling that he has identified Jeff as his interloper and is on his way to Jeff's apartment. The difference, of course, is that in Haneke's conceptual remake, Jeff, the likable would-be detective, turns out to be a monster, whereas the suspicious Thorwald is revealed to be completely innocent—a devoted, hard-working husband whose wife suddenly left him for another man. My point here is that our alignment with Georges is no less galvanizing that our alignment with Jeff and that our identification with both characters, along with the escalation of their respective conflicts, develops around a series of masked-off blind spots. And although it would be unthinkable for Hitchcock's Thorwald to climb to the roof of the apartment building and leap to his death, Haneke delivers an analogous moment of impossibility. In *Caché,* it takes a jarring, frame-shattering instant of violence to convince us that the man in the mysterious apartment "across the way" has done nothing wrong and that the film's ostensible protagonist, having misinterpreted everything he has seen, has been the real menace from the outset.

Even after the suicide, however, Georges cannot seem to fathom that Majid did not "want" something from him. Moreover, no explicit reason for the suicide is ever given; it is left wholly open to interpretation. Majid's experience in custody is only ever talked about, never seen, except for a few seconds in the police van. Yet if we presume Majid is innocent, his experiences following the initial meeting with Georges must have been terrifying, subject as he was to explicit persecution and physical detainment. It is easy to imagine Majid's line of thinking: *As a six-year-old child, he ruined my life once, and now he is a powerful and wealthy adult; why wouldn't he be able to do exactly what he is promising—destroy my life once again?* Yet, to be clear, Majid's point of view is precisely what the film categorically omits, and even the aftermath of his suicide fails to produce the kind of satisfying, easy answer that Hollywood thrillers have led us to expect.

If the video is, as Georges characterizes it, "dumb," in retrospect it is impossible to miss the way in which the video's dumbness is both his/our own, and at the same time a mask that lures him/us in, motivating a desire for answers. Later in the film, however, we get a slightly different account of things. After watching the second plastic bag video—a nearly identical nighttime shot of the house—Anne says, "It's dumb, but it scares me." The difference between the first and second assessments tells us why the nonconfirmation of the Other tends to incite violent escalation and not a more efficacious, rational response. Our defensive response to the gaze will always exceed the mark—in some cases spiraling out of control—because, as Haneke makes clear, where the gaze is concerned there is no "mark." In other words, there is no such thing as excess when faced with a rival that refuses to show itself, dumbly refusing to answer. At its core, this is precisely the problem with apparatus theory: it presumes that a wise, manipulative rival is structuring our desires, rather than a stupid, inert one. Richly developed by Haneke, what we might call *"cache theory"* resolves this contradiction, and it is easy to imagine his films becoming a conduit for new psychoanalytic theory in the same way that Hitchcock's films have served it in the past.

## *Conclusion: Undoing the Impossible*

Counter to the common sense, humanist readings of Georges's motivations that dominate most critical assessments of *Caché*, a psychoanalytic account would insist that Georges does not seek to avoid a realization of the Other's desire but instead to solicit such an encounter. The apparently contradictory fact that he effectuates this encounter by way of a defensive posture is, according to psychoanalysis, no contradiction at all. The key is to push this reading to account for the interstices of the narrative—the many years between Georges's youth on the country estate and his present-day existence as a public television personality. We need not be too specific about chronology: between 1961 and the present day, Georges has unconsciously structured his entire waking life—especially his career as a public figure, broadcast into homes nationwide—as a means of luring Majid back into the picture, back into contact, to answer the question of the Other's desire once and for all. Yet, as the film repeatedly stresses, the goal of such a lure can never be fully realized, except perhaps in the kind of tragedy that plays out in the film's third act. In many of Haneke's films, television—or better, televisuality—implies a comfortable but ultimately illusory distanciation between the viewer and a mediated object. In *Caché*, a series of video recordings bring about the collapse of this distance. Having attained real nearness—in effect having teleported Georges into

Majid's reality—the result is not clarity and understanding, as one might idealistically hope. Rather, when Georges comes face-to-face with his object of desire, the other (small "o") he encounters cannot do anything but disappoint, pathetically imploding under the weight of the Other (capital "O") he is expected to be.

As the narrative nears its conclusion and the audience is set up for a kind of epiphany—recognizing on some level that the gaze and the look are not the same—it becomes clear that, despite his tribulations, Georges has utterly failed to make this same realization. Early in the film, upon seeing himself walk directly past the ostensible "camera" in the first video, Georges remarks, "How come I didn't see him?" He quickly concludes, "It'll remain a mystery," and indeed Georges remains invested in the notion of Majid's involvement in a mysterious conspiracy to the bitter end and beyond, even after his rival appears to have been vanquished. He remains convinced that his actions were justified because someone *was* looking, entirely missing the structural necessity of his own blindness. To share any part of Majid's perspective would result in a complete breakdown; in McGowan's words, "Though we can accomplish the impossible, we can't do so without simultaneously destroying the ground beneath our feet."[21] As in Lacanian theory, for Haneke the impossible is indeed possible; in other words, it is both doable and an experience one occasionally endures. The impossible is not, then, a violation of physical laws but a violation of a particular subject's symbolic network—the set of unquestioned ideological "givens" that condition each subject's everyday practices. In taking a couple of sleeping pills at the end of the film (our vantage makes it very clear that he ingests only two, not a suicidal overdose—the other obvious option for him), Georges opts not to do the impossible but in effect to *undo* it, drifting back into his role as a respectable and profoundly repressed bourgeois subject.

Despite all the news footage that appears on the Laurents' television screen, Haneke's film presses beyond a positivistic assertion that Western capitalist oppressors need to raise their consciousness about exploited, warring peoples in developing nations. *Caché* is much more radical and, frankly, more bleak than this. Instead, in both its narrative and its style, *Caché* makes clear that for any desiring subject certain recognitions are constitutively impossible, beyond any hope of realization except in the form of an ego-shattering, perhaps revolutionary breakdown. Even having witnessed Majid's suicide face-to-face, any final encounter with the desire

## "Comment ça, rien?": Screening the Gaze in Caché

of the Other remains unrealizable, both for Georges and ultimately for the viewer as well. The symbolic framework in which Georges exists, and in which he was raised—the set of parameters that constitute his sense of the possible—are simply too rigidly ossified to admit any other options. Because he is a good Cartesian subject, Georges cannot read the inert glare of the Other as anything other than intent, and as the film ends we presume he will go on behaving as he has since his childhood on the country estate, all too willing to demonize, and perhaps to banish, what he fails to understand.[22] In this way, Georges's naked retreat into his dark, womblike bedroom at film's end represents neither a victory over the gaze nor a defeat but merely a much-needed rest after having endured some temporarily uncomfortable circumstances. This gesture in no way mitigates Haneke's position that radical transformation is possible for individual subjects; the key is to not follow Georges's example and instead to risk everything on doing the impossible, however difficult or traumatic this may be.

Beyond this, we are left with the mask structure of the film's final shot—another mute, highly ambiguous static long take, this time depicting Majid's son (Walid Afkir) and Georges's son, Pierrot (Lester Makedonsky), chatting on the school steps. What we see could be a concurrent event in the waking world or Georges's dream of a better future. It could also be yet another plastic bag video, or even a flashback that predates the arrival of the first tape, revealing the beginnings of a heretofore unsubstantiated conspiracy between the young men. Whatever ending we would like to see, the shot's masklike structure overrides any possibility of a finally satisfying easy answer, suggesting that Haneke would, at the very least, impose some qualifications on the newfound "hope for the future" some critics have attributed to the film's conclusion (especially in light of the seemingly amicable tone of the exchange on the steps). Counter to this rosy picture, *Caché* places the human subject in a vicious deadlock with the big Other of the symbolic order. If the film is right, our only hope for meaningful contact with individual others must come by way of a recognition of our own necessary misrecognition that the Other exists. In this resistance to easy resolutions, as in his carefully wielded inertness of style, perhaps Haneke would not at all object to being aligned with Lacan. Both are philosophers and theorists whose positions are inextricable from their practice. More to the point, however, both are antihumanists in the best possible sense, which is to say unapologetically, even brazenly insistent on the power of nothing.

## *Notes*

1. Todd McGowan, *The Real Gaze: Film Theory after Lacan* (Albany: SUNY Press, 2007), 7.

2. André Bazin, *What Is Cinema?* vol. 1, trans. Hugh Gray (Berkeley: University of California Press, 1967), 105.

3. Though lacking the cryptic brevity of the English-language title *Hidden*, *Caché* might better be translated as "Masked Off" or "Blotted Out," two phrases that more properly evoke the gaze-producing structures in the film.

4. Mladen Dolar, *A Voice and Nothing More* (Cambridge: MIT Press, 2006), 39. The other "paramount embodiment" of *objet petit a* is, of course, the voice, and Dolar's book is the definitive work on this subject.

5. McGowan, *Real Gaze*, 6.

6. We could easily write off the excessive duration of "Plastic Bag Video #1" as a signifier of surveillance at its most banal—something akin to a convenience store security tape or a weather camera atop a cellular tower—were it not for the fact that our first encounter with the video is at the very beginning of the film and thus lacks any contextualizing frame. So far as any first-pass viewer is concerned, the opening shot *is* the film called *Caché*. In this way, the seeming endlessness of the video is very much like the live feed from the window-camera in *Benny's Video*, mechanically reproducing the banality of the outside world on screen but never intended to be actively scrutinized by the one who engineered the setup.

7. Jacques Lacan, *The Four Fundamental Concepts of Psychoanalysis*, trans. Alan Sheridan (New York: Norton, 1978), 67–78.

8. Michel Chion, *Kubrick's Cinema Odyssey*, trans. Claudia Gorbman (London: BFI, 2001), 139.

9. Laura Mulvey, "Visual Pleasure in Narrative Cinema," in *Film and Theory: An Anthology*, ed. Toby Miller and Robert Stam (Oxford: Blackwell, 2000), 483–94.

10. Todd McGowan, "Looking for the Gaze: Lacanian Film Theory and Its Vicissitudes," *Cinema Journal* 42, no. 3 (2003): 34.

11. Lacan, *Four Fundamental Concepts*, 89.

12. Jacques Lacan, *Écrits: The First Complete Translation in English*, trans. Bruce Fink (New York: Norton, 2006), 690.

13. Lacan, *Four Fundamental Concepts*, 84.

14. This directorless inertia is in no way undermined by two later videos that are shot from inside a moving car. Because the camera's movement is tied directly to the car's movement, its status as a compliant passenger overrides any sense of a subject who is running the show. We sense that "it moves," rather than "he/she is moving it." The exception to this, of course, is when the driver picks up the camera and turns it, revealing Georges's boyhood home. This marked formal departure is baffling in its randomness, and the question, Why the anomaly? itself becomes a sort of gaze.

15. Perhaps the most deliberate homage to Allan Grey's coffin ride is the "Perfect Day" overdose sequence from *Trainspotting* (Danny Boyle, 1996).

16. Joan Copjec, *Read My Desire: Lacan against the Historicists* (Cambridge: MIT Press, 1995), 36.

17. Slavoj Žižek, *Looking Awry: An Introduction to Jacques Lacan through Popular Culture* (Cambridge: MIT Press, 1992), 114.

18. McGowan, *Real Gaze,* 6.

19. For a more detailed discussion of Spielberg's *Duel* in relation to the Lacanian gaze, see McGowan, "Looking," 33–34.

20. John David Rhodes, "Haneke, the Long Take, Realism," *Framework* 47, no. 2 (2006): 18.

21. McGowan, *Real Gaze,* 177.

22. When Georges attempts to explain to Anne why Majid was sent away as a child, his account is full of unfounded judgments: the family doctor who examined Majid and found no illness was an "old fool"; the rooster Georges told Majid to kill was a "cranky bird . . . evil, always attacking us." In this ongoing fantasy of persecution, Georges clearly misrecognizes how his desires remain structured around his subject-forming separation from the (m)Other, an originary trauma that fueled his childhood jealousy of Majid's adoption. The series of videos, inscrutable and always surprising Georges with their arrival, causes this same separation anxiety to return full force in Georges's adult life.

*The Piano Teacher* (2001): Erika as "keyhole."

Fatima Naqvi and Christophe Koné

# The Key to Voyeurism
## Haneke's Adaptation of Jelinek's *The Piano Teacher*

European reviewers warmly greeted the release of Michael Haneke's film *The Piano Teacher* (*La Pianiste*) in 2001—to be expected, perhaps, considering the number of prizes the film garnered at the Cannes Film Festival the same year.[1] To many, *The Piano Teacher* represented a successful adaptation of Elfriede Jelinek's acclaimed 1983 novel by the same title, a fascinating translation from one medium to another. Their reactions, on the whole, lent testimony to the maturity of the discourse surrounding films based on literary predecessors, in that few were interested in the film's supposed "fidelity" to the original novel's contents.[2] In fact, numerous critics stressed that Haneke had profoundly departed from the original to allow a shift in focus. The trajectory these commentators charted for the transfer from novel to film involved the movement from the sociogenesis of female sadomasochism in Jelinek's case to the impossibility of normal intimacy in an emotionally "glaciated" West in Haneke's. (A few with dissonant opinions objected to Haneke's elision of the concrete social and political setting of Jelinek's text in his parodic melodrama of "boy meets girl."[3]) One particularly discerning Austrian reviewer, Klaus Nüchtern, remarked on the specific change that had occurred in the adaptation concerning voyeurism: while Jelinek's novel allows the main character no other choice but to be an intensely controlling *voyeuse,* Haneke's film emphasizes the impossibility of controlling this voyeuristic gaze.[4] This aspect of the film, as it relates to the key and keyhole leitmotif and the topological construction of space, is our focus in this essay.

## The Keyhole and the Keyholder

Haneke's *The Piano Teacher* explores the key and keyhole as symbols for phallic power, repressed female sexuality, and voyeurism at the same time as the film complicates the binary oppositions that an optical metaphor of keyhole as peephole implies (actively voyeuristic subject versus passively viewed object). Ultimately, the film transcends the psychoanalytic paradigms to which it lends itself so readily—and thus fits into Haneke's larger concern with what he perceives as omnipresent explanatory models that have somehow aged and are not quite up to par with the historical moment. Indeed, in the discussion that follows, the prevalence of 1970s film theory, relying heavily on psychoanalysis, should be unsurprising. Both Haneke (born 1942) and Jelinek (born 1946) come of age when these theories had their heyday; however, they both are aware of the theories' limitations once they have become accepted belief. As such, both artists incorporate elements from depth psychology and simultaneously seek to get beyond it.

On one level, the key and keyhole function in the film as a metaphor for genitalia and intercourse, in accordance with the dream symbolism Sigmund Freud outlines in *The Interpretation of Dreams* and in *The Introductory Lectures to Psychoanalysis*.[5] The film revolves around fantasies of violent penetration—penetration that is only accomplished via cuts in flesh (with the razor blade or the kitchen knife), however, or with rape. On another level, the key is also generally associated with the pianist Erika Kohut's overbearing mother, mapping the power relations of patriarchal society—Jelinek's and Haneke's bugaboo—onto the relationship between mother and daughter.[6] The mother can be read, as John Champagne has written, as a "(phallic) Lacanian pre-Oedipal mother, the mother who is both adored and feared by the child because of the child's dependence on her and its closeness to her body."[7] Mother Kohut only relinquishes her power over the key when the suitor Walter Klemmer "overthrows" her during Erika's violation. She is, to a large degree, Lydia Perovic argues, Julia Kristeva's "mythic mother of psychoanalysis," who must be overcome.[8]

The opening of the film already establishes the key as symbol for the power that Erika (Isabelle Huppert) attempts to appropriate from her mother. We are confronted with a medium shot of a closed door from the inside of an apartment. Erika, shown in a medium shot, discreetly opens the door, inches her way in, and carefully closes and locks the door with the safety chain. By doing so, she already signals that there is no way out

## The Key to Voyeurism: Haneke's Adaptation of The Piano Teacher

of this claustrophobic interior and that the spectators will be hostages, forced to witness the ensuing argument between Erika and her mother over the fact that she has returned home late. Heading through the hall to her bedroom, Erika is caught; her mother's reproachful voice from offscreen stops her. Her disembodied interdictions stand in contrast to her diminutive size when she does enter the picture. Tyrannically interrogating her daughter, the elderly mother (Annie Girardot) appears on the screen, blocking her daughter's way into her room and pushing her back into the hall, until Erika completely turns her back on the viewers. Erika's mother grabs the bag from her, searches it, and discovers a dress. Throughout this vehement disagreement, spectators hear the clinking noise of the keys that Erika holds in her gloved hand before throwing them away onto the chest in the hall and rushing to her bedroom closet. Through this gesture, she signifies that she gives up the argument with her mother, for the little girl cannot measure up to her all-powerful progenitor. After returning to the hall where the two women struggle for the dress, Erika, in an outburst of anger, gets into a physical fight with her mother. (The "hole" [*trou*] that she tears into her mother's hair, as Frau Kohut puts it, allows for a moment of tearful reconciliation.)

Interestingly, similar scenes are repeated later, suggesting that this ritual of violence between mother and daughter constantly plays itself out within a restricted space of partially closed doors.[9] Thus spectators follow Erika in her daily routine beginning in the twenty-fourth sequence, when she leaves the apartment in the morning, quits the conservatory in the afternoon, goes to the drive-in theater in the evening, and finally comes home late at night. The first part of this later sequence can be read as the reverse of the film's opening scene. This time, Erika, shown in a medium shot, is getting ready to leave for the conservatory. While talking to her mother, present again only as a voice emanating from offscreen, Erika closes the door of her room and heads to the hall, holding her bag and a Hermès scarf in one hand, her keys and gloves in the other. She stands in front of the mirror, throws keys and gloves on the chest to tie her silk scarf with a key pattern (a version of the *Les Clefs* model with myriad keys) around her head, and finally grabs the keys again before giving her mother instructions and a sullen good-bye kiss. A tone of command is now in her voice; the symbol-laden keys are tied around her head and in her hand.

When Erika returns home in the thirty-third segment, a shift in perspective happens, and the same mise-en-scène from the film's beginning recurs: rather than the more open space of the hallway, it is again the same shot of the closed door from the inside of the now familiar apartment that Erika shares with her mother, which gives way to a similar scene of physical violence between mother and daughter (with slapping now instead of hair pulling). This doubled scene gives the viewer a clearer insight into the peculiarly repetitive behavior of the two women. The daughter invents excuses to escape the mother's gaze and to carve out a private space where she can appropriate the role of the voyeuse rather than the watched object; the mother punishes her daughter for escaping her gaze by tearing apart the daughter's couture clothing. There is an obvious lack of space in the cramped apartment—closed spaces seem to open onto more confined spaces as an illustration of their suffocating relationship. Catherine Wheatley has pointed to the sense of claustrophobia the film engenders: "The claustrophobic décor of the mother and daughter's home and tight close-up framing of the exchanges that take place between the two women within it functions as a visual representation of this excessive closeness."[10]

Although Erika has the keys to the apartment, she rings the bell when she returns home on time, that is, at the time when her controlling mother expects her to be back home, whereas she uses her keys to get in the apartment when she is coming home late—probably in the secret and vain hope of sneaking past her mother, who always stays up until her daughter is back, watching television and drinking. When Walter (Benoît Magimel) follows Erika into the staircase of her building, she rings the doorbell. By doing so, she acts as if she does not have the keys, indicating her presence to her mother and demonstrating her regression to a little girl, precisely what she had warned her mother against in the twenty-fourth sequence. (Significantly her red hat makes her look like an antique porcelain doll and is removed by Walter before his attempt at a kiss.) After boldly imposing his presence on the mother, who in astonishment opens the door to the couple, Walter follows Erika into her room. There, in order to have some privacy, they must push a dresser against the door to prevent Erika's mother from intruding, for Erika does not have the key to her own room nor does she sleep there. Spectators rarely glimpse the keys that Erika holds in her hands; by and large, they only perceive their clinking noise. For the one who dwells in the realm of sound like the piano teacher, it is apparently appropriate to have ghostlike, purely acoustic keys. During the late-night visit that Walter pays Erika, forcing his way into her apartment, he makes sure to emphasize this fact with a tinge of irony. "At least this one has a key. How about one for your daughter's room?" ("Eh bien voilà! Ici au moins il y a une clef! Ça serait bien que votre fille en ait une aussi pour sa chambre, vous croyez pas?"), he smirks, while he is locking the mother in the bedroom to have his way with the daughter in the entry hall. While the mother carries the keys as an attribute of power, the daughter merely wears them as a fashion accessory akin to the Hermès silk carré that she uses as a headscarf when she goes to work in the conservatory and later in the drive-in theater. Significantly, she ties her scarf around her head, which the later "key"—the letter to Walter—is supposed to metaphorically unlock. As the seat of rationality, her mind has the upper hand, she warns, over any supposedly heart-centered emotions. "I have no feelings" ("Je n'ai pas de sentiments"), she warns Walter when she gives the letter to him: "Get that into your head. If ever I do, they won't defeat my intelligence" ("Vous feriez bien de vous mettre ça dans la tête. Et même si j'en ai un jour, ils ne triompheront jamais de mon intelligence").[11] Erika, deprived by the phallic mother of any key(s), compensates her lack of power with its pictorial representation but simultaneously relies on symbolism to guard against any real power. In many ways, the protagonist, although middle-aged, appears as a female child with penis envy who must disavow her castration.[12]

Images of key and keyhole are present in the sequence that takes place at the drive-in theater, where Erika prowls at night to spy on couples having sex in cars. Significantly, Haneke's adaptation shifts this episode of voyeurism from Jelinek's Prater Park to a drive-in, to Austria's only "Autokino" on the periphery of Vienna. By utilizing this setting, Haneke not only suggests a criticism of the Hollywood blockbusters filling European screens (the 2000 action films *Frequency* and *The Skulls* are being shown) but more importantly establishes a link between cinematic voyeurism in general and the consummation of consumers. As explosions fill the screen, the audience "comes." The other effect of this setting is to reverse the inside-outside nature of the film viewing experience: as Erika attempts to escape her enclosure (she compares her home to a "cage"), she moves into the strangely public-private space of an open-air theater, where viewers can be more private in their cars than they could be in a regular cinema. As such, she is on the one hand engaged in a privately public voyeurism, in which we all are when we go to the movies. On the other, she assumes the position of an exhibitionist, who also undermines the distinction between public and private. She is seen masturbating her admirer in the bathroom of the conservatory, stalking copulating couples, and fellating Walter in the storage room of the ice rink—always wearing the trench coat that has become the exhibitionist's clichéd trademark. Erika puts on a show for the spectators, but to their great discontent, it is never the exciting performance that they want to see.

Accordingly, Haneke continues his interrogation of the role of cinema as institution, which, in a metaphor particularly befitting our discussion, has been itself compared to a "hole" in the societal fabric. As film theorist Christian Metz already wrote in the 1970s:

Going to the cinema is one lawful activity among others with its place in the admissible pastimes of the day or the week, and yet that place is a "hole" in the social cloth, a *loophole* opening on to something slightly more crazy, slightly less approved than what one does the rest of the time.

[Aller au cinéma est un acte licite parmi d'autres, qui a sa place dans l'emploi du temps avouable de la journée ou de la semaine, et cette place est pourtant un "trou" dans l'étoffe sociale, un *créneau* qui ouvre sur quelque chose d'un peu plus fou, d'un peu moins approuvé que ce qu'on fait le reste du temps.][13]

The spectators' voyeurism within the institution cinema always retains something of this prohibited character of the primal scene, where it "is always surprised, never contemplated at leisure" ("celle-ci est toujours surprise, jamais contemplée à loisir"). The titillation of transgression is not to be underestimated: "The permanent cinemas of big cities, with their highly anonymous clientele entering or leaving furtively, in the dark, in the middle of the action, represent this transgression factor rather well" ("Les cinémas permanents des grandes villes, à public foncièrement anonyme, où l'on entre et d'où l'on sort furtivement, dans le noir, en plein milieu de l'action, figurent assez bien ce coefficient de transgression").[14] The mise-en-abyme in Haneke's drive-in sequence implies the cinemagoers' furtive desire for a kind of vicarious phallic *jouissance* via Metz's "hole"; to this effect, Erika is here identified with the motif of the key and keyhole. As she leaves the snack bar to wander around, the medium close-up of her head, juxtaposed against numerous screens behind her, makes the pictured keys on her headscarf distinguishable. Additionally, Erika herself appears in silhouette as a keyhole, filmed in a long shot while walking through the drive-in theater. The shot clearly identifies the spectators as voyeurs, no different than Erika, with similar desires.[15] Significantly, the images of keys and keyhole that are found on the female body appear on the screen precisely when the female character stands outlined against the movie screen.

*The Key to Voyeurism: Haneke's Adaptation of* The Piano Teacher

It is through this female keyhole that the spectators watch and get an eyeful. The spectators' male gendering is here reintroduced; woman is reduced to the empty space of the hole in the process.

We mentioned earlier that Erika transcends the voyeur's (or voyeuse's) position. Of course, Erika's disavowal of her impotence is connected to her voyeurism, for watching through the keyhole gives her a phallic *jouissance*.[16] To illustrate this, the whole sequence where she is walking through parked cars in the drive-in, looking to satisfy her voyeuristic desires, and finally comes closer to one vehicle for a better view, is her point-of-view shot. The spectators are indeed watching random people having sex in the backseats of their cars through her (eyes) and with her.[17] As Wheatley notes: "[While] she spies on a copulating couple at a drive-in movie, Erika urinates as she watches, an act which can possibly be interpreted as a form of female ejaculation."[18] Her face, shown in a close-up, displays all the signs of orgasm: her lips part, and the sound of the woman's panting seems to be emanating from her. Tears stream down her face as she crouches down for the release. Erika identifies with the sexual object of the same gender during the act of penetration, namely, the woman moaning in pleasure, who is indifferent to Erika's presence. As the psychoanalyst Otto Fenichel writes about the role of identification during the process of looking: "Anyone who desires to witness the sexual activities of a man and woman really always desires to share their experience by a process of empathy, generally in a homosexual sense."[19] The transformation of the novel's capitalized ethnic Other—a Turk is having sex in the Prater with an Austrian woman in Jelinek's book—into a well-known Austrian film actor, Georg Friedrich, who usually plays lower-class, proletarian characters, also has significant implications for the sexual pleasure Erika attempts to achieve in this sequence.[20] It is not only the woman's pleasure that interests her (as Fenichel points out, looking at an object involves both identification with one's gender and alienation from it). We actually do not see anything of the sex but are privy to the man's growing awareness of Erika's presence. In contrast to the subservient Turkish man, who quickly becomes quiet again and gives up his futile search for the stalker, Friedrich's rage burns, and he pursues Erika. We witness the shot/reverse shot where their gazes meet at close range. His anger is due to the fact that she is watching him secretly and that she has arrogated the right of the male moviegoer; he is indifferent to the woman's supposedly superior class. The cinematic space reserved for "licit" voyeurism of Laura Mulvey's 1975 kind (where woman is objectified in her "to-be-looked-at-ness") has thus become a surveillant space of openly perverse pleasure—for a woman, no less.[21] The woman in the Burberry trench coat *exhibits* her voyeurism, trying to control the male gaze by displaying herself as keyhole and making use of it simultaneously.[22] Furthermore, Erika is little interested in the vicarious pleasure of what is to be absorbed from the screen in this scene. Indeed, the similarity between the porn booth and the drive-in theater lies in the possibility of having a nearly tactile relationship to the object of her gaze (Freud refers to looking as analogous to touching).[23] In the porn booth, Erika grabs tissues filled with sperm and inhales them deeply; at the open-air movie theater, she comes very close to the car to get a good look. A kind of immediacy is reintroduced, the mediation of cinema downplayed.

Although Haneke has no interest in catering to the audience's curiosity or in conceding pleasure to it or reassuring it, he nonetheless seeks to engender an awareness of the theoretical implications of its position—and to show that the immediacy of the cinema is a mirage.[24] By manipulating the viewer's expectations (as in his notorious 1997 film *Funny Games*), the director challenges the spectators with the multiple implications of their voyeurism.[25] The overt symbolism of this scene carries repercussions for the entire film. As Maria van Dijk notes, Haneke's construction gives the film a definitive teleology, one absent or more tenuous in many of his earlier works such as *71 Fragments of a Chronology of Chance* (*71 Fragmente einer Chronologie des Zufalls*, 1994) or later films such as *Caché* (2005): "Haneke constructs for us a position as voyeur, a third party to Erika's frenetic descent." Precisely because of the lack of diegetic dialogue or offscreen narration, Erika is left "doubly alienated" within the film, from herself and from the viewers.[26]

In the process of doubly alienating us, the director's hand in the spectators' captivity is moved into the foreground. Ultimately, Haneke controls the image. As such, he assumes the stance of *deus absconditus* in his film, one that has not been adequately analyzed in the discussions centering on his clinically detached visual style. It is often equated with impartiality or limited neutrality rather than omnipotence.[27] Psychoanalytic paradigms, as we indicated at the outset, go only so far toward explaining the film's many difficult scenes and especially the director's authorial stance. For Haneke, there is never the "double denial" that Metz sees in the cinema's functioning. First, the story does not hide its discursive construction—that is, what is seen *knows* that it is seen, to rephrase Metz—and, second, this knowledge informs the audience's awareness of itself. It cannot quite hide from its own voyeurism. The Metzian interpretation of this "double denial" reduces the voyeur to the "brute fact of seeing," which the theorist associates with the functioning of the "narrator God" and the "spectator God."²⁸ However, Haneke is actually far more interested in playing with this assumption on the part of the viewers; in effect, his film is about the recalcitrant image, from which the viewers must to some degree be excluded by the "auteur God."²⁹

In a different context—but one that we hope to show is pertinent to Haneke's *Piano Teacher*—Roland Barthes discusses the viewers' exclusion from the image itself. In regard to the wounds suffered on the (battle)field of love, the French critic and theorist maintains that they arise from something seen rather than from something known. In other words, the wounds stem from a disavowal ("I know very well, but all the same").³⁰ In *A Lover's Discourse* (*Fragments d'un discours amoureux*), he writes under the entry for "image": "the most painful wounds are inflicted more often by what one sees than by what one knows" ("les blessures les plus vives viennent davantage de ce que l'on voit que de ce que l'on sait").³¹ Barthes argues that any visual experience may have an exclusionary aspect to it, precisely because it depends on the viewer's vivid sense of clandestinely cowering at a keyhole and being wounded by what he or she sees. The keyhole allows only very limited access to the forbidden scene, imposing its contours on the abrogated image. Barthes writes:

The image is presented, pure and distinct as a letter: it is the letter of what pains me. Precise, complete, definitive, it leaves no room for me, down to the last finicky detail: I am excluded from it as from the primal scene, which may exist only insofar as it is framed within the contour of the keyhole. (132)

[L'image se découpe; elle est pure et nette comme une lettre: elle est la lettre de ce qui me fait mal. Précise, complète, fignolée, définitive, elle ne me laisse aucune place: j'en suis exclu comme de la scène primitive, qui n'existe peut-être que pour autant qu'elle est découpée par le contour de la serrure. (157)]

Here Barthes follows Metz, who three years earlier tied the spectator's voyeurism to the primal scene in *The Imaginary Signifier*. In a more explicit fashion than the purposefully elusive Barthes, Metz describes the primal scene with its "scenario of castration" as a symbolic drama representing the human condition of real and imagined loss; hence its surreptitious viewing becomes applicable to cinematic spectatorship.³² However, more important than the transgressive element that is, paradoxically, socially sanctioned according to Metz (which we have already discussed in the drive-in sequence), there is the perceived exclusion of the viewer from the image he sees in Barthes's case. For Metz, the film itself disavows the presence of the viewer, particularly in classical cinema with its erasure of its discursive basis. For Barthes, the individual unit of the image shuts out the viewer on account of his intense interest. Barthes continues his reflections with a definition of the image:

Here then, at last, is the definition of the image, of any image: that from which I am excluded. Contrary to those puzzle [rebus—F. N., C. K.] drawings in which the hunter is secretly figured in the confusion of the foliage, I am not in the scene: the image is without riddle. (132)

[Voici donc, enfin, la définition de l'image, de toute image: l'image, c'est ce dont je suis exclu. Au contraire de ces dessins rébus, où le chasseur est secrètement dessiné dans le fouillis d'une frondaison, je ne suis pas dans la scène: l'image est sans énigme. (157)]

According to Barthes, the image is without a riddle because the "I" is aware of the fact that it is excluded from the image. While looking at an image it knows that it is not a part of it. There is a necessary distance between the subject-viewer and the object-viewed.

Perhaps it is in this regard that Haneke's most classically fashioned film to date (with its increased use of continuity editing and more mobile camera vis-à-vis his earlier works) still retains its discursive basis and draws attention to itself. Many elements of voyeuristic satisfaction are undercut. This is done not only by the constricting framing—the "keyhole's" contour prevents the whole image from appearing—and the disorienting use of music that juxtaposes profane and sacred, high and low culture. By mixing genres and different types of images, Haneke, as has been often noted, reflects on images and on their use in Western culture. For instance, the television is always on in the Kohuts' apartment and imposes its presence through sound as well as image. Erika's mother constantly watches television documentaries about wildlife, organ trafficking, cowboys, and so on while waiting for her daughter. The only scene where Erika watches television, however, is when she visits the sex shop, and a generic shift suddenly takes place within the film. While selecting a porn movie to satisfy her scopophilia, the spectators watch not just one but four pornographic images side by side. They are confronted with a myriad of obscene scenes from a point-of-view shot before Erika selects one film. Throughout the remaining scene, the spectators are with Erika, watching a woman on a table lying on her back fellating a man, and watching Erika watch as well as smell discarded tissues. We are doing precisely what Erika strives to do throughout the *Piano Teacher:* watch an image as well as watch the object of our gaze watch an image—but without having the object watch us. The film explores the loss of subject-object boundaries since Erika is as much the subject of the gaze as the object of our gaze, as are the spectators, who are recurrently seen by Erika in some frustrating head-on shots, caught in the act of peeping on her. This might be one of the further functions of the scene in the porn booth: mixing high and low culture, "legitimate" and "illegitimate" images, shows the similarities between the two and how both converge on the spectators' scopophilia. The only time where we finally see the sex we want to see, we feel a certain kind of malaise and put the blame on Erika's deviant nature—yet our viewing pleasure is by implication as perverse and deviant as hers. In addition, pornography and bourgeois high culture are deeply intertwined: Schubert, whose *Winterreise* is often part of the diegesis, including in the porn booth sequence, died of syphilis that he most likely contracted from a prostitute (*pornê* means "prostitute" in ancient Greek). To a certain extent, Erika herself functions as a prostitute on the cinema screen, where she is placed in front of our eyes and is supposed to give us visual pleasure (as in the word's etymology, where to "prostitute" oneself means to "stand in front of").[33]

However, the film also thematizes the process whereby the spectators are shut out from the image. They are often aligned with Erika in terms of point-of-view shots, and her desire to control the view as well as her inability to do so is abundantly obvious. The melodramatic tragedy of this woman is that she wants to be the subject and the object of the gaze at the same time: she wants to be seen, and at the same time she wants to escape the controlling gaze of the mother; she wants to see without being seen while watching porn or live action; she wants to be seen while directing and controlling Walter's (and our) gaze. In this, she is very much like the director himself. In the fortieth sequence, for instance, the young piano student of whom Erika is jealous cuts her hands on the glass shards Erika has put in her pocket. We see a close-up of Walter's shocked face rather than the girl's, as an authoritative man's voice intones from offscreen: "Don't stand here. There's nothing to see" ("Ne restez pas là. Il n'y a rien à voir").[34] Immediately thereafter, the camera follows Erika into the lavatory, only to have the door shut on it, while it focuses squarely on the red "locked" sign (in contradistinction to the earlier matching sequence in the porn shop, the locked door is not transcended to share Erika's space inside the stall). In the resplendent white bathroom, Erika also commands Walter to look at her, not his penis, as she masturbates him. The spectators are barred from any view, since Walter is shown either from the back or the waist up. Here too the light does not imply greater clarity. Instead, it is a blinding whiteness, as it will be when Erika stumbles onto the white ice rink after fellating Walter. In this later scene, Erika admonishes Walter not to look while she vomits up his sperm.[35]

While Erika's ability to "direct" and control the gaze is challenged, however, the real director's is not. He can suddenly pull up a camera to a locked door, making us well aware that the role outlined for the vacant spectators of classical cinema does not apply.[36] The spectators cannot possibly have the sense that they are the subjects of enunciation—as would be the case in classical cinema—and immediately identify with the camera itself.[37] This may be one way of reading the film: by dint of excessively controlling and directing the spectators' gaze there is nothing to see anymore. Ironically, this is how the film ends. We stay in front of the Vienna *Konzerthaus* that Erika has left, and there is nothing to see but the rigid lines of the façade, emulating the bird's-eye views of the piano keys that recur throughout the film.

For Barthes, the wounding image delineates itself clearly against the outlines of the metaphorical keyhole, "pure and distinct as a letter" ("pure et nette comme une lettre"). The letter Erika writes to Walter functions as a key, for it opens the door to Erika's fantasy, reveals her secret desires, and also unleashes violence. This scene takes place in her room and shows Walter sitting in an armchair near her, reading aloud her weighty missive. Significantly, the Hermès scarf with its key pattern is flaccidly wrapped around a hanger on the closet's door, visible in the background of the two figures. Among the precise instructions contained in the letter on how to tie, beat, slap, and punch her in the stomach, she expresses her dearest wish: Walter should take all the door keys with him and should not leave a single one in the apartment. The scenario of bondage, pain, and humiliation should be acted out in a situation where her mother cannot intervene. In fact, Erika fantasizes a reversion of the roles that the two women play: she wishes her mother to be deprived of the key(s) and therefore to be forced to watch through the keyhole while her daughter enjoys the phallus—her masochistic fantasy putting her in a position of power. In her letter Erika lays bare her desire that shocks and frightens Walter.[38]

Incensed, for the letter does not match his conventional conception of love and romance, Walter reacts with rejection and dismissal. He disparages her missive by calling it "shit" and asks her in an angry tone what this may "open" up for him: "What will this open up for me? Huh?" ("Ça va ouvrir quoi tout ça pour moi? Hein?"). As a reply to him, Erika literally opens up.[39] First she lies down on the floor and reaches under the couch to pull a box from its hiding place. She opens it and shows Walter her unused sex toys. After confessing to him that the urge to be beaten has been in her for years, she gets up and heads to her closet, whose doors she opens wide (opening wide a closed space). This time, the shot of her standing in front of her closet full of clothes, where a corner of the Hermès scarf is visible, is Walter's, allowing spectators to identify with him. His voice offscreen speaks for the audience when he expresses his disgust and dismissal toward her. By telling Erika that she is sick and in need of treatment, he indirectly answers the question she asked him previously. For her previous question, "Do I disgust you?" ("J'te dégoûte, hein?"), confronts the spectators; it is not merely directed at Walter but also at the audience in an irritatingly centered close-up shot of her head. Within a phallocratic social order men are most likely the ones who would engage in masochistic pleasure, since they can get a safe "thrill," temporarily conferring power on the traditionally powerless woman within a sexual game. Here the traditionally powerless woman fantasizes about being dominated and abused by the powerful man, which makes her look even more revolting in the eyes of the audience. As Robin Wood points out: "Were I disgusted by Erika, I would have also to be disgusted with myself," since the film imposes self-reflexivity on the spectators and therefore puts them at its center (more about the implied optics later).[40] If Erika's masochistic fantasy that takes form in her letter is disgusting, then the audience that watches conventional melodramas depicting masochistic heroines with pleasure is in fact disgusting.[41] Erika makes female submission and denigration—the flipside of female idealization in cinema—within the patriarchal order appear even more unbearable.

## *Efforts at Control*

In regard to his godlike stance, Haneke's revival of the auteur touches on Jelinek's own reflections about her writing. While the contrast between his reduced and tightly framed images and stark editing symmetries and her word cascades—her texts are filled with ironic allusions, idiomatic expressions with an unexpected twist, high and low cultural references, and so on—is emphasized over and over again, the similarities between their expressed intentions and their styles have been little noticed.[42] Particularly in the Nobel Prize winner's works of the 1990s and the first decade of the new millennium, she has emphasized the role of the author as the giver of language, even when that language escapes her control.[43] Georg Seeßlen has been the only one to remark on this similarity between author and director. He writes: "But if there is such a thing as a gruesome comedy of language in Jelinek, which always speaks along with her: I am language, then there is a gruesome comedy of film in Haneke, which always also shows: I am cinema" ("Aber wenn es bei Jelinek so etwas wie eine grausige Komik der Sprache gibt, die immer auch mitspricht: Ich bin Sprache, so gibt es bei Haneke eine grausige Komik des Filmischen, das immer auch mitzeigt: Ich bin Kino").[44] Jelinek herself, from the vantage point of 2001, speaks about this aspect of her 1983 novel in an interview:

Basically, I am an author who even gives her voyeuse instructions about *how* she is to see something. Thus it is a double arrogation: not only toward the father, but also toward God. Now there is no one against whom I can rebel anymore. This impulse arises out of the feeling of not being able to speak as a woman.

[Ich bin im Grunde eine Schriftstellerin, die einer Voyeurin auch noch Anweisungen gibt, *wie* sie etwas zu sehen hat. Es ist also eine doppelte Anmaßung: Nicht nur gegenüber dem Vater, sondern auch gegenüber Gott. Jetzt gibts niemand mehr, gegen den ich aufstehen kann. Wobei der Impetus schon aus dem Gefühl kommt, als Frau nicht sprechen zu dürfen.][45]

The statement that the author attempts to control Erika's views and her viewpoint is vividly corroborated by episodes from the novel such as the following. A little way into *The Piano Teacher,* Erika visits a live peepshow rather than a porn booth:

She does not walk into the employee section, she steps into the section for paying guests—the more important section. This woman wants to look at something that she could see far more cheaply in her mirror at home. The men voice their amazement: They have to pinch every penny they secretly spend here hunting women. The hunters peer through the peepholes, and their housekeeping money goes down the drain. Nothing can elude these men when they peer.

## The Key to Voyeurism: Haneke's Adaptation of The Piano Teacher

[Sie geht nicht in die Abteilung für Angestellte des Hauses, sondern in die Abteilung für zahlende Gäste. Es ist die wichtigere Abteilung. Diese Frau will sich etwas anschauen, das sie sich zu Hause viel billiger im Spiegel betrachten könnte. Die Männer staunen laut, weil sie sich das Geld vom Munde absparen müssen, mit dem sie hier heimlich auf Frauenpirsch gehen. Auf dem Hochstand, diese Jäger. Sie lugen durch die Gucklöcher, und das Wirtschaftsgeld verbraucht sich schnell. Nichts kann den Männern beim Schauen entgehen.][46]

This passage also utilizes the hunter-image that Barthes introduces in his definition of the image. Barthes, however, turns on its head the traditional dichotomy of the active stalker/hunter and the passive object/prey. For him, the hunter emerges when the voyeur glimpses a puzzle whose contours he may or may not be misinterpreting. In Jelinek's case, she literalizes the cliché of voyeur as hunter-stalker. This becomes clear when one looks at the German original, with its emphasis on the positioning of the men as hunters ("On the raised stand [*Hochstand*], these hunters") and their erections (the implied slang "Ständer" in *Hochstand*). The voyeurs are metaphorically located above the woman at whom they peer through the peephole. The narrator comments on the godlike omniscience their panoptic position affords: nothing escapes their gaze. Jelinek seems to then undercut the image of the men as hunters fixating on their prey; Erika too enjoys the vantage point from the raised stand. When she usurps this perch, she can look down on women and men alike. However, the plenitude of sexualized vision implicit in the men's viewing is turned into nothingness in Erika's case, a nothing that is semantically contiguous with the earlier mention of woman's "lack" (*Mangel*):

All Erika wants to do is watch. Here, in this booth, she becomes nothing. Nothing fits into Erika. . . . Nature seems to have left no apertures in her. Erika feels solid wood in the place where the carpenter made a hole in any genuine female. . . . But Erika doesn't want to act, she only wants to look. She simply wants to sit there and look. Look hard. Erika, watching but not touching. . . . Even when Erika cuts or pricks herself, she feels almost nothing. But when it comes to her eyes, she has reached an acme of sensitivity. (51–52)

[Auch Erika will nichts weiter als zuschauen. Hier, in dieser Kabine, wird sie zu garnichts. Nichts paßt in Erika hinein. . . . Die Natur scheint keine Öffnungen in ihr gelassen zu haben. Erika hat ein Gefühl von massivem Holz dort, wo der Zimmermann bei der echten Frau das Loch gelassen hat. . . . Erika will jedoch keine Handlung vollführen, sie will nur schauen. Sie will einfach still dasitzen und schauen. Zuschauen. Erika, die zuschaut ohne anzustreifen. . . . Auch wenn Erika schneidet oder wenn sie sich sticht, spürt sie kaum etwas. Nur was den Gesichtssinn betrifft, hat sie es zu hoher Blüte gebracht. (53–54)]

The recurring mention of the verb *schauen* (four times in four sentences), the explicit reference to woman as "lack" and to scopophilia (*Schaulust*, 56) in the context of Erika's watching other women clearly makes reference to psychoanalysis. However, scoping is divorced from love or pleasure, "schauen" cut off from any "lust." Erika is a voyeuse whose gaze does not afford her any particular sexual and sensory pleasure. This is in contradistinction to Haneke's film, where Erika's sexual pleasure is connoted by way of the related registers of sound, smell, and hearing (her auditory seduction by Walter's piano playing, her deep breaths when she inhales the smell of sperm in the booth, her proto-orgasm when she spies on the couple in the movie theater). The sense of sight becomes an end in itself for Jelinek to emphatically stress the ocular models inherited from Euclidean perspective, according to which God's—or, in Jelinek's case, man's—overpowering and omnipresent eye looms at the vanishing point of converging perspectival lines.[47] As such, all efforts at control through the keyhole are related to spatial regimes of above-below, front-back, and inside-outside in the text.

## *Updating Voyeurism for the Undead*

Jelinek returns to the voyeuse's position at the peephole in her magnum opus from the mid-1990s *Children of the Dead* (*Kinder der Toten*) to problematize these spatial regimes and their implicit hierarchies.[48] One of her typical zombie-like characters, a student named Gudrun, peers through a keyhole. What she sees is a mutilated, decomposing image of herself engaged in a sexual encounter with another undead figure, where penetration—figural and literal—is particularly disorienting because bodies pass through each other and themselves, combining, dissolving, rearranging in fragments. No spatial coordinates are fixed, and everything is in flux. Not only does the ground give way below Gudrun's feet, but the entire inside-outside, up-down model of space is inverted, folded into and through itself into a model of topological space: "the modalities of surfaces, volumes, boundaries, contiguities, holes, and above all the notions of inside and outside, with the attendant ideas of insertion, penetration, containment, emergence and the like" are discredited.[49] No longer can gender be ascribed to spatial configurations, as was possible in *The Piano Teacher*. As Juliane Vogel writes about Jelinek's 1995 novel, the surface of the mountainous, sodden landscape reveals everything, doing away with our general perception that the truth lies "below." The fluctuating, self-generating landscape has clearly hermaphroditic and metamorphotic implications for gender:

The "softening" stones are, additionally, covered with a "damp coating" or "with pillows of moss," . . . implying the fertility of the surface, and if they are overgrown, finally, with a "dark damp grass," . . . then the folds of the mountain chain become the sex of a gigantic female body. The folded ground in Jelinek's work always has the superficial structure of the female genitalia that becomes a topological object of the first order and prepares a birth, which transpires each time through self-metamorphosis: as a "growth" or a nodal structure . . . it is born and birthing simultaneously, a female fold, that simultaneously turns itself into a penis and thus brings itself into existence.

[Wenn die "weichenden" Steine außerdem mit einem "feuchten Belag" bzw. mit "Moospolster beklebt" sind, . . . deutet sich die Fruchtbarkeit der Oberfläche an, und wenn sie zuletzt noch "mit dunklem feuchten Gras" bestanden sind, . . ., dann ziehen sich die Falten des Gebirges zum Geschlecht eines riesenhaften weiblichen Körpers zusammen. Der gefaltete Boden besitzt bei Jelinek immer auch die Oberflächenstruktur des weiblichen Genitals, das zu einem topologischen Objekt ersten Ranges aufrückt und eine Geburt vorbereitet, die jeweils durch Selbstverformung vonstatten geht: Als ein "Gewächs" oder Knotengebilde . . . ist es geboren und gebärend zugleich, eine weibliche Falte, die sich zugleich als ein männliches Glied hervorstülpt und damit selbst auf die Welt bringt.[50]

In such a space of endless transformations, the student Gudrun cannot get any "grip" on what she sees. Voyeurism in *The Children of the Dead* is also divorced from excitation or stimulation; instead, as Gudrun bends down to the keyhole, she seeks respite and relaxation.[51] However, the experience nonetheless becomes bewildering when the firm ground separating the viewer from the viewed gives way. The fantasy of seeing without being seen becomes a phantasmagoria of alteration through perception—the voyeuse is transformed into the supposedly separate object of her vision. The narrator does not hesitate to link Gudrun's state to the general condition of humanity today: "As if we were endlessly condemned to become what we see" ("Als wären wir endlos verurteilt, das, was wir sehen, auch selber zu werden") (115).

In this apocalyptic novel, the mutation of the undead proceeds according to the dictum that what we see is what we become, and this what is always already a decomposing, morphing, multiple self. This scene in *Children of the Dead* offers a negative appraisal of what Slavoj Žižek defines as fantasy: "Fantasy proper is not the scene itself that attracts our fascination, but the non-existent imagined gaze observing it, like the impossible gaze from above."[52] For Žižek, the popularity of "survivor" television shows attests to a significant change in the relationship to this gaze and the concomitant fantasy of being seen. Anxiety now arises from the prospect of not being exposed to the Other's gaze at all times, which has become an "ontological guarantee" of one's being.[53] In Jelinek's scenario described earlier, however, the television viewer has become the prototype for all voyeurs, and the imagined Other's gaze does not guarantee any ontology—quite the opposite. "The viewer has mutated into his own television image," the readers find out when Gudrun bends down to the keyhole ("Der Zuseher ist zu seinem eigenen Fernsehbild mutiert") (115), an image that flashes by. The omnipotence once ascribed to God is now Gudrun's, prostrating herself before the Highest ("dem Höchsten"). In such a situation, God hypocritically maintains that he is the one that created humankind, the narrator comments ironically—in effect, however, the scene is about the solipsism of self-genesis via voyeurism.[54]

Gudrun's vision, before becoming grossly materialistic and sexual, first opens up on to an expanse of whiteness, with snowlike crystals stretching to the horizon. The blinding whiteness represents the space (and time) warp that has resulted from the changes in spatial (and temporal) perception today. "Spaces once conceived of as separated, segregated, now overlap," writes Victor Burgin. For him this is a result of the televisual perception to which all humans are now prone, placing side by side the microscopic and macrocosmic. "To contemplate such phenomena," he continues, "is no longer to inhabit an imaginary space ordered by the subject-object 'standoff' of Euclidean perspective." For him, the best analogies for spatial coordinates are topological ones, where "apparently opposing sides prove to be formed from a single continuous surface."[55]

Haneke, like Jelinek, problematizes the ocular models that have been correlated to psychoanalytic theories of spatial representation, depicting changes in the subject-object "standoff" that revolve around the sense of sight. When Erika breaks out of her phallic power games and is surrounded either by a blinding whiteness (when she stumbles through the unlocked doors of the skating rink) or an ultimate blackness (when her bloodied face is shown against the backdrop of the closet), Haneke's film dissolves the spatial regime to which she has subjected herself through her voyeuristic games. In those moments, we might want to imagine a change flickering across her face, demonstrating both her subjection to the keyhole as well as her ability to go beyond it.[56] However, where would this transcending be possible? Haneke updates the voyeuristic scenario along the lines proposed in *The Children of the Dead*, countermanding any such reading: when Erika lies prone under Walter's thrusts, she resembles a corpse against a dark background, and his rape becomes an instance of necrophilia in a topological space. The undead are in a nonplace that concretizes the meaning of "utopia" but robs it of liberating, utopian potential. In this, Haneke's film remains truest to its acerbic original: there is no there there for all the characters, women and men alike.

## Notes

1. For positive reviews see, for example, Simone Mahrenholz's review: "Der barocken verbalen Sintflut von Jelineks Vorlage begegnet Haneke mit einem kühleren, rationaleren Ton. Doch beide treffen einander in dem schonungslos sezierenden, urteilsfreien Blick auf menschliche Grausamkeit und auf einen Eros jenseits der Konventionen." Mahrenholz, "Erika im Bade: Aufdringliche Wahrheit: Michael Hanekes Die Klavierspielerin," *Die Welt*, October 11, 2001, www.welt.de/print-welt/article480695/Erika_im_Bade.html (accessed January 10, 2008). See also Wilfried Wiegand, "Ausgedehnte Abendspaziergänge in den Sexshop und in die Verzweiflung," *Frankfurter Allgemeine Zeitung*, May 17, 2001, Nr. 114, 49; and Dietrich Kuhlbrodt, "Die Klavierspielerin," *Filmzentrale*, www.filmzentrale.com/rezis/klavierspielerindk.htm (accessed January 10, 2008). One English reviewer preferred the film to the novel; this has to do, no doubt, with Jelinek's inaccurate reputation as a "misanthropic polemicist." See Stuart Jeffries, "No Pain, No Gain," *The Guardian*, May 24, 2001.

2. On the issue of adaptation, see in particular Robert Stam's three-book series *Literature through Film: Realism, Magic, and the Art of Adaptation* (Malden, MA: Blackwell, 2005), *Literature and Film: A Guide to the Theory and Practice of Film Adaptation*, edited with Alessandra Raengo (Malden, MA: Blackwell, 2005), and *A Companion to Literature and Film*, edited with Alessandra Raengo (Malden, MA: Blackwell, 2004). See also James Naremore, ed., *Film Adaptation* (London: Athlone, 2000). On the issue of Haneke's adaptations, see Fatima Naqvi's article "A Melancholy Labor of Love: Film Adaptation as Translation in Michael Haneke's *Drei Wege zum See*," *Germanic Review* 81, no. 4 (2006): 291–315.

3. See Christina Bylow, "Die allgemeine Krankheit der Frau: Der Regisseur Michael Haneke verfilmt einen Roman von Elfriede Jelinek: Die Klavierspielerin," *Berliner Zeitung*, October 10, 2001, www.berlinonline.de/berliner-zeitung/archiv/.

bin/dump.fcgi/2001/1010/feuilleton/0006/index.html (accessed January 10, 2008); and Claus Philipp, "Hochleistungs-Sportstück mit Huppert: Elfriede Jelineks Roman, verfilmt von Michael Haneke-ein Missverständnis?" *Der Standard*, August 2, 2004, http://derstandard.at/?url=/?channel=KULTUR%26ressort=KINO2000%26 id=776316 (accessed January 10, 2008). See also Katja Nicodemus, who argues in the *taz* that Haneke reduces the sociopolitical aspects of Jelinek's novel to the farcical personal pathology of one woman. In her view, however, Isabelle Huppert's acting style restores the dignity and tragedy of the original. Nicodemus, "Der Ekel im zuckenden Mundwinkel," *taz*, October 10, 2001, www.taz.de/index.php?id=archivseite &dig=2001/10/11/a0126 (accessed January 10, 2008). Jonathan Romney maintains that the adaptation elides the context that makes Erika what she is and cuts away the linguistic energy of the original, in "It's All a Question of Technique," *Independent*, November 11, 2001. Finally, Stefanie Maeck in "Schmerz, oh Schutz vor dir!" claims that Haneke does not manage to create a specific filmic language for the masochism Jelinek describes: "Der einzigartige Sprachrausch, er findet zu keiner eigenständigen, filmischen Grammatik." See Maeck, "Schmerz, oh Schutz vor dir!" *Filmtext*, www.filmtext.com/start.jsp?mode=1&key=315 (accessed January 10, 2008).

4. See Klaus Nüchtern, "Wenn Frauen schauen," *Falter*, November 7, 2001, 22–23.

5. While rooms represent the womb, the key becomes a symbol for the penis (Sigmund Freud, *Gesammelte Werke* [Frankfurt am Main: Fischer, 1999], 2–3:359) that can gain entry to the door of the female genitalia (ibid., 11:157–58, 160).

6. See Jelinek's comment in an interview: "Basically it's a homosexual relationship between men: The daughter is the mother's phallus" ("Im Grunde ist es eine homosexuelle Beziehung zwischen Männern: Die Tochter is ja der Phallus der Mutter"). Qtd. in Nüchtern, "Wenn Frauen schauen," 22.

7. See John Champagne, "Undoing Oedipus: Feminism and Michael Haneke's *The Piano Teacher*," *Bright Lights Film Journal* 36 (2002), www.brightlightsfilm.com/36/pianoteacher1.html (accessed January 10, 2008).

8. See Lydia Perovic's review, "The Passion According to Erika," *Critical Sense* (Spring 2005): 131–40, esp. 139.

9. For a reprint of the German version of the screenplay, see Stefan Grissemann, ed., *Haneke/Jelinek: Die Klavierspielerin* (Vienna: Sonderzahl, 2001), 33–114.

10. See Catherine Wheatley, "The Masochistic Fantasy Made Flesh: Michael Haneke's *La Pianiste* as Melodrama," *Studies in French Cinema* 6, no. 2 (2006): 121.

11. See the screenplay in Grissemann, *Haneke/Jelinek*, 84.

12. The furious mother's compulsive tearing apart of her daughter's clothes, which takes place in an intercut segment, can be read as an act of symbolic castration. Erika's desire for the penis expresses itself particularly in the scene that takes place in the conservatory's bathroom, where she insistently masturbates Walter. By doing so, she turns the whole scene into a phallocentric power game—with the use of medium close-ups, Walter's phallus offscreen remains the center of attention.

13. Christian Metz, *The Imaginary Signifier: Psychoanalysis and the Cinema*, trans. Celia Britton et al. (Bloomington: Indiana University Press, 1982), 66, emphasis in

the original; Christian Metz, *Le signifiant imaginaire: Psychoanalyse et cinéma* (Paris: Union Générale d'Éditions, 1977), 91, emphasis in the original.

14. Metz, *Imaginary Signifier*, 65–66; Metz, *Le signifiant imaginaire*, 91.

15. See Robin Wood, "Hidden in Plain Sight," *Artforum International* (January 2006): 4, www.coldbacon.com/writing/robinwood-cache.html (accessed January 28, 2008).

16. Erika's exclamation, "I saw the hairs on your sex," after lifting her mother's nightgown could be read as "I saw, Mother, that you are castrated."

17. "Throughout the film the process of watching is foregrounded," argues Wheatley ("Masochistic Fantasy," 124). The spectator is constantly watching the protagonists either watching television or peeping in on other characters. Erika watches porn and spies on couples copulating; her mother watches television while waiting for her daughter to come home; and Walter, following Erika to the conservatory's bathroom, leaps to the top of the stall and watches her urinating.

18. Ibid., 125.

19. Quoted in Victor Burgin, *In/Different Spaces* (Berkeley: University of California Press, 1996), 68. In a later scene, Erika literally jumps on her mother and tries to rape her.

20. In the porn shop, the three men observing Erika before she enters the booth seem to be Turkish.

21. On surveillant space, see Thomas Y. Levin, "Rhetoric of the Temporal Index: Surveillant Narration and the Cinema of 'Real Time,'" in *CTRL [SPACE]: Rhetorics of Surveillance from Bentham to Big Brother,* ed. Thomas Y. Levin, Ursula Frohne, Peter Weibel (Cambridge: MIT Press, 2002), 578–93.

22. See also Burgin, *In/Different Spaces,* 62.

23. Ibid., 71.

24. See Wheatley: "As with all Haneke's works, the real protagonist is not on the screen but in the audience" ("Masochistic Fantasy," 125).

25. See also Nina Hutchinson, "Between Action and Repression: The Piano Teacher," *Senses of Cinema* (April 2003), www.sensesofcinema.com/contents/03/26/piano_teacher.html (accessed January 15, 2008).

26. See Maria van Dijk, "Alienation and Perversion: Michael Haneke's *The Piano Teacher,*" *Bright Lights Film Journal* 36 (2002), www.brightlightsfilm.com/36/thepianoteacher.html (accessed January 15, 2008).

27. See Wheatley, "Masochistic Fantasy," 119.

28. See Christian Metz, "Story/Discourse: A Note on Two Kinds of Voyeurism," *The Imaginary Signifier* (1982): 89–98, esp. 97.

29. A number of commentators have remarked on the tightness of Haneke's framing technique, which adds to the characters' trapped nature. See, for example, Stefan Grissemann "In zwei, drei feinen Linien die Badewannenwand entlang," in *Haneke/Jelinek*, 11–32, esp. 19.

30. Metz quotes this definition of disavowal from Octave Mannoni in *The Imaginary Signifier* ("Story/Discourse," 76).

31. Barthes uses a quotation from Johann Wolfgang von Goethe's *The Sorrows of the Young Werther* to set the scene for his brief explanation of the image's potency,

citing the moment when Werther espies his beloved Lotte engrossed in a quiet conversation with her betrothed. See Roland Barthes, *A Lover's Discourse,* trans. Richard Howard (New York: Hill and Wang, 1978), 132 (hereafter cited in text); Roland Barthes, *Fragments d'un discours amoureux* (Paris: Seuil, 1977), 157 (hereafter cited in text).

32. See Metz's section "Disavowal, Fetishism" in "Story/Discourse," 69–78.

33. Her ambitious mother also wants to prostitute her, since she wants to place her daughter "in front of" bourgeois society.

34. He is designated as the "Direktor" in the screenplay (Grissemann, *Haneke/Jelinek,* 74); while in German this implies the head of the conservatory, the English "false friend"—the film director—is very suggestive in this context.

35. See Nüchtern, "Wenn Frauen schauen," 22–23.

36. In an interview, the lead actress, Isabelle Huppert, links Haneke with her character in the film rather than the male protagonists. Like Erika, Haneke attempts to "organize the man's pleasure."

37. See Metz's now classic scenario, when he discusses the spectator's identification with the "(invisible) seeing agency of the film itself as discourse, as the agency which *puts forward* the story and shows it to us. Insofar as it abolishes all traces of the subject of the enunciation, the traditional film succeeds in giving the spectator the impression that he is himself that subject, but in a state of emptiness and absence, of pure visual capacity. . . . As far as all these traits are concerned it is quite true that the primary identification of the spectator revolves around the camera itself" ("Story/Discourse," 96–97).

38. Slavoj Žižek interprets *The Piano Teacher* in light of the Lacanian impossibility of sexual relations. According to him, the film illustrates the clash of incompatible fantasies between man and woman and shows how detrimental the actualization of fantasies is for the desiring subject. See Žižek, *Welcome to the Desert of Real!* (New York: Verso, 2002), esp. 20–21.

39. The German screenplay leaves out the reference to opening, present in the English subtitles of the French (see Grissemann, *Haneke/Jelinek,* 90).

40. See Wood, "Hidden in Plain Sight," 4.

41. Thus, Erika's letter is the key that opens a reflection not only on spectatorship but also on melodrama as genre. As Wheatley points out, "masochism is everywhere within the melodrama, and this is certainly true of Haneke's film" ("Masochistic Fantasy," 122). Significantly, Haneke repeatedly stresses in interviews that his film is in fact a parody of melodrama (see Scott Foundas, "Interview: Michael Haneke: The Bearded Prophet of *Code Inconnu* and *The Piano Teacher,*" *IndieWire,* December 4, 2001, www.indiewire.com/people/int_Haneke_Michael_020329.html ([accessed January 28, 2008]). *The Piano Teacher* contains different elements that are typical of the melodrama: the story takes place in a middle-class society, Schubert's *Piano Sonata D9* and *Winterreise* give the movie its musical motif, and numerous scenes take place on staircases, where enamored and infatuated Walter chases after cold and distant Erika. The female protagonist's behavior shows some of the melodramatic heroine's typical comportment: hysteria, desire, and muteness. However, Haneke updates the melodrama and confers on it the cold and colorless look of repression, at

odds with melodrama's supposed visual excessiveness (Wheatley, "Masochistic Fantasy," 119). Erika's letter, which reaches its peak in her excessive and exhaustive list of sexual demands, offers an uncompromising reading of the suffering role assigned to women in melodrama. As Wheatley observes: "By foregrounding the masochistic drive that underpins the traditional melodramatic narrative in the women's film, the film effectively deconstructs it, troubling the generic standard that has spectators finding pleasure in the sight of an ultimately frustrated feminine desire shown on screen" (ibid., 122). Although Erika's letter with its masochistic content problematizes the roles of victim and perpetrator, the rape definitively asserts the dominance of the male over the female as well as the hegemony of patriarchal society. Walter subdues and punishes through sexual violence the woman who cannot conform to his normal and traditional sexual desire.

42. Jelinek herself speaks of her text as "a real rubble of metaphors" ("ein richtiges Metapherngeröll"). Quoted in Nüchtern, "Wenn Frauen schauen," 23.    4 3 . See Fatima Naqvi's chapter on Jelinek's godlike stance, "Cognitive Dissonances," in *The Literary and Cultural Rhetoric of Victimhood* (New York: Palgrave, 2007), 169–92.

44. See Georg Seeßlen, "Grenzüberschreitung," *Strandgut* (October 2001), www.strandgut.de/Archiv/Film/fk011001.htm (accessed January 15, 2008).

45. Quoted in Nüchtern, "Wenn Frauen schauen," 23, emphasis in original.

46. Elfriede Jelinek, *The Piano Teacher*, trans. Joachim Neugroschel (London: Serpent's Tail, 1988), 51 (hereafter cited in text); Elfriede Jelinek, *Die Klavierspielerin* (Reinbek bei Hamburg: Rowohlt, 1983), 53 (hereafter cited in text).

47. See Astrid Schmidt-Burkhardt, "The All-Seer: God's Eye as Proto-Surveillance," in Levin, Frohne, and Weibel, *CTRL [SPACE]*, 17–31.

48. Elfriede Jelinek, *Die Kinder der Toten* (Reinbek bei Hamburg: Rowohlt, 1995) (hereafter cited in text; our translation). See Stefan Grissemann's review, in which he describes the "nonplaces" Haneke's figures traverse, "Auflösung der Körper, Blutlust," *Die Presse*, May 15, 2001.

49. Bruce Morrisette's article "Topology and the French Nouveau Roman" is quoted in Juliane Vogel, " 'Keine Leere der Unterbrechung'—*Die Kinder der Toten* oder die Schrecken der Falte," *Modern Austrian Literature* 39, nos. 3–4 (2006): 15–26, esp. 18.

50. Ibid., 19–20 (our translation).

51. See the opening of this section in Jelinek, *Kinder der Toten:* "Gudrun ('The Student') bends down to the insect-shaped hole in the door to rest a bit, to cozy up with the sight that she will be privy to, and she nearly falls, eyes first, into the room" ("Gudrun ["Die Studentin"] beugt sich zu dem kerbtierförmigen Loch in der Tür, um sich ein bißchen auszuruhn, an den Anblick, der sich ihr bieten wird, zu schmiegen, und schon fällt sie, Augen voran, beinah ins Zimmer hinein") (115).

52. See Slavoj Žižek, "Big Brother, or the Triumph of the Gaze over the Eye," in Levin, Frohne, and Weibel, *CTRL [SPACE]*, 224–27, esp. 225.

53. Ibid., 225.

54. See Jelinek, *Kinder der Toten*, which describes Gudrun's vision as follows: "[She sees] herself in the mirror of creation, as she prostrates herself before the High-

est, and he still maintains that it is he who explains [lays out] humans to himself" ("[Sie sieht] sich selbst im Spiegel der Schöpfung, wie sie sich gerade dem Höchsten vorlegt, und dieser behauptet tatsächlich immer noch, daß er es sei, der die Menschen sich selber auslegt") (116).

55. See Burgin's chapter "Geometry and Abjection" in *In/Different Spaces*, 39–56, here 44.

56. Indeed, it is tempting to read her final act of "penetration" with the knife and her exit via the keyless doors of the *Musikverein* as a liberating departure.

*Caché* (2005): The film's final shot and also its most ambiguous.

Mattias Frey

# The Message and the Medium
## Haneke's Film Theory and Digital Praxis

In the 1990s, Michael Haneke cultivated a reputation as one of Europe's most controversial and radical feature filmmakers. His first theatrical releases, *The Seventh Continent, Benny's Video, 71 Fragments of a Chronology of Chance,* and *Funny Games,* shocked audiences with their reflexive levels, distanced aesthetics, and treatments of violence. Haneke delighted at disturbing. Swiss authorities initially banned *Benny's Video.* Wim Wenders was one of the many celebrities to publicly exit the screening of *Funny Games* at Cannes.

At the time, critics often saw Haneke as part of an emerging explicitness in continental filmmaking that included Rémy Balvaux's *C'est arrivé près de chez vous* (*Man Bites Dog,* 1992), Mathieu Kassovitz's *La Haine* (*Hate,* 1995), Virgine Despentes's *Baise-moi* (*Rape Me,* 2000), and Gaspar Noé's *Seul contre tous* (*I Stand Alone,* 1998) and *Irréversible* (2002), not to mention much of Catherine Breillat's work. The European cinema of violence surely has many roots and antecedents. It speaks most immediately to (or reacts against) the allure of Quentin Tarantino's *Reservoir Dogs* (1992), Hong Kong and other Asian action flicks, and Oliver Stone's *Natural Born Killers* (1994). The European directors test the limits of spectatorship and the boundaries between "legitimate art" and exploitation, voyeurism, and complicity in violence (and, often, violent sexuality).

Where Haneke departs from the others, however, is the sophistication with which he has theorized his own work in interviews, public appearances, and writings. Appearing on Alexander Kluge's television program, Haneke kept up with the most intellectual filmmaker Germany has ever produced. In conversation with journalists, Haneke betrays his bourgeois upbringing and classical training in music and philosophy with élan. He cites Theodor Adorno, recites Bertolt Brecht, lauds Blaise Pascal, and alludes to Jean-Louis Baudry. Commentators have written persuasively on how Haneke mobilizes and recuperates European high culture in his literary adaptations (Bachmann, Rosei, Roth, Kafka, Jelinek) and use of music (J. S. Bach versus John Zorn).[1] Haneke's pronouncements on the *Hochkultur* are often downright romantic. "If one deployed music as a means of communication," the director of a 2006 engagement of *Don Giovanni* at the Opéra national de Paris says, "we would be able to solve conflicts much more easily."[2] Despite protests to the contrary, Haneke seems to fear and loathe technology: "I have nothing against technology nor computers. They make life much easier, even if the computer is a Trojan horse. If the systems crash, the so-called civilization is paralyzed. It could become a reason for war, destroying the other's systems. The more technological the world, the easier it is to be destroyed."[3]

Europe's most radical director is in crucial ways its most conservative. His Austrian "glaciation trilogy" is classic *Zivilisationskritik* (civilization critique), portraying lives deformed by media, technology, and generational disconnect. This thinking runs through Haneke's film theory, expressed programmatically in his essay "Violence and Media."[4] According to Haneke, violence has belonged to the motion picture since the time of its origins, and this subject matter defines the major genres, such as the horror movie, gangster pictures, war films, and adventure stories. Because of film's special connection to reality, furthermore, the filmic representation of violence is judged by other criteria than literature or painting. Formal matters are critical. Whereas photography and painting show the result of violence, film portrays it in action. The movie's relentless temporality, its simultaneous assault on eye and ear, and the cinema's "larger-than-life" proportions realign structures of sympathy. The still picture encourages an identification between the spectator and the victim. The motion picture, however, connects spectator to perpetrator.

Therein begins a normative critique of how film represents violence. Mainstream forms exaggerate or aestheticize violence. Otherwise, they make it ironic or seem unreal. According to Haneke, three major tactics serve to render violence acceptable:

1. Disassociation. By this, Haneke means portraying violence in a setting or time far from the spectator's normal life (for example, the Western,

science fiction, horror).

2. Moral justification. Providing situations in which violence is the only logical choice—for instance, in war, rape-revenge, and vigilante films—excuses violence.

3. Embedding violence within comedy or satire (for example, in slapstick, the Spaghetti Western, or Tarantino's cynical pastiche).

Although Haneke begins his comments with the assertion that one must move away from treating violence as a moral issue (accusing someone guilty) toward questions of form, later in the piece he assumes an ethical stance and predicts a dire future. Violence has increased in quality because of advances in special effects and has increased in quantity with the proliferation of new media. Furthermore, the "similarity" of representational forms has produced a leveling between real (for example, news reports of war) and fictional violence. Recalling Jean Baudrillard's contemporaneous work, Haneke wonders if the only difference between *Star Wars* and the media event "Blitzkrieg in Kuwait" was its television time slot.[5] In fact, children growing up today may be unable to distinguish between the two. Forms must be found to represent violence in a way that respects victims, returns pain to the representation of violence (rather than aesthetic pleasure), and allows viewers to identify with the victims rather the perpetrators. Elsewhere, in a squib called "Film as Catharsis," Haneke outlines the shape of this formal program: "[My films] are intended as polemical statements against the American barrel-down cinema and its dis-empowerment of the spectator. They are an appeal for a cinema of insistent questions instead of quick (because false) answers, for clarifying distance in place of violating closeness, for concentration rather than distraction, for provocation and dialogue instead of consumption and consensus."[6]

In "Violence and Media," Haneke worries about the interaction between real violence and screen violence and in general mourns the erosion between the real and its representation. Temptation would stop one here to deem Haneke a prophet of the postmodern, a nostalgic naysayer and doomsdayer in step with Baudrillard, Paul Virilio, and Marc Augé. I have done this before.[7] But does such a dialogue account for all of Haneke's filmmaking? Does it even telegraph the force behind his film theory? The early Austrian features might constitute an indictment of the western European bourgeoisie and media critique in the vein of Baudrillard and Virilio. Examining Haneke's writings more closely and scrutinizing his more recent features, however, complicates this image and, at the same time, helps to reconcile the competing prospects of this radical, conservative filmmaker.

## *Terror and Utopia of Form*

Before addressing Haneke's films, let us turn to another of his major essays, "Terror and Utopia of Form." In this love letter to Robert Bresson, Haneke recounts his early experiences with cinema. His first screen memory is leaving *Hamlet* (1948), screaming. For the young man growing up in Wiener Neustadt (a suburb of Vienna), going to the movies was a "rare, unusual, and thus precious experience."[8] (Let us not forget that, although Haneke first achieved serious critical notice in the 1990s and international scholarly attention in the first decade of the twenty-first century, he was born three years *before* Rainer Werner Fassbinder and Wim Wenders.) The account of these years reveals a nostalgia for the golden age of cinema-going and the anxiety that children coming of age today are lost in a surplus of images and at the mercy of television's pejorative influence: "The knowledge of that magic power of living images—evoking terror and rapture in equal measure—has largely been forgotten in a world in which newborns are used to the constant presence of virtual reality in the guise of their home TV set." Haneke finds it hard to communicate these special moments in the cinema to the generations for which a society without "the eternal presence of competing floods of images" is no longer imaginable (137).

One such special moment came in *Tom Jones* (1963) when the title character stops his chase and turns to look at the audience and offers an ironic comment. For Haneke this was an "epistemological shock": the sensual discovery of the audience's "victim[hood]" by (rather than partnership with) "those who 'entertained' us for money" (138). This epiphany produced a hunger for a "film art, which preserved the experience of being directly moved, of the wonderful enchantment of my childhood cinema, but which nonetheless would not turn me into the intellectually immature victim of the narrative or narrator" (139). Haneke found this perfect film art years later in the "hitherto most precious of all cinematic jewels" (142), *Au hasard Balthazar* (1966).

Bresson's film depicts "a life of little joys and great efforts, banal, unsensational, and inappropriate for cannibalization on the movie screen on account of its depressing prosaicness . . . an ass has no psychology, only a fate." Haneke is drawn toward the cinema of examples that Bresson's title promises: "Accidentally, by way of example, Balthazar." In these descriptions, one recalls *The Seventh Continent, Code Unknown,* and *71 Fragments of a Chronology of Chance,* which offer, instead of heroes, "a surface of projection, an unwritten paper, whose only task is to be filled with the spectator's thoughts and feelings" (142). Indeed, one sees *L'Argent* (1983) in the first third of *The Seventh Continent* and in the city montage sequences of *Benny's Video. Diary of a Country Priest* (1951) haunts Anna's letter to her husband's parents in *The Seventh Continent* and much of *71 Fragments of a Chronology of Chance.* The parallels between *Au hasard Balthazar* and Haneke's television project *The Rebellion* are not to be missed.

In "Terror and Utopia of Form," Haneke probes above all Bresson's treatment of humans. Far more than Jean-Luc Godard's films, whose "cerebral fireworks and high jests" derive from "the rakish 'naturalness' of young actors," the cinema of Bresson offers a liberating experience to a large degree because of his nonprofessionals, whose "availability is reduced to mere presence" (143). These figures—"models" or "human models," in Bresson's parlance—are central to Haneke's subsequent close reading of *Au hasard Balthazar* and foremost in his appreciation of the French director.[9] "The characters move in marionette-like equilibrium," Haneke writes, "no movement is led by emotion, no tear disposes the swelling sorrow and yet, or just for this reason, we as spectators feel the depth of desperation in all characters more strongly than in refined melodrama appealing to our emotions." Bresson preserves "the polyvalence of true life" (146–47).

Just as Haneke's entire piece is prefaced by a quotation from Heinrich von Kleist's "Über das Marionettentheater," so too does this section allude back to that essay. Perhaps the most important aesthetic statement by a German man of letters from the early nineteenth century, Kleist's essay supposes that the very intention to produce beauty or grace in art renders these virtues unreachable. Intention is for Kleist already the imitation of the natural and thus artifice. (Compare Schiller's concept from 1793, "Über Anmuth und Würde," which maintains that there exists a unity between the attempt to achieve grace and beauty and those qualities themselves.) The marionette is, in Kleist's understanding, the emblem of grace and beauty. Its innocent beauty can never be replicated by its opposite, the human dancer. Conscious reflection, characteristic of humanity since the original sin, has destroyed the human ability to reach full grace.

Haneke sees Kleist's theory in the Bressonian nonactors. Reviewing Bresson's aphorisms from *Notes on the Cinematographer* (for example, "Nothing rings more false in a film than the natural tone of the theatre copying life and traced over studied sentiments"; "Radically suppress *inten-*

*tions* in your models" [18, 25]), the connection between "marionettes" and "models" seems not so far-fetched. Kleist's crisscrossed logic reappears in Bresson. The "production of emotions," as Haneke quotes Bresson, is "produced by a resistance against emotions."[10] So too Bresson's style: its beauty lies in the "dirty image," the exactitude and "necessity" of each image and sequence, borne out of Bresson's resistance, Haneke speculates, against his cameraman Pasqualino De Santis's beautiful pictures (144–45).

Besides the relationship with characters/performers, Bresson's attitude toward his spectators wins special praise from Haneke. Bresson's stylistic distance from the spectator is in fact a measure of the filmmaker's appreciation of him or her. Unlike mainstream films, which do not allow "the necessary dialogical perspective between art product and recipient," Bresson's work betrays "the author's almost corporeal aversion against any form of lie, in particular against any form of aesthetic deception" (144). Bresson's films are important because they take the spectator seriously and because of what they reduce and leave out: the gesture of persuasion that emotional identification requires, causal explanations founded on psychology or sociology, the pretense of a unity between the human with its representation, the exceptional. "In its gesture of refusal [*Verweigerungsgestus*]," Haneke explains, this respect for the human being offers "more utopia than all bastions of repression [*Verdrängung*] and cheap comfort together" (152–53).

"Terror and Utopia of Form" resists easy classification. It is at once memoir and hagiography. As a filmmaker's manual, it champions a minimalist dramaturgy, a spare style, and "nonpsychological" characters. It delves into spectatorship theory and ethics. Along the way, Haneke creates a hierarchical canon of postwar international film history: duplicitous drivel, exciting and true films—"Pasolini's *Salò* (1975), Tarkovsky's *Zerkalo* (*The Mirror,* 1975), individual films by Ozu, Rossellini, Antonioni and Resnais, Kluge's *Artisten* (*Artists under the Big Top,* 1968), Straub's *Chronik* (*The Chronicle of Anna Magdalena Bach,* 1968) and a handful of others" (151)—and, at the highest level, Bresson. The argument subscribes to both auteurism (Bresson prevailing against De Santis) and a functional idea of national cinema: successful films "are as different as the authors and cultural circles from which they originate" (151).

Nevertheless, one might distill a major preoccupation in Haneke's theory. In dour prescriptions like "Violence and Media," squibs like "Film as Catharsis," as well as the often rhapsodic "Terror and Utopia of Form," his writings focus on questions of ontology and realism. The first essay, as we recall, expounds on how violence has remained an essential constituent of cinema since its inception and continues to define the major genres. Indeed, movie violence's particular dilemma pertains to film's—as opposed to literature's or painting's—indexical relationship with reality. This ontological property necessitates Haneke's subsequent ethics of the image. Although the title of the essay references "media" as a collective, the director is very specific about which forms bear what sort of responsibility for the violence problem. Reasonably educated adults of (Haneke's) age should be able to differentiate reel and real violence. Television's ensemble of channels, whereby reportage and rerun are supposedly interchangeable for today's youth, represents the true fall from grace.

Likewise, this ontological "original sin" runs through "Terror and Utopia of Form" as a motif, appearing already in the essay's epigraph (from Kleist): "Hence we would have to eat again from the tree of knowledge in order to fall back to the state of innocence?" (135). Harking back on his youthful cinephilia, a halcyon time when images had an absolute value, Haneke bemoans the visual flood that television has left in its wake. The visual surfeit, the author repeats, has produced an aesthetic relativity. Moreover, ethics and aesthetics go hand in hand: the televisual aesthetic relativity has yielded a moral relativity. This equation innervates yet another, the filmmaker's oft-repeated demand for the absolute "identity of content and form" (151). He shares this belief with his idol: "Nothing more inelegant and ineffective," Bresson noted, "than an art conceived in another art's form."[11]

In sum, medium specificity, the doctrine by which film's essence "indicates, limits or dictates the style and/or content" of film, underpins Haneke's theoretical writings: the message is the medium.[12] His films demonstrate how this theory works in practice and, in particular, how the terms—but not values—of medium specificity have changed productively over the course of his oeuvre.

## *Film Praxes*

Haneke's cinema has always rewarded, indeed required, careful spectators attuned to a subjective notion of medium. In *Code Inconnu,* for instance, the viewer must ponder the image produced by a static camera to derive its importance to the narrative. We peer interminably at an airplane cabin door, before the Kosovar woman without papers suddenly appears in police handcuffs. We do so without any devices that, according to Hugo Münsterberg, contribute to the cinema's special "involuntary attention," such as a cut or a close-up.[13] In a later scene, like a game of Where's Waldo? we find Amadou in a crowd of drummers nearly hidden in the frame. These moments take to an extreme what André Bazin writes about neorealism in "An Aesthetic of Reality": "Whereas the camera lens, classically, had focused successively on different parts of the scene, . . . [i]t is no longer the editing that selects what we see, thus giving it an *a priori* significance, it is the mind of the spectator which is forced to discern, as in a sort of parallelepiped of reality with the screen as its cross-section, the dramatic spectrum proper to the scene."[14]

In the classical scopic regime of the movie theater (the one that Bazin's theory assumes and Haneke's writings fondly recall), the director controls the length of this contemplation. But it is increasingly clear that Haneke is no longer making films that can be adequately perceived in one sitting at the cinema. His films respond to changed spectatorship conditions with fresh demands on the audience. *Caché* seems to require a DVD viewing after one or multiple viewings on the big screen. Built into the film is on the one hand a need to stop, rewind, and repeat—in other words, to manipulate cinema's traditional time values. On the other hand there is a virtual requirement to see the film in a large, movie theater format—that is, a requirement of space and setting that partially returns to Walter Benjamin's conception of painterly spectatorship in the era before mass reproduction.[15] Viewing *Caché* for the second time, for instance, the spectator searches in vain along Majid's cluttered wall in the effort to discern the hidden camera filming the action. *Caché*'s final image, in which Pierrot converses with Majid's son, is an example of this second form. This polysemous image has the potential to alter dramatically the spectator's sense of narrative cause and effect—that is, if he or she actually detects the inconspicuous meeting in the corner of the frame just before the credit titles. This is perhaps only possible on a cinema screen or with privileged paratextual knowledge.

There is an irony to this approach when considered across Haneke's oeuvre. *Benny's Video* presents a figure who is unable to differentiate between several layers of mediated reality and unreality. These are nonevents that can be easily rewound and reexperienced at any time. *Funny Games*, furthermore, has its preppy sadists turn the remote toward the audience and rewind the proceedings. By *Caché*, Haneke produces a narratological, philosophical, technological, and market-commercial situation for which the viewer must rewind and review. Comparing *Benny's Video* and *Caché*— two films with related thematic designs—foregrounds the way in which a change of medium produces an altered philosophical basis for Haneke's cinema.

The first sequences index the theoretical shift. *Benny's Video* begins with a buzz and a bang. The television screen snow-shower opening credit yields to an amateur video of a pig being slaughtered on a farm. The title character, the loner son of wealthy Viennese parents, repeatedly rewinds and reviews the sequence and then re-creates the scenario upon a schoolgirl, whose murder he commits and records. Later, he channel surfs through RTL news reports of the August 1992 neo-Nazi assault on asylum-seekers in eastern Germany, war movies, toy commercials, and footage from the military conflict in the Balkans. The effect creates a flat line of reality or unreality, a total conflation of the actual and the virtual. Benny experiences news, commercials, feature films, the pig video, and finally his slaying of his classmate as all equally unreal. Benny inhabits a society of pure transit points and temporary abodes, not unlike Marc Augé's *surmodernité*, a world completely mediated through video and saturated by spectacle. This setting seems in keeping with the writer of "Violence and Media."

*Caché* begins in a less assuming manner: for five minutes a long shot captures a quiet street in Paris's thirteenth arrondissement called rue des Iris, during which the credits superimpose and fill the frame. Yet, the shock in this sequence is ontologically rather than graphically violent. As a male and female voice begin to argue from offscreen and fast-forward lines blur the frame, the spectator realizes that the characters are watching this image along with him or her, that his or her perspective is aligned with theirs, and that the film itself has not quite begun.

Surely, the introductory sequence to *Benny's Video* provides a model for this VCR logic. Indeed, already in *Code Unknown* Haneke toys with the spectator by employing a film within his film. In these earlier works, however, he lets the viewer in on the joke. The amateur handheld camcorder images make Benny's video legible as a different aesthetic and phenomenological layer. The careful viewer would immediately detect the high-rise death scene in *Code Unknown* as a fake: whereas Haneke shoots all other scenes in long takes, this scene deploys conventional continuity editing.

The initial sequence in *Caché* is the first of many instances in which Haneke destabilizes point of view. Later, a car trip to a public housing project on the outskirts of Paris—following sequentially Georges's departure from his mother's house—turns out to be another video. A variation comes after Georges's television show. What appears to be the camera taping the show for televisual broadcast (or what might in fact be television itself) seamlessly tracks Georges receiving a phone call off-set. What might be the province of one camera eye is revealed as omniscient. Even the tapes that Georges receives are sometimes shot from positions illogical within the fiction (the rue de Iris would have to have been outfitted with a crane).

Of course, these concerns could be classified under the rubric of Haneke's stated project: "a cinema of insistent questions instead of quick (because false) answers."[16] But *Caché*'s philosophical conundrums are produced, unlike in his prior films, by a technological solution: Haneke's first use of high-definition digital video for an entire film. *Benny's Video* functions by maintaining a strict medial division of camcorders, surveillance monitors, television news and commercials, and the 35mm "film"—modes of viewing that the spectator could differentiate and that Benny somehow could not. *Caché* depends on the seamlessness of all these forms on the same digital medium, which destabilizes the spectator with a desubstantiated image.

## *The Desubstantiated Image*

In *Reading the Figural*, D. N. Rodowick outlines a theory of "desubstantiation," which in terms of representation means the "disappearance of visible and tactile support from both image and text."[17] He notes the shift in semiotic environment implied by the displacement of the analog and the leveling of all representational forms "to the algorithmic manipulations of binary code" (210–11). In particular, Rodowick foregrounds the "transformation of the orientation of the eye" as an important effect of desubstantiation. In other words, in an age when the digital-photographic has lost its direct indexicality and has become so easily manipulable, we have a new relationship to all images. This idea may be a good point with which to sort out the nuances between "desubstantiation" and the approaches toward the value of the image in the late twentieth century advanced by Baudrillard and Virilio.

Baudrillard regards representation in the most radical respect: simulation is the opposite of representation. Rodowick distances himself from Baudrillard's doomsday scenario. Representation has not become more and more immaterial and insubstantial. Rather, the eye and hand have gradually withdrawn their powers and relinquished them to machines. The concept of interface is coming to define, both figuratively and literally, digital culture's machinic connectivity (214). In this way, Rodowick stresses what is truly at stake in the so-called digital revolution: not a reversal or death of representation à la Baudrillard, but rather a "transformation of perspective," a new division of labor between humans and machines. On this point Rodowick approaches Virilio. Virilio, after all, also deems a defining feature of the audiovisual development to be not only the proliferation of surveillance but above all the "splitting of viewpoint," which he defines as "the sharing of perception of the environment between the animate (the living subject) and the inanimate (the object, the seeing machine)."[18] Despite these similarities, one must recognize whither these contiguous observations lead. For Virilio, splitting of viewpoint is one feature of a world in the throws of a genuine "crisis in perceptive faith . . . that is threatening our understanding." To Rodowick, although surely concerned about the new ways of seeing, Virilio's conclusion that our society is "sinking into the darkness of a voluntary blindness" (150) is not necessarily foregone. Unlike both Baudrillard and Virilio, Rodowick acknowledges potential positive consequences from the digital: "At the same time, the powers of transformation in representation are radically augmented, thus motivating a shift in aesthetic function" (212). Thus, the Rodowick model provides a more flexible scale to weigh the trade-offs of digital culture than Baudrillard and Virilio.

The notion of the "desubstantiated image" enables a better understanding of the paradigm shift in Haneke in two major ways. First, the idea that digital culture has leveled representation to the flat line of binary code bears out—in opposite ways—across the two films. *Benny's Video* has its main character leveling all permutations of actual and virtual to the same level of unreality—a move that intends to make these various levels all the more distinct and discrete to the viewer, and thus all the more important. This is a film that still mourns Virilio's splitting of the viewpoint. *Caché*, on the other hand, plays a game of legibility and illegibility precisely with the harbinger of the desubstantiated image, digital footage. Because of the consistency in medium it is always, initially at least, impossible to differentiate between the various perspectival levels, whether television, home video surveillance tape, or Haneke's film itself. It is the very consistency of medium and, one might venture, the 2005 viewer's new weariness to all images, which destabilize. The viewer of *Caché* is cast into the role and position of Benny.

Second, desubstantiation, with its connection between digital's augmented powers of transformation and shifts in aesthetic function, explains the arc of Haneke's films. In theory and interview, he has always insisted that his work revolves around the coldness of Western bourgeois society, the representation of violence through media, and an interrogation of the real. He wishes to put the spectator in a bind, to lure and lock the viewer into a self-reflexive voyeurism, in his own words, "to rape the spectator into autonomy and awareness."[19] Certainly, *Caché* also works as a critique of the Western bourgeoisie. Recall the dinner party sequence, in which the Laurents' guest holds forth for an extended anecdote, and especially the book-release party, where Anne's telephone conversation competes on the soundtrack with a tipsy guest name-dropping Proust, and yes, Baudrillard. But, *pace* Haneke's rhetorical theatrics and his own nods to Baudrillard in essays and interviews, it is precisely these references that make a productive dialogue between Virilio's or Baudrillard's apocalyptic thinking and *Caché* untenable. For all of Haneke's social critique, despite Georges's visit to a cinema to numb his conscience after witnessing Majid's suicide, and for all critics' assertions that Haneke's films lack redemption, his cinema finds its creative redemption precisely in the binary flat line of the new media he has so vociferously denounced. The desubstantiated image becomes a muse for the most stubborn media critic and one of the most passionate defenders of celluloid among European filmmakers. Nevertheless, this is not to say that Haneke's recent practice contradicts his earlier theory. In a way, he has become ever more consequential, pursuing medium specificity and the identity of form and content even into the digital. If the moving image has lost its indexical quality, according to Haneke's logic, so too must the audience forego its grasp on what is "real" and what might not be. Even as the medium has changed, the message remains.

## *Notes*

Part of this chapter appeared in an earlier form as "*Benny's Video, Caché*, and the Desubstantiated Image," *Framework* 47, no. 2 (2006): 30–36. All translations are mine, unless otherwise noted.

1. See, for example, Christopher Sharrett, "Michael Haneke and the Discontents of European Culture," *Framework* 47, no. 2 (2006): 6–16; or Roy Grundmann, "*Auteur de Force:* Michael Haneke's 'Cinema of Glaciation,'" *Cineaste* 33, no. 2 (2007): 3–9.

2. Thomas Assheuer, *Nahaufnahme Michael Haneke: Gespräche mit Thomas Assheuer* (Berlin: Alexander, 2008), 71–72.

3. Ibid., 62.

4. Haneke presented these thoughts before a screening of *Benny's Video* at the Marshall-Theater in Munich in 1995. They are published as "Gewalt und Medien"

in ibid., 155–63. An abridged English version (with many errata) appears as Michael Haneke, "Violence and Media," ed. Gerhard Larchner, Franz Grabner, and Christian Wessely, *Visible Violence: Sichtbare und verschleierte Gewalt im Film* (Münster: Lit, 1998), 93–98.

5. Compare Jean Baudrillard, *The Gulf War Did Not Take Place,* trans. Paul Patton (Bloomington: Indiana University Press, 1995).

6. Michael Haneke, "Film als Katharsis," in *Austria (In)felix: zum österreichischen Film der 80er Jahre,* ed. Francesco Bono (Graz: Blimp, 1992), 89.

7. See Mattias Frey, "Benny's Video," in *The Cinema of Michael Haneke: Europe Utopia,* ed. Ben McCann and David Sorfa (London: Wallflower Press, forthcoming).

8. Michael Haneke, "Schrecken und Utopie der Form: Bressons *Au hasard Bathalzar,*" in Assheuer, *Nahaufnahme Michael Haneke,* 135–53 (hereafter cited in text). The essay first appeared in Verena Lueken, ed., *Kinoerzählungen* (Munich: Hanser, 1995).

9. See Robert Bresson, *Notes on the Cinematographer,* trans. Jonathan Griffin (Copenhagen: Green Integer, 1997), especially 14ff.

10. Haneke, "Schrecken und Utopie der Form," 145; Bresson, *Notes on the Cinematographer,* 126.

11. Ibid., 65.

12. Noël Carroll, *Theorizing the Moving Image* (Cambridge: Cambridge University Press, 1996), 50, and quoted in D. N. Rodowick, *The Virtual Life of Film* (Cambridge: Harvard University Press, 2007), 35.

13. See Hugo Münsterberg, *The Photoplay: A Psychological Study* (New York: BiblioBazaar, 2007).

14. André Bazin, "An Aesthetic of Reality," in *What Is Cinema?* vol. 2, trans. Hugh Gray (Berkeley: University of California Press, 1967), 28. For more on the connection between Haneke and neorealism, see John David Rhodes's contribution to this volume.

15. Benjamin writes, "Distraction and concentration form polar opposites which may be stated as follows: A man who concentrates before a work of art is absorbed by it. He enters into this work of art the way legend tells of a Chinese painter when he viewed his finished painting. In contrast, the distracted mass absorbs the work of art." Walter Benjamin, *Illuminations,* trans. Harry Zohn (New York: Schocken, 1968), 239.

16. See Haneke, "Film als Katharsis," 89.

17. See D. N. Rodowick, *Reading the Figural, or Philosophy after the New Media* (Durham: Duke University Press, 2001), 212 (hereafter cited in text).

18. Paul Virilio, *The Vision Machine* (Bloomington: Indiana University Press, 1994), 134 (hereafter cited in text).

19. Quoted in Mattias Frey, "A Cinema of Disturbance: The Films of Michael Haneke in Context," *Senses of Cinema* (September–October 2003), www.sensesofcinema.com/contents/directors/03/haneke.html.

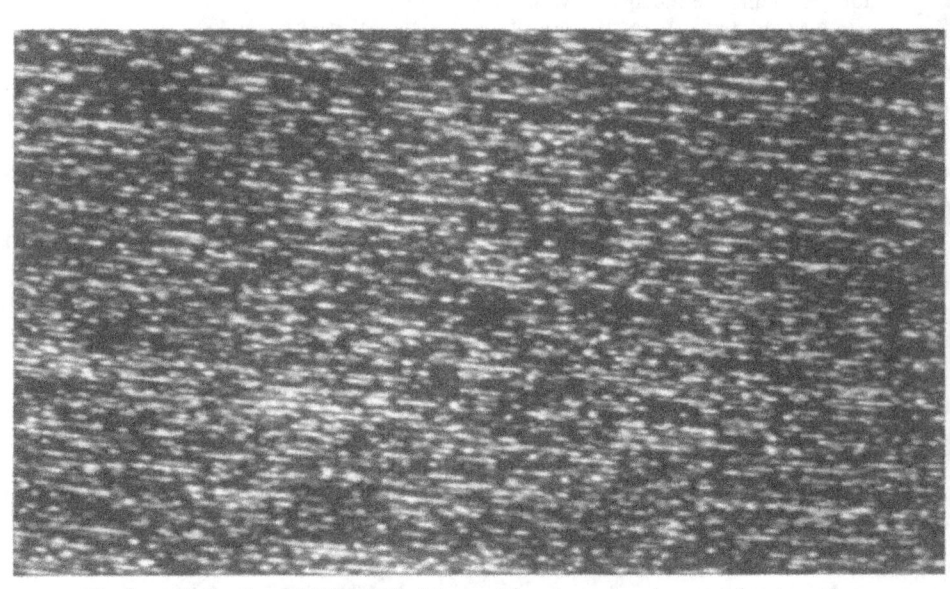

*The Seventh Continent* (1989): Television as "the phenomenal space of a séance."

Meghan Sutherland

# Death, with Television

In 1935, almost a decade before American broadcast television began to air on a regular basis, it would have been difficult for the young medium to effect much of anything. Still, the mere prospect of its emergence already loomed large enough in the popular imagination to inspire a B movie, starring Bela Lugosi, with a title that now sounds like a forensic classification for all the social and psychic ills attributed to it since: *Murder by Television*.[1] Despite the sweeping evocations of this title, one of the great charms of the film is that the murder mystery it enacts takes care to draft a more precise autopsy of its victims. By the end we learn that it is neither the molecular warp of the electronic image nor the hypnotic power it holds over masses of viewers that does the killing but rather the president of a broadcast network who fears losing his monopoly claim to a patent on television technology—a charged bit of social criticism at a moment when RCA executives were securing just such a monopoly.[2] Television, the film seems to quip, does not *do* anything; it takes an executive to execute.

The prospect of death by television has generally taken a more amorphous form as a figurative threat in the discourse of mass culture, casting a broad shadow of doom over twentieth- and twenty-first-century cultural theory, middlebrow criticism, popular punditry, and social scientific analysis of the Left and the Right. Depending on which commentators and theorists one consults between the years of 1943 and the present, television is responsible for the waxing and waning of any number of indices charting the decline of Western civilization—whether the endpoint of that decline is posited as good old-fashioned godlessness or a capitalist regime totalizing enough to smother any remaining fire left in the world. To be sure, some arguments posit good effects for television, and some focus more specifically on, say, advertising or cartoons; some are more warranted or more thoughtful than others. For instance, a wide gulf of concerns separates Fredric Jameson's worries about the fate of the political unconscious in "Video: Surrealism without the Unconscious" from the battery of social scientific experiments that connect violence or obesity to something called "television" (why not conglomeration? or fascist parents? or war machine?).[3] Still, the grounding assumption of all such discourses is ultimately the same: television, or alternatively, "the media"—an epithet that speaks well to the vagueness of such talk—*does something* to us and to society. In addition to *affecting* reality, it *effects* reality. While the nature of the effects and the scale on which they occur remain a matter of energetic debate, their existence is more or less taken for granted both in the academy and in many of the same living rooms where television is apologetically declared a guilty pleasure. Television is the social, cultural, and political equivalent of smoking: we *know* it will kill us and that it is unbecoming moreover, but out of either defiance or gluttony we refuse to quit.

It must be said, however, that television is not entirely like cigarettes. In particular, it does not result in physical asphyxiation, and it does not directly promote the growth of cancerous cells that colonize bodies in a new state of death. So it is worth asking a question that is seldom, if ever, taken very seriously: What would it mean for television to have an *effect* on the existence of democracy, or intelligence, or our bodies? What would the nature and terms of *responsibility*—something that suggests a certain concrete causality—even be for a *medium*? And furthermore, what would it mean to take seriously the ultimate effect—death—as a potential effect of watching television? This question is in many ways preliminary to the more familiar kinds of discussions about ideological subjects and good or bad representations. It simply asks, What is the ontological status of television, which is to say, the ground on which it exists in relation to our existence? Or even more simply, How does television intervene in reality?

Perhaps because behavioral social scientists have pursued these foundational kinds of questions with such uncomplicated zeal, in the last few decades television and new media scholars have eschewed them altogether. In fact, if the humanities-based practice of media theory has any ontological discourse of death by television at all, it is both ad hoc and de facto, consisting of only two possible utterances that are quietly taken for granted even when they run afoul of one another. For instance, the more nihilistic among us might answer these questions with a reference to Jean Baudrillard's 1983 treatise *Simulacra and Simulations*, where the poles separating media images from material reality fundamentally "implode" in the nuclear abyss of postmodernism, and no ontology is either possible or necessary.[4] Here, the phrase "death by television" should be understood in the simultaneously causal and diagnostic terms of a bad infinity, a metaphysical outcome that is by definition unthinkable.

Of course, as Friedrich Nietzsche reminds us, true nihilists are rare. So it is hardly surprising that virtually all of the major television scholarship of the last twenty-five years rests on a much less gruesome premise, that is, the field-defining model of hegemonic media discourse that Stuart Hall made famous with the 1980 essay "Encoding/Decoding." In this pathbreaking formulation, Hall describes mass-communications discourse as a "complex structure in dominance," where mystifying media images compete for hegemonic realization in concrete social practices.[5] Hall does not explicitly address or thematize the ontological significance of this structure. And yet, the essay clearly attempts to describe the nature of the relay between the mystifications of ephemeral media images and the comparatively material discursive productions of social reality—a relay that Hall breaks down into five "linked but distinctive" moments.[6] The only two "determinate" material moments of this relay come at the beginning, when a media producer "encodes" an ideological message about social reality into a text, and at the end, when a media consumer "decodes" this message in complicit, negotiated, or resistant interpretations, and in turn either reproduces or challenges the ideology of the message in other material social acts and practices. The image itself is thus indecisive and ineffective by definition. Although it attempts to capture something meaningful about social materiality by nudging the viewer to accept the reality it posits—that is, to *affect* this meaning in a way realistic enough to *effect* this meaning in the actions of the viewer—it is not as yet real; it is simply the immaterial midwife of reality, a "medium" whose very *lack* of existential definition is also precisely what allows it to channel this supra-ontological communication between two different realms of being. If death by television should come, then, it will only do so by way of the latter's ghostly proximity to the former; television itself is nothing more than the phenomenal space of a séance between the immaterial spirit world and the leap into material history, whether we see that leap as angelic or demonic.

I know of no television studies work that addresses the ontological significance of Hall's scenario, let alone any work that attempts to evaluate or reconsider the implicit premise at the latter's core.[7] And yet, this premise has served as the unspoken ontological ground of virtually every major trend in the methodological repertoire of late-twentieth-century television studies scholarship, from reception studies and institutional research to that infamous practice of "reading against the grain." So in my estimation, it is fair to say that scarcely any media theorist has grappled with the ontological question of television either as earnestly or persistently as Michael Haneke has in his films. If there is a poet laureate of death by television in the world of contemporary cinema, he is it. Consider the infamous premise of the 1992 film *Benny's Video:* Benny, a video-obsessed adolescent, records a farmer's execution of a pig by pneumatic gun during a weekend in the countryside. He replays it endlessly alongside violent American movies from the video store. Having stolen the gun and brought it to his videolair, he then half-heartedly reenacts the execution for his camcorder with the same pneumatic gun, only this time he kills a girl he meets at the video store instead of a pig. When Benny's father asks him why he did it—having worked up a philosophical mood by hacking the girl's body to pieces for disposal—Benny gives an apathetic answer that Baudrillard or Jameson could have anticipated and diagnosed in full: "I don't know. I wanted to see what it feels like . . . probably."

Haneke's nearly identical Austrian and American versions of *Funny Games* (1997 and 2007) do not put a finer point on the link between death and television. This pair of films is most often read as a critique of violent movies. After all, it plies its viewers with a protracted narrative of family-style torture—exacted by two young men who appear fresh from a shopping spree at the J. Crew outlet store—only to jeer the audience for enjoying the carnage occasioned by their presence at the film. But it is worth noting that the strongest self-reflexive moments in *Funny Games* are expressed through distinctly televisual tropes. For instance, valuable discussions have been devoted to the fact that when one of the torturers kills the first family member—the child—he does so in the offscreen space of a long take that shows a comparatively quotidian domestic scene.[8] However, it is less often noted that when this long take ends its deferral of the scene of violence, it abruptly cuts not to the dead body of the child but to a tightly framed shot of the family's television set drenched in blood; the images onscreen idle by like nothing has happened. As if to make the point of this pun unequivocal—the blood is "on" television, so to speak—when the matron of the family later manages to shoot one of the assailants in a bid for escape, the other responds with a gag worthy of a clever nineties sitcom.

He simply grabs the family's remote, rewinds the film we are watching, and forestalls the revolt so that the narrative may continue to unfold toward the family's inevitable execution, which has been made inevitable precisely by the temporal power that television's capacity for time-shifting promises even to cinema.

With these and many other death scenes from throughout Haneke's oeuvre in mind—and a television set is implicated in virtually all of them—it is hardly surprising that both popular and academic critics characterize Haneke's apparent antipathy toward "the media" in terms of postmodern theory.[9] For one thing, distributors' synopses of the films almost uniformly solicit such readings. Kino's gloss on the DVD cover of *The Seventh Continent* (1989)—which begins the "glaciation trilogy" completed with *Benny's Video* and *71 Fragments of a Chronology of Chance* (1994)—promises "a meticulous dive into the postmodern disregard of affect . . . and a stark look at lives severed from feelings." The same text describes the trilogy in general as a statement on "the intersections between media, alienation, and violence." The films do not necessarily *fail* on this promise. And yet, I would argue that the technological abyss of information, simulation, and irony that generally goes by the name of postmodernism hardly describes what they show us or ask us to think about. Indeed, to look closely at even a few of Haneke's many stagings of death by television without determining their postmodern status in advance is to see a considerably more nuanced philosophical exploration of how television helps constitute our social and political existence. And what is more, this exploration provides suggestive cues for a new conception of the relation between these two terms, as well as our place in it. After all, this relationship has for far too long been reduced to one of two basic models: either the postmodern model of simulation, where the difference of representation is nullified along with reality, or British cultural studies' version of media hegemony, where every claim that media make on the representation of society and the world can and must finally be "demystified" and is thus also denied any substantive claim on existence. Since both of these discourses of media effects ultimately eradicate television's relationship to what actually exists—one makes it a simulacrum and the other makes it an economic epiphenomenon—such a consideration promises to yield a very different vantage on the politics of representation.

Fittingly enough, Haneke's first film, *The Seventh Continent*, offers a good place to begin. The skeletal events of the film and the emotional void of consumer accumulation that attends them do much to explain

Haneke's postmodern reputation. The first hour or so gives us a series of matter-of-fact tableaux showing Georg and Anna, two decent-looking and well-off middle-class parents, and their young daughter, Eva. As we watch Georg and Anna find growing success at work and in their finances, they linger around the edges of baroque scenes that are most properly focused on household goods, and indications of deep emotional repression accrue. In other words, the film displays a robust selection of postmodern indicators: the rise of an apathetic irony, a world of surfaces and goods, a loss of meaning. The last half-hour shows the family after the parents have made an entirely unsentimental decision to alleviate the emptiness of their existence by quitting their jobs, literally flushing their money down the toilet, destroying *almost* all of the household goods, and committing collective suicide. Again, these scenes focus almost entirely on the objects—the fastidiousness with which the family obliterates them. It is thus difficult to ignore the one object that not only survives this consumption holocaust but also subsumes the entire last frame of the film. That object is a television set, still turned on but blaring with the violent snow of a failed signal. Of course, this television screen does not just subsume the frame; it also implicitly subsumes the consciousness of the last living consumer, Georg, who in the penultimate shot stares at the camera with the equivocal blankness of either coma or death.

Because this scene positions Georg's two-dimensional television set in a mise-en-abyme with the viewer's own three-dimensional screen or set—so that a very material screen contains the mere *image* of a screen within its limits, creating the dizzying reproductive effect of a screen-within-screen—it already proposes a certain kind of relation between media representation and what exists more concretely. But what is this relationship? A closer look suggests just how interesting this trope of mise-en-abyme will be for our consideration. The set first appears in the frame as the reverse-shot object of Georg's dead gaze, which is to say, as his only companion in death. However, from here the shot slowly tightens on the screen so that the white noise it broadcasts back to both the viewer's and the dead man's gazes gradually absorbs the very limits of the film's field of vision—an especially strong effect when viewed on a television set. And when the camera completes its hypnotic voyage into the onscreen snow—having been interrupted in its progress only by rapid-fire glances back at preceding scenes from the film, and perhaps Georg's own consciousness—the two frames and gazes become consonant with each other; our eyes are Georg's as well. What is more, these frames and gazes all converge at the very moment in which the white noise of the screen finally ceases to admit any more interruptions from the film's repertoire of images for Georg's memory. The television screen seems to broadcast Georg's loss of consciousness, but it is hard to say why: Because it is *responsible* for this loss? Because it is a metaphor for this loss? Or because it just happened to serve as the only witness that would abide a friend's suicide? In this sense, the film ends with an enactment of death by television that blurs the literal and figurative meanings of the phrase "death by television" itself. Or rather, it literalizes the figurative notion of such a death by reveling in the gray area between the transitive and prepositional meanings of the word *by.*

It would be almost effortless to read this final elision of screens and consciousnesses as a statement on the very postmodern abyss that the film's synopsis promised to render: we are lost in a televisual void of consumer objects where no plane of existence or meaning can be found to take precedence over another. Our screen is Georg's screen or any other. We are all now free to ease back off into a group coma that elides consciousness with death—a coma exacted by either television or its role as ceaseless witness to our gravest ways of being, which is to say our nonbeing. However, to read the scene in this way is to completely disavow the visual logic that the trope of mise-en-abyme enacts, and to ignore in turn the figurative relation that it asks our eyes to think. For mise-en-abyme describes a *profusion* of frames-within-frames, and not one that ever resolves neatly in the latters' canceling out one another entirely. (This latter scenario might simply be recognized as mise-en-scène, or whatever else one wants to call the kind of scene that appears to be an *unsituated* one without any defined border but that nevertheless *is* precisely because it was situated thus in a particular frame.) One could certainly argue that the final headlong shot into the blizzard of the television screen effectively performs the scene of this canceling out. And yet, there is indeed still one remaining frame for this mise-en-abyme of screens. Whether we are watching the film in a theater or on a television, mise-en-abyme by definition insists that there is always *one more frame* anchoring our relation to it; it is simply the "real" frame that marks the limits of representation. And in this case, that frame is either a real movie screen or television console that is itself filled with that more limited plot of snow. In this sense, mise-en-abyme rhetorically compels us not to deny the existence of limits or ground as such but rather to reflect all the more earnestly on the limits that order and ground our own experience of what *is,* and the nature of the boundary that so neatly separates it from the *what is not* of a representation. Accordingly, the film does not so much ask the viewer to identify with the dead man, to experience the meaningless feeling he felt, or to freeze to death in a blizzard of postmodern emptiness. Quite the contrary, it asks us to take seriously the question already before us: What is the status of television's seemingly mediate and *im*mediate relation to our living and dying? What is the nature of the boundary between the world confined to its representational economy—or for that matter, any representational economy—and what spills into our own social and political economies of being, defining the limits and modes of that being in the process? How, in short, is a medium responsible for the fate of our existence?

In many respects, these are the same basic questions that Martin Heidegger raises about technology in the landmark essay "The Question Concerning Technology." Observing that "we are too easily inclined either to understand being responsible and being indebted moralistically as a lapse, or else to construe them in terms of effecting," Heidegger concludes that the instrumentality of technology is itself related to the concept of causality, and thus, one must gain a deeper understanding of the concept of responsibility in order to understand what modern technology is.[10] He then goes on to argue that responsibility should most fundamentally be understood as a "bringing-forth" into "revealing," and that modern technology should in turn be understood not as a mere means to an end but as "a way of revealing" existence.[11] But it is not just any way of revealing; it is an "en-framing" or "destining of revealing"—one that orders in advance and thereby forecloses the potential realities it purports only to "bring-forth," creating a "standing-reserve" of facts, beings, and resources available at our convenience. Seen this way, both representation and technological mediation in general play a pivotal role in constituting the very ground of being and necessity that we perceive as the total horizon of the world; they organize all the contingent possibilities of this world's existence into a manifest order that appears fixed, and in doing so, they effect being by affecting it.

As Oliver Marchart has rightly insisted, this formulation of being in terms of "necessary contingency" entails a significantly different understanding of mediated existence than the universe of indeterminacy for which postmodernism has become the shorthand.[12] Indeed, a world denuded of any stable ground or fixture—truth, fate, and all the other reliable things that postmodern media technology are said to subsume—is quite a different prospect than a world that, despite the impossibility of such grounds, nevertheless requires them as the bases for its existence. For in this latter sort of world, the fixed order of necessity on which the existence of any ground at all depends is simply produced from the contingent materials of a given moment, so that provisional representations of existence seem only to "reveal" the truth when in fact they constitute the latter's ability to materialize as such. Or rather, processes of representation define the grounding effects through which we understand the materiality of "truth" and "existence" in the first place. While disorder constitutes the violence of the former scenario—think of Jameson's mourning for "cognitive mapping"—it is order that constitutes the violence of the latter scenario.[13] Ernesto Laclau's aesthetic formulation of hegemony—a synecdoche in which a contingent particularity takes on the appearance of a necessary totality—demonstrates this sort of violence well, and also the ambivalence of its force.[14] For although this sort of order makes the world possible in the first place, it does so at the risk of reducing what it produces to the "standing-reserve" of a dominant ideology. It was more or less this same basic threat that Heidegger had in mind when he warned about the "supreme danger" of technology's claim to reveal and indeed order the total facticity of the world, writing, "As soon as what is unconcealed no longer concerns man even as an object, but does so, rather, exclusively as standing-reserve, and man in the midst of objectlessness is nothing but the orderer of the standing-reserve . . . then he comes to the point where he himself will have to be taken as standing-reserve."[15]

One could say that Georg and his family decide to kill themselves because they have met this very fate. After all, Heidegger's conception of being bestows a distinctly constitutive effect on representation, and Georg's expiration appears consonant with the expiration of the television image. What is more, Heidegger conceives of this fate in terms of an image, that is, as a "world picture"—a plenitude of visibility that exhausts the existence of every material being in the process of marshaling it for ready use.[16] Along these same lines, Georg and his family seem to choose death by television precisely because they recognize themselves as the mere wardens of a meaningless capitalist order, so much so that they must count themselves among the "objectless" objects to be destroyed. And yet, it must also be noted that while Heidegger's account of technology resonates with Haneke's scenario in important ways, it does not quite manage to account for the remainder with which we are left at the end of Haneke's mise-en-abyme: that stubborn final frame of a television that remains *on* and *with* us in static, even if it remains so without an image. Indeed, if all technology essentially reduces the world to a picture—which is to say, as an immediately graspable "standing-reserve" of facts that conceal their own mediation—then the inevitable remainder of both Haneke's televisual mise-en-abyme and mise-en-abyme in general foregrounds the fact that visual media technology would necessarily redouble this effect. That is, because the purported function of television and film technology already explicitly consists of "bringing-forth into appearance" a picture of the world as given, it immediately, even proudly, avows Heidegger's most gruesome charge: Television brings forth the world! Or, as the announcers for the NBC morning show *Today* put it, "*This* is *Today.*"

It is for this reason that the Marxist tradition of television studies has expended so much energy "demystifying" the medium's hegemonic illusions at the level of *content;* if the contents of *Today* do not necessarily coincide with the contents of "today," then the impulse to distinguish the ontological status of the two—one is presumably material and the other is not—makes a certain amount of sense. And yet, it is also for this reason that so many scholars working in this same tradition take it for granted that technological *forms* of mass media forge different scales of "imagined communities," "technoscapes," and/or "mediascapes," all of which indeed constitute the existence of the social world in some important sense. Since the variously scaled industrial technologies of print capitalism, television, and the Internet help forge social connections in what can safely be described as material social space, there is never much need to question whether this "effect" is also part of material reality; the ontological status of television technology can simply be cleaved apart from that of the image it displays.[17] For the most part, these conversations do not go on at the same time or in the same place, or on an explicitly theoretical register, so there has not been any concern about either the tension or the reciprocity between them; nor has there been any rigorous theoretical attempt to conceptualize their relationship. As a result, though, neither of these accounts sits easily enough with the other to explain that peculiar doubled quality of television's mise-en-abymic place in Georg's end. More precisely, neither accounts for the complicated way that the scene relates, on the one hand, the frame of television technology—a persistent form of connectivity that shapes our consciousness of real spaces and communities—and on the other hand, the particular hegemonic content or image through which this frame also seals the fate of the world in a very specific sort of picture.

If Haneke were not so profoundly invested in tropes and their relation to the literal—an investment well in evidence in the scene of Georg's death as well as the gag about "flushing money down the toilet"—one could simply disregard this peculiar problem, as well as the figure of mise-en-abyme that raises them.[18] We could declare Georg a victim of postmodernism or, alternatively, of the "world picture" and leave it at that. However, Haneke uses precisely the same trope to render the relationship between death and television over and over in the course of his films.[19] Indeed, while John David Rhodes has written suggestively about Haneke's tendency to exhaust the frame of long-take cinema—and along with it, the latter's storied claims to provoke the active engagement of the spectator with the visible plenitude of the image—I would add that Haneke's preoccupation with framing and the limits of visibility almost invariably builds into a staging of the multiple frames that constitute mise-en-abyme.[20] In virtually every scene of violent death that Haneke renders it is an elaborate staging of mise-en-abyme that relates the ontological planes of film screen, television screen, and the three-dimensional domain most commonly associated with what actually exists. Though this last domain is certainly the one where technology's ability to "bring-forth" into visibility has most properly and implicitly been recognized, Haneke's use of mise-en-abyme expressly destabilizes this border by making visible as well the doubled sort of "enframing" that technologies of visibility open up for being. That is, because Haneke so reliably positions the murdering television screen as both the content and the form of our own screens—the subject of the image and the real technological object on which this image appears—it raises the very question of what mediated technology might actually do to the world. By extension, it raises altogether new possibilities for thinking about the relationship this intervention brokers between the ontologically quarantined categories of media technology as form, on the one hand, and media content, on the other. And so, if we take Benny's half-hearted explanation of his crime to his father with any seriousness at all, then it would seem that Haneke's insistent restagings of both mise-en-abyme and murder by television might compel us to rethink the relation between being and technology for visual media, and in the process, to rethink as well the relation between television and our own social and political existence.

It is difficult to imagine a film better suited to this task than *71 Fragments of a Chronology of Chance*. The film is not only structured as a mise-en-abyme at every level—from shot to shot, scene to scene, and beginning to end of the narrative—the relationship between death and television comprises the entire horizon of its events. And as the title perhaps already makes obvious, the progress of these events takes shape according to an order that resonates strongly with the notion of necessary contingency. The first frame of the film consists of a written text on a black background stating that on December 23, 1993, a nineteen-year-old student walked into a Viennese bank, shot four people, then killed himself. The rest of the film is comprised of a series of scenes, each separated decisively by a dead black interval. Without any real sense of causal or informative logic, these scenes assemble a disjointed succession of tableaux from the strange and often stagnant itinerary of chance events that bring the characters together to die—as required by the fate sealed in the epitaph with which the film begins. Maximilian Le Cain puts it well: the film simply and singularly "deconstructs the process whereby people pass from their own realities into media-related facts."[21]

In this much alone, the structure of the film could be understood as a mise-en-abyme because it unfolds a real event that is not explicitly counted as a fragment—the nonfictional text that occasions the images—into a receding economy of embedded frames of fiction. And while these frames will fold back into that event by the end of the film, they will also exceed it by opening a series of visible windows into the lives of the victims, none of which are resolved by the gruesome fate they meet. Indeed, these seemingly very ordinary lives remain utterly unresolved by the film's ending, open to the permeable border that the film stages between being and representation, media event and real event, our world and its encapsulation on any number of screens sitting in front of our eyes. Of course, the effect of this mise-en-abyme of windows or frames is only redoubled by the fact that many of the film's "fragments"—most notably, the first and last—are comprised strictly of Viennese television news segments taken from the days recounted in the film's progress toward the shoot-out.

The first fragment consists of a segment from the television news of October 13, 1993, which we pick up amid the airing of footage from the war territory of the former Yugoslavia. However, the screen displaying this footage quickly peels back in a "page-turning" effect to reveal an anchorman in yet another screen discussing the failure of the UN-brokered truce in Somalia, which then peels back to reveal footage of American troops both bombing Somalia and declaring its friendly intentions, which then peels back once more to a screen illustrating UN and U.S. "efforts" to foster democracy in Haiti. The fragment ends abruptly right here. Much like the narrative structure of the film that I have already described, then, it establishes a televisual economy of violence that seems at once to propose a tenuous logic uniting the various violent conflicts underway in a thousand screens cast across the global world (the totalizing entities of the United Nations, the United States, and global ethnic warfare, for instance). At the same time, though, the news segment also seems to eschew a holistic or causal relation between these events—that is, one that might extend beyond their simple chronological positions in the news segment. For all intents and purposes they are strictly proximate, and they recede from view as quickly as they reappear to regenerate the ground of visibility anew and indefinitely. The status of this fragment in the film itself feels much the same. It is tenuously meaningful to the total effect of the film and causally related to the point we are supposed to make about violence and media at the abrupt end of the narrative. However, it is also quite obviously removed from the precise determination of violence in a Viennese bank that concerns the film and its characters—and perhaps in excess of it as well.

The final fragment of the film further multiplies this effect. Following just after the scene for which every viewer has been readied—when the fateful shooter shoots—this fragment consists of a television screen showing footage of the tragic event, with passersby wondering after motives for such a "senseless act of violence" in the days leading up to Christmas. Then the page-effect peels back this screen to reveal a female anchor reporting on the failure of a UN-brokered cease-fire for the holidays in Bosnia and from there peels back again to show footage that has been recycled from a newscast we watched in an earlier segment of the film. The first part shows remixed scenes of Bosnians expressing gratitude for food if not a Christmas tree; the second segment shifts directly into a familiar story about Michael Jackson's claims of innocence despite damning evidence against him in a child molestation case. Both the segment and the film end abruptly with the newsfile footage showing Jackson gyrating on stage, and the reporter's voice-over beginning a sentence that will not be finished: "His career . . ." Simply put, the deaths finally become part of the televisual order, tenuously linked to the violence in Bosnia and the spots on Michael Jackson's penis. They are next to themselves and to the total scope of the world now—somehow remote from its causal order of explanations and motives even as they continue to order and unfold as constituent fragments of the world and its onscreen life. As in *Benny's Video* and *Seventh Continent,* then, television implicitly outlasts the death it marks—only this time it also mocks the comparatively arbitrary expiration of the film that attends it.

While these glimpses from *71 Fragments* make the film's interest in connecting murder and television quite plain, they do not make the terms of the connection so immediate. The film's self-avowed chronological narrative certainly positions the fragments in a causal relationship leading directly to the event of violence, so television's place among them makes it responsible too. But in what way? One relatively literal answer to this question can be found in the only scene of the film that connects the fated characters together without the "fragmenting" black partitions. Here we see an old man who has just been bickering on the phone with his estranged daughter as he watches a television news broadcast discussing both Bosnia's Christmastime deprivation and a Romanian orphan, living homeless in Vienna, whom we have been following in parallel. In the next fragment that features the old man we will watch him go directly to the bank (along with the shooter) to give his daughter, an executive there, a Christmas gift for his grandchild. But in this fragment, the shot of the old man watching television cuts in close to the full scale of the screen showing the orphan. When the shot cuts to a medium distance again, we find ourselves in the living room of a couple we have also been following, and they too are watching news of the orphan. In the next fragment from their lives, we watch the mother driving with the orphan—apparently now her ward—on her way to the bank, where she will also encounter the shooter. With this pivot through the screen in mind, then, we could perhaps say that television does its violence in the film primarily as a technological *formation,* in the way it connects people socially while also isolating them. However, to do so would ignore the very sentimental response to *content* that drives both of the connections that we see unfold in the more literal scene of violence—namely, the woman's emotional impulse to adopt the orphan, which leads her to the bank that day, and the old man's presumable reflections on children in need of Christmas gifts amid a violent family war.

As this enfoldment of form and content already suggests, if the question of television's deathliness holds any interest at all it is only because of the very complicated answer that the mise-en-abymic structure of the film demands in reply. For it is this structure that gives sensual aesthetic form to the conceptual proposition of the film—"a chronology of chance"—by aerating the film's total narrative progress toward death with its neatly counted but still inconclusive fragments. These successively staged fragments grow out of one another, layer upon layer, to produce a sense of narrative causality leading to the totalization of both the film and the lives it animates. But as the dead space between them constantly reaffirms, they are not necessarily bound in any stronger causal order; they are also simply fragments, partial and proximate glimpses into lives that fail to offer any commensurately totalizing explanation for their end. As I have already tried to suggest, the scenes do not offer any deep psychological explanation for the event. We see several signs of stress in the killer's life—a nagging mother, Christian schoolmates who are into competitive gambling, a rather demanding table-tennis coach, and of course, the purchase of a stolen gun—but no event save the shooting itself is decisive. If the figure of mise-en-abyme can be said to have a causal order, then, it is surely the very order of fatality that Greek tragedy taught us so well. To be more precise, it is a zig-zagging, inverted, and enfolding movement, a retroactively established chronology of chance that never forgets its fragmentary status, even as it declares an aesthetic limit point just as decisive as death: the frame around *it*.

When posed this way, the mode of responsibility that mise-en-abyme implies also resonates strongly with the notion of necessary contingency. Indeed, the film appears to be a set piece for the realization, or "bringing-forth," of this concept. Along these lines, we could say that Haneke presents both the text of the film and the notion of fatality that orders it as twinned scenes of hegemonic violence. For as Laclau has explained, the construction of any order of differences as a hegemonic totality depends on the erection of a comparatively violent frontier—a difference that is explicitly outside this totality—in order to forge a sense of holistic unity among those less important differences.[22] Along similar lines, the abrupt ending of the film, which comes midsentence in the anchorman's address, seems to perform this very function, highlighting the relatively arbitrary violence of a representational totality right as it coincides with an actual death.

While I would not really disagree with this basic reading of the film, it does little to explain why television seems to hold such a prominent place in the film's violence.[23] Much as Heidegger's original formulation does, the film would necessarily present all causality and all being as a scene of necessary contingency. Television would thus impinge on the necessity of death in exactly the same way that any other sort of contingency might; it would be no more decisive than the event of the shooter's running out of gas and going to *that* bank across the street. At best, one could note that television is itself a source of representational order and read Haneke's decision to represent the final event of the shoot-out entirely through its screen as an enactment of a Heideggerian world picture. Television technology, in this scenario, would automatically effect death on every event it reports, giving each an existence within the hegemonic economy of the visible world's events while making invisible every other contingent realization of the world's contents and possibilities. In the process, it would also give the human beings subject to whatever violence it makes visible through this textual form of violence a sense of "objectlessness" and invisibility. Simply put, the total visibility that television technology repeatedly promises to viewers—and television news most of all, as the self-avowed "window on the world"—would have to be understood as the effective executor of fate, where what *appears* congeals as what *is*.

It is worth noting that this scenario coincides almost exactly with the antipathy toward representation that still haunts the discourse of necessary contingency in contemporary continental philosophy. Indeed, with the possible exception of Laclau, the consensus among the array of philosophers that Marchart has identified with the "postfoundational" strain of political thought seems to be that representation is as much a necessary evil as totality itself, and is even coincident with it in its more terrifying effects.[24] Jean-Luc Nancy—who has devoted years of thought to the invisibility of obviousness in Heidegger's world picture—offers only the most rousing and explicit version of this sentiment in *The Creation of the World or Globalization*, where he writes:

A representation of the world, a worldview, means the assigning of a principle and an end to the world. This amounts to saying that a worldview is indeed the end of the world as viewed, digested, absorbed, and dissolved in this vision. The Nazi *Weltanschauung* attempted to answer to absence of a cosmotheoros. And this is also why Heidegger, in 1938, turning against Nazism, exposed the end of the age of the *Weltbilder*—images or pictures of the world.[25]

Having succinctly reduced representation in general and visibility in particular to Nazism, it is no surprise that Nancy concludes just as succinctly, "It is in all respects not only reasonable, but also required by the vigor and rigor of thought, to avoid recourse to representations: the future is precisely what exceeds representation."[26]

Nancy's imperative captures very well the extent to which the idea of a "world picture" has itself become codified in contemporary political philosophy, serving as a convenient trope for the convergence of some ultimate bad politics with the ultimate "bad" representational form.[27] Because the unusually well preserved trope of the world picture still makes its effortless elision of visibility, order, and totality, it does more than just harbor a quiet scopophobia. It also obviates the need for political philosophy to bother thinking more carefully about how mass media help produce our social and political totalities, declaring the latter antithetical to the very domain of the political, not to mention thought itself. For instance, it is hardly a coincidence that in Alain Badiou's *Ethics*—which tries to reconceive ethics on the terrain of necessary contingency—Badiou also replaces the trope of Nazism with equally totalizing tropes of representation, treating "representability" as a negative space around which to define the singularly unrepresentable domain of ethical "truths."[28] Few variations on this theme are as bizarre as Badiou's attempt to formulate a notion of ethics that is useless in the mediated world that occasions it. At bottom, though, they all carry the same implication where the uniquely public medium of television technology is concerned. In promising to deliver "the world" to our eyes, it polices the hegemonic borders of mass visibility and, in turn, serves as a warden to the necessity of what is in a world filled with more radical possibilities. It is the very engine of fate, and the end of political possibility.

I have not taken this brief detour into the scopophobic discursive underpinnings of necessary contingency just to make contemporary philosophy play the straw man for Haneke. On the contrary, I have done so because I believe that it is only in the context of this discourse that we can fully perceive just how carefully Haneke amends it through the explicitly visual staging of mise-en-abyme, and indeed, how suggestive this staging could prove for a more philosophical thinking of visual media. After all, the film's causal structure certainly does present the shoot-out out as an expression of the violence that all totalizing forms of order visit on contingency—television being just one convenient trope of such an order and the text of the film being another. But as one might expect, this mise-en-abyme has one more layer still, and this layer gives television a more complicated place in the violence at hand. Because the fragments from the television news broadcasts manifest the structure of a mise-en-abyme in their own right—as the segmented aesthetic of television news typically does—the peeling layers of images that they successively present to the viewer condense into one fragment the same causal order that the film's title proposes for the violent act it restages. That is, they move from one evening's story to the next with no apparent sense of causal progress, and yet, in the process they affect a relatively arbitrary but still effective "program" through which to picture the fact of world events and their relation to one another. Television thus becomes thinkable—or at least visible—in much the same terms that contemporary philosophy has positioned the bad totality of the world picture: it is a trope of contingency's death through the construction of a visible order. And yet, at the same time the mise-en-abymic structure of the film refuses television this totalizing role by also reducing it to a contingent image layered against a thousand other images leading up to this end result. Consider the way in which the final television broadcast seems all at once to consummate the totality of the film's violence—reducing the lives of the victims to the status of one more image among others—while also exhausting this film totality quite explicitly as it regenerates indefinitely beyond the latter's textual limit: "His career . . ." In this sense, it would be more accurate to say that the aesthetic and technological form of television technology effectively encapsulates the film's totality as a mise-en-abyme of necessary contingency, but at the very same time, it fails to exist as anything more than a fleeting partial picture of—and within—that fatal order. That is, if the film posits mise-en-abyme as the very trope of fatality, then television can only be understood as the figurative stutter *of* and *within* this trope, where total necessity and total contingency visibly reverberate. Accordingly, if we understand television as a representational production of death, then its visible oscillation here between the role of executioner and witness—necessity and contingency—requires us to call it not just death but *death, with television.*

Perhaps the best way to express the peculiar sort of relationship that Haneke stages here between death and television would be to say that television visits death. Just as it does at the end of *Seventh Continent,* here television both abides and effects death. It is the reaper whose very appearance is also an act of reaping; it is both proxy and producer, the beside and the because, the most reliable consolation and the violence that demands consolation in the first place. Television visits space in a similar sense, giving ground to the remote world it visualizes while simultaneously refusing us more than a tourist's touch. By extension, then, we might also describe the figurative relation of mise-en-abyme that makes this relationship visible and thinkable at once as a trope of visitation.

Reformulating the relation between media and being along these lines holds powerful implications for both philosophy and politics. First and foremost, the trope of visitation gives us a way of conceptualizing some of the more confounding ways in which visual media technologies transform the work of enframing by layering at least two hegemonic productions of order over one another: on one register, the "imagined communities" that they connect as social formations and, on another, the particular representations of the world that immediately appear as characterizations of those formations. This process of layering—where the content of the television image serves as the unstable guarantor of its own technological form—is one of the most underthought aspects of how the medium helps produce the world. While the connective tissue of media technology effectively vouches for a social whole of fluctuating scales that is cut to its measure, whether national or global, the images actually appearing onscreen provide their own particular embodiment of a nation, world, and society cut to an array of different measures at once. In other words, television hegemonizes the order of the world both inside the screen and around it, and precisely because it stutters in the relay between the two. Though television theorists have always divided these two registers of hegemony from each other, the trope of mise-en-abyme suggests the urgency of thinking of them together—at least if we hope to understand the peculiar way in which media constitute the existence of society while also rendering it provisional in a thousandfold flux of layered and unlayered screens. For indeed, as I have discussed at greater length elsewhere, it is surely no coincidence that the trope of mise-en-abyme inverts the relation between part and whole in precisely the same way that Guy Debord's notion of spectacle does, appearing at once "as society itself, as a part of society and as a means of unification."[29] Mise-en-abyme is itself the aesthetic trope through which spectacle produces society as such, withdrawing it from our grasp only to dump it back out into three dimensions.

This way of thinking about television's role in our social existence has implications for political philosophy too. Perhaps most generally, I would like to suggest that Haneke's sustained use of mise-en-abyme poses a provocative challenge to the scopophobic tendency lingering in the otherwise vital philosophical discourses it takes up. Indeed, by giving to the eyes the very problems of visibility that necessary contingency raises, the relation he enacts between being and image effectively problematizes the rather pat opposition that postfoundational thinkers have constructed to divide the ambivalent political possibilities of representation between, in effect, the forms that affect necessity and the forms that affect contingency. For instance, while Jacques Ranciere has drawn a decisive distinction between totalities that police and totalities that found politics—where the former purports to represent a whole that exhausts every difference and the latter claims the name of whole for one disproportionate fragment—Haneke's mise-en-abyme effectively reconfigures these two political trajectories in a necessarily *différantial* and visual relation.[30] For indeed, the peculiar sort of totality that television constructs when it "pictures" the world always hovers somewhere between these two claims; it is always effective, but also something and somewhere else. Just as the television scenes of *71 Fragments* serve at once as figures of the film's form both in part and whole, regenerating necessity anew in each frame, representation more generally could be said to set these same two vectors of possibility in the endlessly inverted relation of mise-en-abyme. In this much, Haneke's use of mise-en-abyme might serve to open the question of media and being to political ontology in ways that the fatal tropes of "necessary contingency" and "world picture"—not to mention the traditional conception of hegemony—have long foreclosed. Of course, it also offers a reminder that is simpler and perhaps more politically urgent for our social and political survival today: since we must live out our political lives between a screen we see before us and a screen that we have always already forgotten is receding behind us, the only real risk we face of a collective death by television is to forget that looking, far from repelling our thought and our action, only ever demands more of it.

## Notes

1. It was the genius and skill of my friend Phil Hallman that brought me to this film. As curator of the incomparable Donald Hall Collection in the University of Michigan's Film and Video Program, Phil's insight, originality, and thoroughness as a collector have surely inspired many more scholars than just me. He deserves copious thanks.

2. The most thorough treatment of this intensive period of media-corporation warfare can be found in William Boddy, *Fifties Television: The Industry and Its Critics* (Urbana: University of Illinois Press, 1994).

3. Some of the most famous examples include Fredric Jameson, "Video: Surrealism without the Unconscious," in *Postmodernism, or the Cultural Logic of Late Capitalism* (Durham: Duke University Press, 1991), 67–96; Jerry Mander, *Four Arguments for the Elimination of Television* (New York: Harper Perennial, 1978); and Cass Sunstein, *republic.com* (Princeton: Princeton University Press, 2002).

4. Jean Baudrillard, "The Precession of Simulacra," in *Simulacra and Simulations,* trans. Sheila Faria Glaser (Ann Arbor: University of Michigan Press, 1995), 9–10. It should be emphasized that Baudrillard does not link his formulations of the simulacrum to the more substantive ontological treatment of the term that Gilles Deleuze develops throughout his oeuvre.

5. Stuart Hall, "Encoding/Decoding," in *Culture, Media, Language: Working Papers in Cultural Studies, 1972–1979,* ed. Stuart Hall et al. (London: Routledge, 1992), 128. This version of Hall's argument is, of course, the condensed recapitulation of his prior writings and presentations on the subject—all of which, it must be said, grew out of an ongoing engagement with the work that Ernesto Laclau and Chantal Mouffe were doing to elaborate a discursive ontology for the political. I will say more about their work later on; for now, suffice it to say that Hall's "Encoding/Decoding" essay represents the most widely disseminated version of his attempt to import some of the philosophical debates about ontology into the domain of media theory.

6. Ibid.

7. I should mention that I have also discussed the significance of "Encoding/Decoding" for media theory (both good and bad) in my book *The Flip Wilson Show* (Detroit: Wayne State University Press, 2008), and I comment at much greater length on the relationship between Hall and Laclau's respective approaches to discursive production, as well as the theoretical implications of their differences, in my dissertation, "Variety, or the Spectacular Aesthetics of American Liberal Democracy" (PhD diss., Northwestern University, 2007).

8. See John David Rhodes, "Haneke, the Long Take, Realism," *Framework: The Journal of Cinema and Media* 47, no. 2 (2006): 17–21; Brian Price, "Pain and the Limits of Representation," *Framework: The Journal of Cinema and Media* 47, no. 2 (2006): 22–30.

9. For instance, Mattias Frey both recounts and enacts this tendency in two overlapping essays: the "directors" entry on Michael Haneke at the online journal *Senses of Cinema*, www.sensesofcinema.com/contents/directors/03/haneke.html, and "*Benny's Video, Caché,* and the Desubstantiated Image," *Framework: The Journal of Cinema and Media* 47, no. 2 (2006): 30–36. Drawing on Baudrillard's notion of the "digital narcissus," Marc Augé's idea of *supermodernité*, and D. N. Rodowick's account of the "desubstantiation" of images, Frey advocates using the shifts in Haneke's own use of media technology—from celluloid to digital—as a conceptual guide to the postmodern theories most apropos to the films' critiques of media.

10. Martin Heidegger, "The Question Concerning Technology," in *The Question Concerning Technology and Other Essays*, trans. William Lovitt (New York: Harper and Row, 1977), 9.

11. Ibid., 11–12.

12. See Oliver Marchart, *Post-Foundational Political Thought: Political Difference in Nancy, Lefort, Badiou, and Laclau* (Edinburgh: Edinburgh University Press, 2007), 11–13.

13. See Fredric Jameson, "Architecture: Spatial Equivalents in the World System," in *Postmodernism*, 97–131.

14. Laclau and Chantal Mouffe discuss this conception of hegemony at length in the landmark *Hegemony and Socialist Strategy: Toward a Radical Democratic Politics* (London: Verso, 2005), but Laclau develops the tropic dimension of representation just in evidence here most fully in *On Populist Reason* (London: Verso, 2005).

15. Heidegger, "Question Concerning Technology," 26–27.

16. Brian Price has already written of the important questions that Heidegger's essay "The Age of the World Picture" would raise for film studies scholars, and I believe the same could be said of television scholars (with the exception on which I elaborate here). Brian Price, "Heidegger and Cinema," in *European Film Theory*, ed. Temenuga Trifonova (London: Routledge, 2008).

17. These respective terms, of course, come from two other works that have quietly served as an ad hoc ontology for media theory without being fully theorized as such: Benedict Anderson's *Imagined Communities: Reflections on the Origins and Spread of Nationalism* (London: Verso, 1991) and Arjun Appadurai's *Modernity at*

*Large: Cultural Dimensions of Globalization* (Minneapolis: University of Minnesota Press, 1996). In both of these well-known instances, technological forms rearrange the ontic contents of society, sometimes producing new social formations in the process, but no serious attempt has been made within media studies to theorize the ontological significance of this technological intervention.

18. Signs of this tropic tendency can be observed in Haneke's nearly invariable decision to name bourgeois couple characters with variations on "Georg" and "Ann," the recurrence of visual tropes including the snow-filled screen, and the almost exact remake in the United States of *Funny Games* (2008). The schematic repetition of all of these gestures renders the entities whose contours they shape in decidedly rhetorical terms.

19. For instance, one should also note Majid's suicide scene in *Caché* and the murder scene in—or should I say, on—*Benny's Video*. This last film begins, rather than ends, with a frame subsumed by a television screen lost in snow.

20. Rhodes, "Haneke, the Long Take, Realism," 17–21.

21. Maximilian Le Cain, "Do the Right Thing: The Films of Michael Haneke," *Senses of Cinema*, www.sensesofcinema.com/contents/03/26/haneke.html.

22. For just one of many discussions on this matter, see Laclau, *On Populist Reason*, 84–85.

23. Brian Price, for instance, has examined Haneke's preoccupation with the violence of order. See Price, "Pain and the Limits of Representation," 22–30.

24. Marchart, *Post-Foundational Political Thought*, 11.

25. Jean-Luc Nancy, *The Creation of the World or Globalization*, trans. Francois Raffoul and David Pettigrew (Buffalo: SUNY Press, 2007), 43.

26. Ibid., 50.

27. It must be said that Nancy does not always speak so broadly of representation. For instance, in *Being Singular Plural*, Nancy himself takes continental philosophy to task for trying to divide a "good" kind of spectacle from a "bad" one. Unfortunately, however, his own way of dealing with this problem reproduces it as a distinction between the image and representation. See Nancy, *Being Singular Plural*, trans. Robert D. Richardson and Anne E. O'Byrne (Palo Alto, CA: Stanford University Press, 2000), 72–73.

28. Arguing that previous notions of ethics fail to posit the latter as anything more than avoidance of the ultimate trope of evil—the Holocaust—Badiou instead effectively opposes the "event" of an ethical truth to a process that is defined almost entirely against equally vague tropes of representational media, ranging from "communicability" to "simulacrum" to "public opinion." See Alain Badiou, *Ethics: An Essay on the Understanding of Evil*, trans. Peter Hallward (London: Verso, 2001), 50–51.

29. Guy Debord describes spectacle in these terms in *The Society of the Spectacle*, trans. Donald Nicholson-Smith (New York: Zone Books, 1994), 12. I discuss this aesthetic conception of spectacle in my work on the figure of variety, another trope of mise-en-abyme. Insofar as this figure structures the aesthetic of variety entertainment—the quintessential popular genre—I argue that it constitutes "the people" of

popular entertainment as a cultural formation while also priming it to fulfill social and political roles as needed. See Meghan Sutherland, "What Is Variety?" *Cultural Studies*, special double issue on Ernesto Laclau's *On Populist Reason*, ed. Robert Harriman and Dilip Gaonkar (forthcoming); Sutherland, "Variety."

30. Jacques Ranciere, *Disagreement: Politics and Philosophy*, trans. Julie Rose (Minneapolis: University of Minneapolis Press, 1999), 9. Laclau also takes up this distinction in *On Populist Reason*, 244–45.

*The Castle* (1997): Kafka in and for the age of television

Bert Rebhandl

# Haneke's Early Work for Television

Most people who are familiar with the films of Michael Haneke know that the director began his career first in the theater, then in television, before focusing his energies on feature-length, theatrically released filmmaking. While the theater productions, by their very nature, cannot be seen again, the films made for television are available for screening—but only if one is lucky enough to gain access to the archives of public broadcasting services in Germany and Austria. Only Haneke's *The Castle* (*Das Schloss,* 1997), an adaptation of the eponymous novel by Franz Kafka, is readily available on DVD for purchase or home viewing. What follows, therefore, are analytical descriptions of and brief commentaries on this seldom seen television work. These accounts are intended to orient readers to an understanding of the consistency of Haneke's formal and philosophical preoccupations across his work, from television to film.

## Und was kommt danach? (After Liverpool)

Haneke was working mainly as a stage director when the opportunity arose to direct his first film for the German broadcasting station SWR. Not surprisingly, he decided to adapt a play for television, *After Liverpool* (1971) by British playwright James Saunders. According to Saunders, "*After Liverpool* is not a play but a suite of pieces to be performed by one or more actors and one or more actresses. The order in which the pieces are played is not specified. Using a musical analogy, the script gives some themes, within and between which any number of variations are possible."[1] Saunders's description might just as easily describe Haneke's early approach to filmmaking as well as the overall architecture of his entire oeuvre. By arranging "pieces" Haneke always envisions a totality of fragments. In the case of *After Liverpool*, this totality is the world of a couple in their thirties; the male is a writer of some sort, and the woman's profession is unclear. They live in a bourgeois apartment, with some modern furniture and remnants of daily life: old newspapers, shelved paperbacks, a poster of Jean-Luc Godard's *Masculin, féminin* above their small kitchen table.

Haneke used a German translation of Saunders's play by the established writer Hilde Spiel. The complete title of the film is *Und was kommt danach? (After Liverpool)* (*And what comes after it? [After Liverpool]*). The title sequence is interesting in itself, since it opens with one of the most famous riffs of rock and roll: Keith Richards's guitar, followed by Mick Jagger's voice in "(I Can't Get No) Satisfaction" by the Rolling Stones. Haneke's sound-image design uses the quintessential popular music of the 1960s, but he deconstructs it simultaneously by using the song to accompany images of a Beatles concert, as if no true authorship, let alone authenticity, inhered in the performance of a superhit like "Satisfaction."

Then comes the first shot, the first "piece": a man and a woman, in bed naked, obviously post coitum. "Was I good?" asks the man, starting a conversation that leads into the pitfalls of language. The woman replies with another question. She wants him to phrase his question more precisely: Was he good in comparison to other lovers of hers at certain points in her life? "It's a simple question," he states. Well, it is not, and neither is this other question that haunts couples: Do you love me? The woman and the man go through all the motions of a couple's daily life. Imprisoned by language, they try to communicate but produce only feedback. Obviously language is not the tool that brings people closer together; instead, it alienates. Only in the long last scene does the man open up the situation to another dimension. For the first time (and in a manner that suggests he has been suddenly inspired) he speaks impassionedly of a third person, a blind man he used to observe on the street. It would seem that the film suggests that it is possible to say something about the stranger precisely because this person remains unknown, while it is impossible to say something about ourselves precisely because we claim to know something about ourselves.

Between the pieces, the film returns repetitively to "Satisfaction," accompanied by images of either the Beatles or the Rolling Stones in performance. Inserted into each of these music clips we find a quotation either from song lyrics (mostly by the Beatles) or from writers and thinkers: Ludwig Wittgenstein, Marshall McLuhan, Henry Miller. The first quotation is from Jean-Luc Godard: "The philosopher and the cineaste share a certain life—the view of the world, that is specific to a certain generation." While Haneke rarely seems to think in terms of generations or genealogies, the first part of this statement resonates crucially throughout his work. His view of the world has always been philosophical in the sense that he at least tries to find a way of uniting form and content; in some cases he even goes so far as to make the film image an allegory of thought. In *After Liverpool* the content is quite clearly that of "alienation," which, notoriously and in all its vicissitudes, is the basic fact of Haneke's work. The couple in this film is given no history, neither biographical nor as citizens of a state or as parts of a community. They are abstractions; their fate and our concern for it are philosophical rather than historical. This woman and this man seem to be nothing other than exemplifications of the entire tradition of language skepticism. The film is the first step Haneke takes in exploring the condition of life in a media-saturated environment, and here language occurs as the first medium that alienates people from themselves and their fellow beings. Even the Beatles seem already to have been aware of that, as Haneke quotes the lyrics from "The Word": "Say the word I'm thinking of / Have you heard the word is love." The supposedly genuine expression of love is doubly conditional here, prompted by an interlocutor and hearsay. This quotation constitutes one of the few instances in which Haneke mines popular culture for evidences of his view of the world.

## Drei Wege zum See

Literature is the domain of Haneke's early filmmaking for television; literary adaptations were the medium through he became an auteur in his own right. *Drei Wege zum See* (*Three Paths to the Lake,* 1976) is based on a story of the same name by Ingeborg Bachmann, one of the most influential female writers of postwar Germany and Austria. In this story Elisabeth Matrei, a woman who is exactly fifty years old (the story takes pains to stipulate her age, as it becomes important later), returns to a small Austrian city to spend a few days with her father. On her walks, during which she never arrives at the lake mentioned in the title, she muses about her life and her family, her studies in Vienna, and her career as a photographer in Paris. She also ponders her relationship to a troubled Holocaust survivor from a village that had belonged to Austria until the collapse of the Austro-Hungarian Empire after World War I. The story's narration of the present is entirely permeable to memories of or associations with the past.

Haneke follows the plot of his source very faithfully but simultaneously distances himself from the voice of the story's female author/narrator by employing in the performance of the voice-over a male voice that would have been immediately recognizable to Austrians in the 1970s, that of radio host and filmmaker Axel Corti, famous for making literary adaptations like *Drei Wege zum See*. In fact, Corti's voice was the signature of his own film adaptations of novels like Joseph Roth's *Radetzkymarsch*. The reasons for Haneke's narratorial gender switch remain unclear. Most likely, the constraints of the conventions of national television dictated the use of the male voice-over, a dominant feature of productions like this from the 1970s; Bachmann's female narrator is merely a casualty of televisual "nationalization." The book's cosmopolitan point of view, focalized through a woman who leaves her native country and becomes something like a global citizen, is repatriated within the boundaries of a culture still dominated by father figures.

This repatriation is, of course, also the problem at the center of the plot of *Drei Wege zum See*. Elisabeth's visit to her father's home (where she and her considerably younger brother grew up together) is also a revisiting in memory of all her relationships with men that she has had during her nomadic life as a photographer. For instance, with the despairing Trotta, a man suffering from *Überlebensschuld* ("guilt of survival" after the Shoah), she has a long philosophical dispute about the possibilities of photography (medium of ethical responsibility or pornographic illustration?). Elisabeth claims photography can help to "wake people up." Trotta argues that he does not need illustrations of modern warfare, because he has lived through the war that defined people's lives in central Europe for the rest of the twentieth century.

Haneke does not try to go beyond the limitations of the *Literaturverfilmung* (screen adaptation) save for a few disturbing cuts that break up the overall simultaneity of past and present in the strictly mental dimension of *Drei Wege zum See*. (In one instance Elisabeth runs into a stranger in a hotel bathroom in a scene that remains virtually "alien" within the diegetic world of the film.) Everything we see is filtered through one of three agencies: Elisabeth's (occasionally shattered) perception, the voice of Bachmann's narrator, and Corti's acousmatic presence. These three modes of representing subjectivity are interwoven further through montage (perception), plot (narration), and imaginary (the narrator's "national" voice). Elisabeth is able to leave this context only at the price of cutting herself off completely—the story ends when she has a brief encounter with a possible "lifetime love" at an airport (she leaves the man behind), quits her young French boyfriend, Philippe, and takes on an assignment to go to Vietnam to report from the war.

## Lemminge

With some close-ups of anonymous vandalism on cars and the soundtrack of Paul Anka's 1959 hit "Lonely Boy," *Lemminge* (*Lemmings,* 1979) opens with another nod to popular culture. This was Haneke's most ambitious project to this date, a two-part feature film for television, each part featurelength, the first taking place in 1959 in Wiener Neustadt (the industrial city south of Vienna where Haneke grew up) and the second following up on the same set of characters twenty years later. *Lemminge* can be seen as a generational account of postwar Austria, and while it may not be autobiographical in the strictest sense, it certainly includes a number of parallels with and sources in Haneke's own experiences. (His son David, born in 1965, has a minor role.) The title *Lemminge* is explained by an insert that precedes the film's action and provides encyclopaedic information on the breed of root voles famous for its collective suicidal runs. The people in Haneke's film are also lemmings, albeit in a more existential sense: theirs is a life that lacks all exuberance, a troublesome Heideggerian *Sein zum Tode,* shot through with angst and isolation.

The first part, ironically titled "Arkadien" ("Arcadia"), follows a group of school friends. We have Sigrid (Eva Linder) and Sigurd (Paulus Manker) Leuwen, who live in a large bourgeois villa with their severely handicapped parents. The paralyzed mother never leaves her bed, where she spends the days and nights reading, smoking, and occasionally dozing away thanks to the intervention of a sleeping pill; the patriarch (played by monument of German and Austrian postwar cinema Bernhard Wicki) walks on crutches.[2] We learn later and in passing that both parents were injured during the last days of World War II while using their bodies as shields to protect their children's lives. While Sigurd and Sigrid are well-heeled "rebels without a cause," their story is told alongside that of Fritz Naprawnik, whose working-class milieu is represented in the most iconic manner: tiny kitchen–living room, beer for supper, overbearing father figure. Fritz, who wants to shed his humble class position, has a troublesome affair with the much older wife of his Latin teacher. His good friend Christian is in love with Evi, with whom he joylessly conceives a child, thus dooming the two of them to stay together.

The first part of *Lemminge* is untypical for Haneke, as it offers a surfeit of rather straightforward psychological explanation and historical and social genealogy. The general sense of repression renders futile all the attempts of the younger people to lead an independent life. They fail to find in one another the confidence they never received from their parents. Sex in particular poses an insurmountable problem. Sigrid and Sigurd are clearly drawn to each other incestuously and sublimate their erotic lives by playing music together. While the girls show some tenderness toward one another, none of them chooses to absent herself from the rule of heterosexual law. "Digging in dirt," according to the film's encyclopaedic epigraph, is what lemmings do. Thus, sex is associated with guilt. The film demonstrates that little has changed since the age of Sigmund Freud and Arthur Schnitzler, when the "mysteries of the alcove" were discovered as a main source of personal and social neurosis.

The second part of *Lemminge*, "Verletzungen" ("Injuries"), is, for those of us familiar only with the director's later film work, textbook Haneke. Leaving behind the psychoanalytical and generational explanations of the first part, the film fastens onto an allegorical symptomatology of the age of media contemporaneity and contingency. The protagonists of twenty years ago meet again under the radically different circumstances of 1979. Pregnant and stalwart in her refusal to name the father of her child, Sigrid returns from Munich to find her parents' villa empty. To reinsert herself into the life of her native city, she invites her old pals to a dinner party in the villa's spacious but now derelict living room, a degraded and irredeemable embodiment of a tradition long foreclosed by the catastrophe of fascism and World War II. All the protagonists of the second part of *Lemminge* have middle-class jobs and middle-class problems—sexual frustration, psychosomatic illness, and a general feeling of detachment. When Evi visits Fritz in his modern apartment to start a love affair that seems businesslike from the very beginning, he proudly displays his favorite work of art, a painting by Francis Bacon. Bacon's work, of course, despite its interest, functions as an almost overdetermined sign of alienated, nontranscendent modernity.[3]

Haneke is a believer only in the sense that he registers the void that has been left by religion. When Sigrid, increasingly in despair, seeks the spiritual advice from a priest who could have walked straight out of a Robert Bresson film, the priest utters a typical sentence: "The medieval world is behind us—nobody can take our guilt away from us." What exactly accounts for this guilt (apart from simply having to live the life everybody found themselves in) remains unclear. But it is an overwhelming fact. "My god, what are we doing?" Evi asks at one point. Later, when she says, "I was about to freeze to death," the film offers the first programmatic mention of the metaphor that controls Haneke's first three films for the cinema, the trilogy of "glaciation."

The second part of *Lemminge* poses such heavy questions and utterances with frequency. The story is consumed by the characters' musings about their meaningless lives. At one point Sigrid witnesses several little incidents on a street from her perch in a coffee shop: children fighting, a dead cat, a bricklayer's pot falling from a roof. This little sequence functions as an emblem of the contingency of modern life and its aleatory fatality. *Lemminge* ends in an exercise in classical parallel editing; however, here the film provides no resolution. The film's cutting between the car accident that Christian Beranek had long been planning for himself and his unfaithful wife, Eva, and Sigrid's childbirth does not offer a solution but constitutes rather a desperate attempt to figure an existential crisis that cannot be adequately represented. The hoariness of the choice of parallel editing to figure this unresolvability registers exactly the obdurate nature of the crisis. Christian survives to pose the final question of the film: "What is it that still holds true?" Perhaps some answer is provided by the music of Johann Sebastian Bach that has all but taken over the soundtrack, an entirely different aesthetic and moral register from the rock and roll featured in the film's first minutes. The soundtrack has left the diegetic world, and has traveled from the province of character subjectivity to something much more forbidding. In the three hours of *Lemminge*, Haneke moves from the preoccupations and techniques of a "realist" filmmaker to those of a conceptual film artist. The Bach is the measure of his contemplative distance from his subject.

## Variation. Daß es Utopien gibt, weiß ich selber!

A packed subway in Berlin. A middle-aged man spots a middle-aged woman. The two have met a few days earlier, when she, a journalist, interviewed him, a teacher. The interview has revealed that as a boy the man always thought that angels were watching over everything. *Variation. Daß es Utopien gibt, weiß ich selber! (Variation. That utopias exist, I know very well myself!* 1983) opens with a shot that dives down into the city of Berlin from high above: perhaps a cinematographic movement meant to embody this childhood fantasy. Spatiality is key in this film, one in which all the protagonists try desperately to get close to one another (and to the camera) while still trying to maintain their cool (and the camera its objective overview). *Variation* is Haneke's take on the *bürgerliches Schauspiel* (bourgeois drama), a form easily and frequently adaptable to the conventions of public broadcasting. (This film was, in fact, commissioned by the Berlin station Sender Freies Berlin.)

Georg, the teacher, and Anna, the journalist, are lovestruck from their very first encounter, and their intense and mutual infatuation upsets their everyday lives.[4] But before that, we are introduced to Georg's wife, Eva, when one evening the married couple are shown coming home from a production of Goethe's *Stella*, a piece of domestic melodrama and one of the chestnuts of German classic literature. *Stella* actually exists in two versions. The first 1776 version depicts the utopia of *eine offene Beziehung* (open relationship). The second version of *Stella* from 1806 departs from the earlier version's happy ending and instead closes by way of the *liebestod*, or love-death.

The intertextual reference to *Stella* is appositeness writ large. The *offene Beziehung* was, of course, a subject of much topical, public discussion in 1970s German culture (and in European North American culture more broadly). In *Variation*, Georg and Eva's house is already a *menage*, given that his younger sister Sigrid, a cello player, lives with them. Sigrid is quietly obsessed by her brother, who one day finds her naked on her bed, bleeding to death, or so she claims; in fact, she is menstruating. *Variation*'s epigraph is a quotation from Ingeborg Bachmann: "Life is to beat wounds, and nobody has ever forgiven anybody."

In what might be understood as another reference to German classical literature, the film often seems constructed along the lines of a *Briefroman* (epistolary novel): frequently the soundtrack consists of letters written by the passionate lovers or the partners they have abandoned. *Variation* demonstrates rather even-handedly the variety of ways in which passionate attachments affect the lives of those involved. Anna's partner, Kitty, an actress, reacts aggressively and almost hysterically to the new situation, while Eva, wearing a Hulk tee shirt that she sleeps in, confronts her husband in the bathroom calmly but painfully forthright: "Jealous? No, I don't feel jealousy. I feel longing to the brink of vertigo," she replies to his questions. The therapeutic option seems not to exist for these characters. Talking everything over thinly conceals the aggression barely concealed in the final meeting of the four people involved. (Sigrid, who has survived a suicide attempt, appears only in subjective flashbacks; her incestuous desire seems to banish her to the margins of this tale.) *Variation* ends with everybody going their separate ways. Georg is left alone by Anna, who needs time to "come to terms with herself." The film last presents him eating at a sausage stand before going to see Woody Allen's *Annie Hall* (1977). In Germany this film was released as *Der Stadtneurotiker*, or "the urban neurotic," a term that barely seems to apply to Georg. He seems like a balanced, passionate, calmly assured man who just had to break his wife's heart. There is no solution, no reconciliation. The film's conclusion feels more like that of the momentary pause of an audience before getting up after a movie.

## Wer war Edgar Allan?

The crime plot in *Wer war Edgar Allan?* (*Who was Edgar Allan?* 1984) affords Haneke the chance to make a tender reference to Robert Bresson's *Une femme douce* (1969): the film shows a white scarf gently falling from a window. The woman to whom it belongs never actually appears in this story of a young man from Austria who comes to Venice to throw his life away. A student of art history and in possession of a substantial inheritance, thanks to his father's death, the young man is free to drink and wander through the city. A *Drogenesser* (drugeater), he occasionally meets up with his dealer. This peculiar term is from the classicist language of Austrian writer Peter Rosei, from whose eponymous novella Haneke's *Wer war Edgar Allan?* is adapted.

The intoxicated alienation of the drug addict is quite clearly nothing but a metaphor for the lack of any reliable connection to the subject's world. Haneke bends a rather typical *Künstlerroman* and its preoccupations with the representation of tormented subjectivity to his will, converting it into a theoretical exposition of the mediatization of experience. The student (played by Paulus Manker, a frequent collaborator during Haneke's Austrian years) is trying to make sense of the sensational story he has read about in the papers in which a contessa fell to her death from a palazzo after a drug orgy.[5] A mysterious man he meets in a café soon after these events seems to be involved in this possible murder case, but there is no way for us to distinguish between the increasingly paranoid perceptions of the film's drug-addicted protagonist who occupies his days with insignificant sketch work.

Haneke is also creating similarly fruitless sketches of Venice, a city submerged beneath the surfeit of centuries of images that have attempted to represent it. The protagonist does not get to the "real" Venice any more than Canaletto or Visconti. The film does, however, present a convincing portrayal of a city of the mind: a *Marienbad* of substance abuse. Haneke's use of the protagonist's narcotic paranoia seems to get at the paranoia underlying any effort to represent the world. In his effort to create art out of what is just there, to find the substance of functionless beauty in all things, the film's protagonist both fails and fulfils his vocation at the same time. This old-fashioned understanding of aesthetics is at the core of what Rosei's book deploys as a mode of critical subjectivity at the margins of everyday reality. Haneke takes this transformation of the *Künstlerroman* one step further. His film ends with the image of a fuzzy television screen, an image that will appear with punctual frequency in Haneke's cinema. Rather than a drug fantasy substituting itself for reality, Haneke's conclusion offers the collapse of subjective perception into the substratum of artistic or mediatic representation. The student trying to make sense of the mysteries of Venice is in fact consumed by a completely different realm of virtuality: the nightmarish *Grundlosigkeit* (bottomlessness) of the television image.

## Fraulein—Ein deutsches Melodram

The last film Haneke made for television before he set out to make his first feature, *The Seventh Continent,* was another production for a public broadcaster in the southwest of Germany, Saarfilm of Saarland, the smallest of the provinces of what was then Bundesrepublik Deutschland. It is called *Fraulei—Ein deutsches Melodram* (1986), the words being written slightly incorrectly, the way an American soldier might have spelled it in the 1950s. A *fräulein* is a "miss," an unmarried woman available to the approaches of a stranger. "Fraulein" is also the title of a 1950s song by Bobby Helms that recalls the post–World War II situation during which occupied West German culture rapidly succumbed to Americanization: "Far across deep blue waters, lives an old German's daughter, / By the banks of the old river Rhine. Where I loved her and left her, but I can't forget her. I miss my pretty Fraulein." The subtitle "Ein deutsches Melodram" indicates that Haneke is dealing with genre on several levels. He looks back to the "women's films" of the 1950s as a means of investigating the experiences of a German war widow Anna (Angelica Domröse), the protagonist of his film.

Anna runs the cinema in a small town bustling with enterprise. There is an atomic power plant nearby and a sandpit providing raw material for the production of concrete vital to *Wiederaufbau* (reconstruction). Many years after the war and about halfway through the film, Anna's husband returns from prison. She and the rest of her family go to welcome him at the train station, but he enters town at the main street, like a hero of a Western who has emerged in the wrong time and place. This sense of temporal and generic dislocation or displacement is at the heart of the film: *Fraulein* is about the different temporal and generic regimes that have controlled the conceptualization of the years after liberation and the early *Wirtschaftswunder* (economic miracle).

The film plays with various modes of temporal experience and organization. There is the linear time of Anna's marriage, a union that dates back from the time of the war. There is the intervening and heightened time of Anna's love affair with a French wrestler, a story told in painful flashbacks to the time of her presumed postwar "widowhood." And there is the time of cinema, a temporal regime represented by a poster of Hans Albers, one of the biggest stars of German film during the years of National Socialism and the star of *Münchhausen* (Josef von Báky, 1943). *Münchhausen* was a prestige production from the Nazi period, a fantasy tale shot in Agfacolor whose seeming apolitical content allowed it to continue to be screened even ten years after the war.

One of the first scenes of *Fraulein* shows a projection of *Münchhausen* at Anna's movie theater. Although *Münchhausen* is actually a color film, *Fraulein* shows it in black and white, in accordance with the grim and colorless way in which the 1950s is recalled in the West German popular imaginary. (Most West German films and, of course, all of the nation's television production of the 1950s actually were shot in black and white.) *Fraulein* is not only a story about people coming to terms with postwar situation; it is also an account of a film culture trying to come to terms with itself and the representational legacy it has inherited. Snippets of footage from films of the period, as well as snatches of soundtracks and insertions of *Wochenschauen* (newsreels), all punctuate the film, which is itself a belated melodrama about this period. At the end of the film (and of the fifties), technology is fit for color and *Münchhausen*—this ahead-of-time extravaganza of Nazi cinema—eventually falls into its spot as an object of decidedly apolitical nostalgia.

## Nachruf auf einen Mörder, Die Rebellion, The Castle (Das Schloss)

After the success of *The Seventh Continent* it became easier for Haneke to finance his projects. After his second feature film, *Benny's Video,* he continued to work in cinema but also intermittently went back to television three more times. *Nachruf auf einen Mörder* (*Obituary for a Murderer*, 1991) is a somewhat experimental collage of television footage found while supposedly "zapping" through the broadcasts of several channels on one day. This day happened to be one on which a young man perpetrated a random shooting. Although there is never any statement of a causal relation between this individual and contingent act and the media environment that the young man was surrounded by (and into which, ultimately, his crime is absorbed), Haneke clearly insinuates a connection between televisual consumption and the young man's criminality. If the shooting can be understood as a desperate attempt to make the virtual world real again, then *Nachruf auf einen Mörder* might be said to contain Haneke's theory of mass media *in nuce*.

The two adaptations of literary works that Haneke made in the 1990s are clearly opposed to the culture of consumption and "zapping." *Die Rebellion* (*The Rebellion*, 1993), as well as *Das Schloss* (*The Castle*, 1997), are based on texts by canonical writers from the central European area that used to be the Austro-Hungarian Empire, Joseph Roth and Franz Kafka, respectively. Both Roth and Kafka were Jewish, both wrote in German, and both have become emblematic of the Austrian *Kulturnation* (cultural nation), an entity whose imaginary and political borders were much larger before World War I than they were after.

*Die Rebellion* concerns a veteran returning home from World War I as a cripple. Andreas Pum (Branko Samarowski) fakes a "trembling syndrome" (a typical traumatic reaction to the perils of the war), obtains a licence to play the streets as a hurdy-gurdy man, and meets a widow and marries her. All in all, he seems to have struck it lucky. He makes a crucial mistake when he acts out against dismissive remark made by a rich man on a tram coach. This is the act of the title's "rebellion." In a matter of seconds, Andreas's life is shattered. He goes to prison for insubordination and, following his release, finds works as a cloakroom attendant. Before his death he curses God. By a "mysterious coincidence" he is buried under the number 73, the same number under which he had been imprisoned. Haneke tells this story in a solemn way, guided by the offscreen voice of Udo Samel, who has all the words that Andreas lacks. The historical period is represented through archival footage of workers' marches in Vienna. The film's representations of Andreas's interior world are tinted, only occasionally, by color. What we see is a life wasted by history and redeemed by literature.

*The Castle* is a prestige adaptation of what has been called Kafka's "fragment in prose." Haneke sticks faithfully to the text (going so far even to stop in the midst of a sentence like the book: the voice-over narrator stops midspeech, and the screen turns black) and tries to illustrate as well as he possibly can the impossibility of the protagonist's reaching the castle. The land surveyor K. has encounters with a lot of people but never gets any reliable information on the required procedure by which he might gain access to the castle that seems to be surrounded by a grotesque bureaucracy but that, at its center, is essentially a representational void, or *Leerstelle*, to be filled by any number of allegorical tenors: God after his death? The state in its becoming total? History waiting for the messiah? Haneke, following Kafka, does not privilege any of these interpretations, keeping his adaptation as literal as possible: he shows a man chasing a phantom and becoming an exhausted, confused subject in the process.

## *Conclusion: Television as Antimimetic Laboratory*

Haneke's work for television is the product of a protected environment. Public broadcasting in Austria and Germany up until the late 1980s was without competition from privately run commercial stations. This fairly homogenous media space is frequently referred to in the films themselves, mostly through the familiar voices that were daily companions to people's lives: the voice of the narrator in *Drei Wege zum See,* the voice of a hugely popular fitness instructor during a morning radio show in *Lemminge 2,* the popular tunes of *Schlagermusik* (easy listening) in *Fraulein.* Radio and television were as educational as they were entertaining. Literary adaptations were a major form from this period but differed greatly from their British cousins—those BBC adaptations of Jane Austen, the Brontës, and Evelyn Waugh. In Germany and Austria these *Literaturverfilmungen* were founded on a thoroughly skeptical notion toward the (re)generative capacities of national language and literature. The referential potential of literature is already put in doubt by the very literary texts that Haneke chose to adapt. If there is a sense of "national heritage" at work in his television productions, it is to be found exactly in the lack of equivalence between thought and language, sound and image, idea and its narrative representation.

In Haneke's early work the images are more often than not subject and subjected to language. Such subjection occurs through language that is spoken explicitly from offscreen space or through dialogue that is staged as communicative failure. The relation between the *sujet,* the real (or profilmic), and the audiovisual is not to be described as "the full adequacy between content and form" (as Haneke himself likes to claim) nor as a "negative dialectic" (Haneke's reference to Adorno's notion of the rehabilitation of the objective part of reality over the subjective, idealist predominance of the concept.) Rather, this relation is a modern variant of Plato's criticism of mimesis. Haneke's notion of "idea" is different from Plato's; after all, this is a filmmaker who does concern himself with ontology. If concepts draw on ideas that transcend the real world, then every depiction or artistic creation (every mimesis) is redundant. In Haneke's work in television, and, indeed, in all of his work, a similar criticism of mimesis is at work. His "ideas" are not metaphysical, but they transcend the diegetic world he composes. Haneke's narrative mode embodies an often unbalanced compromise between (factual) contingency and (intellectual) teleology.

In his best films this leads to "conceptual" work in the true sense, like in *The Seventh Continent,* which can be read as a situation borrowed from an American genre movie (a family being taken hostage by some outside force, like in *Desperate Hours*) but that is completely inverted. Similarly, in *Caché* the family is haunted not by ghosts, as in traditional Gothic storytelling, but by the ghosts of history itself taking the form of referential media without a source. More often than not, Haneke sticks to his concepts and renders the characters and situations as mere functions of intellectual presuppositions; his is the work of the allegorist, albeit an allegorist obsessed with the lure of referentiality. His early work in television is the experimental laboratory of a dialectics of language and images that evolves in his cinema into a complex series of negotiations between intellection and imagery, into a mode of antimimesis in the realm of ideas.

## *Notes*

1. "After Liverpool," www.jamessaunders.org/jsafterl.htm (accessed March 27, 2008).

2. Wicki was an actor and also the director of *Die Brücke* (*The Bridge,* 1959).

3. For instance, images of Bacon's work feature in the title sequence of Bernardo Bertolucci's *Last Tango in Paris* (1972) to much the same effect.

4. This is the first use of the names Georg and Anna, names that Haneke employs frequently in his later filmmaking. On the repetitive (and allegorical) use of these names, see Michael Lawrence's essay "Haneke's Stable: The Death of an Animal and the Figuration of the Human" in the present volume.

5. Paulus Manker directed *Der Kopf des Mohren* (*The Moor's Head,* 1995) following a script by Haneke.

Part 3

CULTURE AND CONFLICT

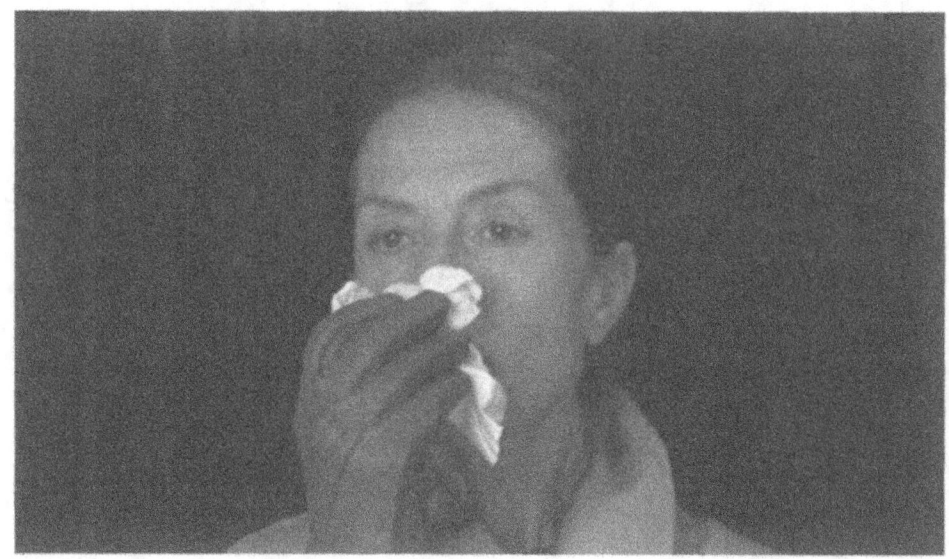
*The Piano Teacher* (2001): Erika watches porn, makes use of discarded tissues.

Christopher Sharrett

# Haneke and the Discontents of European Culture

At the risk of being perceived as pointlessly creating a kind of straw man out of a very distinguished critic, I would like to preface these remarks on Michael Haneke by commenting on Robin Wood's thoughts in *Sexual Politics and Narrative Film* concerning the nature of fascism and what he terms, borrowing from Norman O. Brown, the struggle of life against death, represented by an unrepressed, creative civilization versus fascism and its various institutions that function as agents of repression. In one subsection of his introductory remarks, in which he complements sectors of cultural resistance to the fascist complexion of our current society, Wood writes "In Praise of Yo-Yo Ma," a tribute to the famed cellist whose video of his teaching sessions at the Tanglewood Music Festival Wood screened while writing *Sexual Politics*. Wood is a dedicated student of classical music and a devotee of Bach and Mozart, whose works he counts as among the greatest achievements of humanity. Wood praises not only Yo-Yo Ma's extraordinary mastery of Bach but also his apparent openness and congeniality in the Tanglewood session, an expression, in Wood's mind, of the values antithetical to fascism: "Let him stand as the perfect paradigm of the human being in his/her creative flowering, from which all taint of the fascist mindset is totally absent."[1]

Of course, Wood's appraisal of Yo-Yo Ma began long before the Bush administration, but was there absolutely no evidence with which Wood could anticipate Yo-Yo Ma's joining U.S. Secretary of State—previously National Security Advisor—Condoleeza Rice in concert at the April 2002 National Humanities Medal Ceremony, the two playing the *adagio* to

Brahms's *Sonata for Violin and Piano in D Minor*? Laura Bush introduced the performance, saying that Yo-Yo Ma and "Doctor" Rice would "play it as a prayer for peace." Rice, of course, was a key operative in the U.S. state murder apparatus under Bush, a perpetrator of one of the worst genocidal wars of conquest of recent U.S. imperialism. Did Yo-Yo Ma not understand Rice's relationship to power? Did Yo-Yo Ma, an intelligent man, not know of the ambitions of state power? Did he feign a familiar apolitical posture to maintain his position within dominant culture (one might note that while there is a good argument, one offered by sectors of the Frankfurt School, that classical music is a healthy antidote to a degraded culture industry, the classics have seldom been seen as adversarial in nature, or in any sense threatening to state and private power)?

I have no doubt that Wood would not hesitate to analyze the Yo-Yo Ma/Rice performance and its implications. (Wood is obviously aware, for example, of the co-optation of the classics by Nazism, a point he addresses in his book *Personal Views*.) My point is that Wood's appreciation of Yo-Yo Ma, and many of his well-reasoned appraisals of classical music generally, repeat, to some degree, reactionary and always popular refrains within the intelligentsia about the importance of the Western "canon" and how one's mastery of this culture guarantees the construction of a humane self, a "better person." (Of course, much of this discourse is simply hogwash, its main proponents having little or no knowledge of music or literature; what knowledge they have is narrowly interpreted so as to enforce their conservative agendas.) Wood's praise of the cellist seems to take for granted Yo-Yo Ma's political worldview solely on the basis of his artistic accomplishment, and an attendant congeniality that can hardly be accepted as an index of his humanity.

By no means do I wish to suggest that Yo-Yo Ma alone embodies the terrible compromises and collusion of one of the most reactionary moments of recent history, or the reactionary impulses within aspects of Western art. But it is important to strip ourselves as much as possible of illusions about the consolations of culture and the small island of sanity they supposedly represent, removed from the demands of capitalist power and its state operations. One might also note that Leon Trotsky's formidable book on classical literature is titled *Literature and Revolution,* not, as some postmodern academics might have it, *Literature AS Revolution.* One conceit of the postmodern world, associated with the academic left, is the notion that savvy readings of culture are somehow by themselves a substitute for political action.

Certainly Haneke does not partake of such illusions. His sense of the limits of culture, its role in simultaneously offering awareness while enforcing bourgeois notions of human interaction, is a major concern of all of his films.

I have been reevaluating some of my initial analyses of Haneke's most accomplished work thus far, *The Piano Teacher* (although *Caché* challenges very seriously this ranking); my conversation with Haneke has assisted this reevaluation and disabused me of some assumptions.[2] *The Piano Teacher* may be the most important study of repression and its consequences yet portrayed in narrative fiction film, but while I initially intended this essay to revisit the specifics of Haneke's delineation of the dynamics of repression (two earlier pieces on the film sketch this issue), I find that my understanding of Haneke benefits from mapping the framework of his overall vision, particularly his conception of the crisis of Western patriarchal capitalist society as represented by its culture.[3]

Such a mapping demands attention to Haneke's conflicted view of Western culture and its legacy to humanity. On first glance, it seems Haneke views this culture, as exemplified in classical music, as sustenance for a benighted postmodern civilization. At the same time, he sees this music, and the culture for which it is an emblem, as either deeply implicated in the present crisis or ineffectual in confronting it. These points are most apparent in *The Piano Teacher*, where Schubert's *Winterreise* and to a lesser extent the *Piano Trio in E flat* seem to occupy the healthiest space of Erika Kohut's consciousness and sensibility. Yet while *Winterreise* may be Western music's most compelling depiction of alienation, its use in the film suggests that it is hardly a corrective. Indeed, this composition, and classical culture, may constitute part of the armor that prevents Erika from confronting her pathologies and those of the society that constructed her, as her "tortured artist" self-concept makes her closely identify with Schubert's lonely protagonist. (Although Schumann's work does not appear in the film, Erika cites him as a favorite artist, making a point to emphasize Schumann's madness.) Erika's pathologies are real enough, but she appears to sense that bolstering the eccentricity associated with insanity will give her added authority in masculine culture. Certain scenes of the film are grotesque parodies of Schubert, with Erika offered, it seems, as Schubert's traveler. She emulates the traveler's lonely winter journey in her own journey into torment and sexual alienation; her identification with the traveler holds no hope either for her or, by implication, for the culture that produced her. *Winterreise* recurs in such moments as Erika's distraught flight across an empty hockey rink after her sexual debasement by Walter and also during her visit to a porno shop (Erika's mannered posture is awkward, her studied bearing undercutting a self-assured presence that is basic to her public persona), where she sniffs men's semen in discarded tissues, the *Piano Trio in E Flat* playing nondiegetically in her head, as it functioned diegetically a few moments earlier as she was engaged, if all too briefly, in the social world by practicing the piece with colleagues.

As sound and composition shift in diegetic function, we observe Erika's stiff, authoritarian bearing, unchanged as she seeks pleasure in the porno shop. Schubert apparently provides her with a buffer against the world (with a certain measure of denial, in my view, concerning her own complicity in this world, in particular her cruelty to her students), while also allowing her to reaffirm a superior posture; she is above the degraded male-oriented popular culture of which she partakes. Erika is an enforcer of patriarchal law, not merely through her participation in its sanctioned pastimes (pornography as safety valve for alienated sexual energies), but more importantly through her role as pedagogue. She does not hesitate to chastise her young male students, caught checking out skin magazines at the very shop Erika patronizes. She is an embodiment of the overcompensated, phallicized woman whose pathology ensures her role in policing the codes of patriarchy. One could argue that the benefits of culture shine through in aspects of Erika's humanity, especially her (somewhat cold) consolation to a terrified Anna before the *Winterreise* rehearsal. But at such moments she is merely the benign female patriarch, telling her acolyte to keep a stiff upper lip and jump into the pool and swim. The point is made in the mise-en-scène of her studio, with the imposing heroes of Western music staring from grim portraits. The liberatory function of Schubert, Bach, and others duels with their role as absent fathers (like Erika's own) whose legacy inspires guilt, anxiety, and ultimately madness.

In the porno shop sequence, the *Piano Trio* shifts to the seventeenth song of the *Winterreise,* "Im Dorfe," portraying the traveler's encounter with the cruelty of a middle-class village, the narrowness of which was emphasized by Erika herself during her instruction of the young, diffident female pupil Anna in an early scene, Erika insistently striking the proper piano keys of this extraordinarily sensitive piece. Erika understands the complexity of Schubert, but her instruction suggests not only authoritarianism but also the notion of culture as the possession of bourgeois privilege: there is the strong notion that only the truly enlightened few can *really* understand great art, and by extension how the world works. Haneke undercuts this of course by showing that Erika lacks self-knowledge and that Schubert has taken her into a psychosexual cul-de-sac that cannot be bypassed by cultural knowledge alone.

As Erika watches the videos at the porno shop, the lyrics of "Im Dorfe" playing in her head ("Dogs are barking / their chains are rattling"), the music provides a transition to the next scene. In the context of the porno shop sequence, the "Im Dorfe" song suggests, with considerable pathos, Erika's utter alienation, but the narrative function of the song shifts in the subsequent sequences. When Anna's heartless, authoritarian accompanist sings "Im Dorfe," the moment further emphasizes the distance between artistic mastery and humane sensibility. Like Walter, the accompanist seems a master technician, perhaps one of penetrating understanding of the texts he interprets with Anna, but this mastery hardly conceals the utter bankruptcy of his humanity. Indeed, he is among those of the callous bourgeoisie Erika claims the *Winterreise* cycle castigates. But it would be an error to assume that the accompanist (and Walter) is simply one of the bad guys of the narrative, since the porno shop sequence shows how limited culture is as consolation and instruction. Erika's tragedy raises her far above the accompanist or Walter (as a woman her plight is necessarily more serious in any case), since her artistic accomplishments do little more than remind her of her hopelessness (which is a far greater insight than those achieved by the males of the film).

Erika's lover, the young Walter Klemmer, is a genius at the piano whose understanding of Schubert (and Schoenberg—Walter crosses into modernism) perhaps rivals Erika's, but this strapping blonde Aryan ideal becomes a monster who rapes and comes close to killing Erika, as if Haneke wishes to remind us of the Frankfurt School notion of the implication of Enlightenment thought in the creation of Auschwitz and the number of Nazi state figures who held, as many of the right currently do, that the Western canon must be protected, ensuring the production of right-thinking, moral people. Walter's "democratic" temperament (his graciousness to two young female skaters his hockey team chases off of a rink) reminds us of the façade the bourgeois state needs to maintain its legitimacy. But in this case it is undercut. Walter, as an emblem of fascism, is revealed not only in his brutality but also in small signifiers, such as his red-and-black hockey uniform, his blond-haired, blue-eyed bearing not concealed by his tousled-hair, boyish manner, and above all, in his all-too-common blaming of Erika for being a prick-teaser (he claims) in the horrific scene during which he attacks Erika and her mother, inflicting a beating on Erika that could have easily killed her. Walter's sexual assault of Erika shows us not a sudden eruption of cruelty under a refined sensibility but a rather common assertion of the male will over that of the female in all matters sexual. If Erika has been partially destroyed psychologically by her policing of patriarchal civilization, the destruction becomes complete at the hands of the ideal (if this is the word) embodiment of that civilization and its codes, for whom sexual freedom and joy for the female are proscribed. As Erika longingly watches Walter and his hockey team, she gazes through the bars of an iron fence. It is a representative moment of the melodrama, with the female imprisoned, allowed to observe (and even at points administer) but never fully participate in patriarchal society. (One recalls the use of bars and barriers in melodramas such as *Blonde Venus, The Reckless Moment, All That Heaven Allows, There's Always Tomorrow,* and other films.)

It is perhaps Haneke's greatest achievement in *La Pianiste* that he offers through his exploration of the relationship of culture to the fascist mind a corrective to a dominant conceit of contemporary culture, namely, that culture can take the place of politics and that a good understanding or "reading" of this or that work of art can be seen as a viable substitute for revolutionary activity and social change.

The irrelevance of high culture to the current world is expressed in Haneke's early "glaciation" films concerned with the descent of bourgeois society into an especially profound alienation, represented in his first film, *The Seventh Continent,* in which a bourgeois couple whose married life is a slow-simmering disaster opts for collective suicide, taking their young daughter with them. The story, based on an actual event, poses some of Haneke's essential concerns. The suicide, although seen as such by Austrian authorities, was viewed insistently by relatives as a murder. Why should a well-heeled man and woman kill themselves, killing their child as well? For Haneke, continued existence in the present world might be the clearer indication of pathology, not the acceptance of day-to-day humdrum routine that is the substance of bourgeois life.

In a key moment, the little girl, Eva, accompanies her father to a junkyard, where he disposes of the family car (civilization as a junkyard is a familiar trope well used in this moment, especially in relation to the soundtrack's plangent statement). As the father deals with the owner of the yard, Eva spots a boat departing from a nearby harbor, one of many intimations in the film of a thoroughly unattainable utopia. As she watches the departing boat through the rubble of the junkyard, we hear Alban Berg's violin concerto "To the Memory of an Angel," written on the occasion of the death of the daughter of Walter Gropius and Alma Mahler (widow of Gustav Mahler), a composition that could be read as a deliberately deformed paean to late Romanticism; it is also an eerie deformation of Eva's bedtime prayer ("Dear Lord, make me meek, so that I in Heaven shall Thee meet") and the fragment of a Bach chorale referenced by the father ("I look forward to my death"), which Haneke remarks may be seen as the film's anthem.[4] That Western society is driven by the death wish rather than life and the libido is one implication of *The Seventh Continent*. Neither Bach nor Berg is connected to assisting the child's plight, the one hope for the future, and neither these compositions nor anything else of classical culture are viewed by the world of the film as compensatory, even though the Berg piece is poignant annotation. Children, always linked to bourgeois society's scenarios for the continuation of its repressions and oppressions, are in this case (and perhaps in the more general instance) tied to murder and self-destruction, arguably the real impulse of bourgeois, patriarchal civilization. The couple's decision to self-destruct is not affected in the slightest by any cultural legacy, whose pleasures the two seem well beyond. It is useful to note too Haneke's association of culture with patriarchal will.

The first film of the "glaciation trilogy" makes clear not simply the conflict between contemporary culture and the abandoned Western canon of classic art but the implementation of art by patriarchy and its institutions. Just as glowering portraits of Bach and Schubert stare at Erika from her studio wall in *La Pianiste,* reminding her of the legacy of an art form (one she loves) dominated by men, the Bach allusions in *The Seventh Continent* are tied to male memory and disappointments, even as the female goes along with the spouse's decisions. It is the father who cites the prayers of his past and the father who buys the tools and presides over the family's destruction, finally administering the poison to himself after death has taken his wife and child.

The uselessness of contemporary culture is foregrounded after the devastating scenes of the destruction of the couple's apartment, the husband and wife destroying articles signifying both the cultural past (a clock, a chest of drawers) and present (record albums, magazines, currency). As the husband gives poison to his wife, daughter, then himself, the three settle down in a debris-strewn hallway. As the family awaits death, the pop song "The Power of Love" is performed by a rock group on a not-yet-demolished television set. Haneke has insisted that he dislikes the notion of pitting popular music against the classics, and indeed in this moment his antireductive sensibility, with its fine sense of the dialectics of culture, was never more in evidence. The plaintiveness of the song is never diminished within the scene, but it has no more role than Bach (classical culture) or Berg (modernism) in ameliorating the alienating effects of capitalist civilization in its late phase.

The second of Haneke's "glaciation" (he regrets having used the expression according to 2005 interviews) films, *Benny's Video,* has been to date analyzed chiefly with reference to certain elements of the postmodern age, including the dominance of media and simulation, the associated end of affect, and the dilution of the power of violence due to its overpresence in the media world. These concerns indeed have relevance to any understanding of the film, but *Benny's Video* contains some of Haneke's most devastating remarks about the appropriation and use of high culture by the bourgeoisie. It may be argued that Benny's fixation on video and entrapment by contemporary junk culture (represented best in the pop art–like scenes at McDonald's, including the brief images of the hands of the faceless, ignored cashier, certainly a typically low-paid, undereducated minority employee) and the resultant murder of a young girl to "find out what it's like" form only a portion of the film. The other, perhaps more significant, part of the film concerns a horrific domestic melodrama involving Benny's parents, George and Anna (Haneke, uninterested in psychologizing characters, prefers to use these names for most of the archetypal bourgeois couples of his films), whose need to retain social acceptance and prestige necessitates the father's grisly cover-up of the murder by chopping up and disposing the girl Benny killed while Benny and his mother flee to Egypt (the biblical reference here is important for its use of the Holy Family narrative to demolish the notion of the couple as sacred entity). Although George surely has more affect than his son, his crimes are far more horrible. The "normal" world of the film is open to question, since only Benny's mother is capable of real emotion. Anna is one of Haneke's females implicated in the carrying-out of patriarchal law (in this case the protection of the family name). The cold, calculated act of butchery carried out by George refocuses the narrative; the affectless present embodied in Benny is the legacy of Western civilization embodied in the father.

Before the major action of the film occurs, we see Benny practicing the Bach motet *Jesu, meine Freude* with his schoolmates. The motet is repeated at the end of the film when Benny and his family enjoy a temporary normality—before Benny, for reasons unknown (perhaps to "feel what it's like" and attain illusive affect or to avenge himself on his dissembling father) turns in his parents and himself to the police. The motet is performed at school, then turns into a piece of nondiegetic music as we see a video of a get-rich-quick party, where well-dressed, upwardly mobile couples, many of them clients of George or Anna (he is in high tech; she is an art dealer) stuff themselves as the party sounds turn into the Bach lyrics ("Despite the ancient dragon / despite the gaping jaws of death / despite the constant fear / let the world rage and toss / I stand here and I sing / in perfect calm"). Bach's profession of faith turns into an incredible act of bourgeois defiance, the lyrics expressing a social class's absolute sense of self-assurance. Bach appears elsewhere in the film. As Benny kills time in the Cairo hotel room, he surfs television channels, stopping on a channel broadcasting a performance of the Bach organ piece *Liebster Jesu, wir sind hier.* Benny may or may not recognize the piece—it is certainly more familiar to his ears than the languages of the Egyptian television stations. The music then takes on a nondiegetic function, as the organ, now both plangent and ominous in context, accompanies Benny's video images of the impoverished inner city. Bach now seems as indifferent as Benny to human misery, as well as to the grace of the everyday human world.

George and Anna appear to have plenty of affect: George agonizes over Benny's actions; Anna breaks down and sobs in the hotel room in Egypt during the escape with Benny. Yet their affect expresses solely their need to avoid investigation and public scrutiny, thus having their lives and reputations destroyed. Grief for the dead girl is fleeting at best—its only manifestation may be in Anna's slight, rather horrified giggle as George starts to discuss their troubles and his scenario for the cover-up and her breakdown in the Cairo hotel room, which might be read as simply an expression of overwhelming stress rather than conscience. George mistakes Anna's smile, which she covers with her hand, for hysteria, causing George to command her to get control of herself.

While it is clear that the mother is a tool who must acquiesce in the male's plans, she is nevertheless key to the maintenance of patriarchy's veneer of normalcy. Just as Bach is used to suggest a (mistaken) triumphalism on the part of the bourgeoisie, Anna's world of art conveys a sense of confinement, rather than an enlightened household. The family's dining room, filled with paintings of different periods from Leonardo da Vinci to Andy Warhol, has a very mannered quality, with too many chairs at the long table, as if the couple wishes to maintain a constant formality and sense of social popularity. During the trip to Egypt, Benny and his mother sleep very close to each other; in one scene, Benny videotapes his mother urinating on the toilet, to her not-too-severe displeasure. Tentative destruction of the incest taboo seems to be an element of Benny's undermining of his father's authority (the notion appeared in *Caché*) and the patriarchal law that the mother also enforces, but in the scenes in Egypt there is the sense that Anna's world, that of art and high culture, is perhaps an entrapment that cannot contain the consequences that the couple has produced (Benny, perfectly representative of a generation, is after all their offspring). At the very least, high culture, including the world of antiquity at the roots of civilization East and West, is of no consequence to the monstrous education offered by the postmodern capitalist society that nurtures the parents perhaps more than Benny and friends—George and Anna after all make their living from it. The worthlessness of the past is best portrayed in one of the final images of the film, a video taken by Benny during his Middle East exile, showing a wall of Egyptian hieroglyphs, Benny mugging for the camera.

The conflict/contrast between classical and postmodern culture is extremely marked in the opening sequence of *Funny Games*, with its bourgeois couple, Georg and Anna, and young son driving along a country road in their SUV, playing a guessing game with their CD player. The husband and wife play Handel, Mozart, and Mascagni, each challenging the other to guess the composition and performer. As the main title appears on the screen, the music suddenly shifts to a frenetic piece from John Zorn's *Grand Guignol*, which Haneke has termed *uber*-heavy metal for its sense of commentary on the excess of heavy metal/industrial culture. The detailed knowledge (we cannot say understanding) of classical music by the bourgeois couple does not prevent their slaughter by two yuppie psychopaths, one of whom is postmodernity's version of an intellectual—he discourses blithely on a comic book version of quantum physics as they dispose of Anna's body. As in the instance of *Caché*, the external threat to the bourgeois couple may be read as an exteriorization of the deep internal strife of bourgeois married life, suggested first by their use of culture as insulation from the stresses of the external world (the implication of this isolation could be said to be explored in *Time of the Wolf*, with the bourgeois family returning to their country home to face catastrophe). The situation is, of course, quite explicit in the instance of *Caché*. In that film, Western literature is window dressing for the bourgeoisie, a mark of their respectable façade, and an extension of their smug aspect—Georges and Anne's association with high culture is a mark of their aloofness and self-created insulation from the imperialist terrors their class has perpetrated. More than the couple of *Funny Games*, Georges and Anne of *Caché* suggest how "the bourgeoisie has insinuated itself into cultural history."[5] Far more emphatically than in *Funny Games, Caché* suggests the bankruptcy of bourgeois life on the micro- and macrocosmic levels, since the cultural veneer that is the legitimacy for Georges and Anne hides the bankruptcy of married life as well as the bourgeoisie's tacit or direct involvement in imperialist state policy. Marriage, the venerated "bedrock" of the bourgeois state, today hysterically propped up in the new climate of reaction, is for *Caché* a bedrock indeed: a conditioning institution preparing its members to protect first patriarchal sexual interests, then state interests, always with the mantle of culture offering the mark of respected office. The administration of high culture as an index of the monstrous sexual politics of patriarchal capitalist society becomes clear at several moments. The tension and distrust between Georges and Anne occurs in the film's first moment, during the first discussion of the mysterious videotapes; the tensions escalate markedly when Georges refuses to share with his wife his secret knowledge, setting off her anger that one cannot help but feel has been long festering—distrust in marriage centers first, of course, on issues of sexual jealousy and "fidelity." (As things develop, Georges may be the one who should be jealous.) This question recurs when their son, Pierrot, returns home to his angry parents after a night out. In conversation with his mother, Pierrot offhandedly remarks on her association with her employer, Pierre. That the son and the apparent lover have similar names is a small indicator that Pierrot sees far more than his mother intended, perhaps even more than she was consciously aware of feeling. (With repeated viewings, it seems clear that Pierrot is correct—not only does Anne go to Pierre for comfort, but the solitary figure whom Georges sees leaving their downstairs seems logically to be Pierre.)

The uneasy encounter between Anne and her son portrays both the incest taboo, always on the brink of being shattered, and the lie of Anne's life. The publishing world that she helps to administer, with its snobbish intelligentsia making proclamations on Baudrillard and other intellectual fashions, is largely a cover for her sex life, and yet she feels perfectly justified in her attack on Georges for lack of trust (there is no reason to think that her attack is disingenuous, and Georges's conduct in the Majid affair is indeed reprehensible).

Haneke's statement on the commodity function of culture reaches a refined development in this film. Georges's television literary chat show and Anne's job with a publishing company that entails her hosting wine-and-cheese soirees form crucial centerpieces of *Caché*, suggesting not only the commodification of art but also the traditional role of the commodity in circumscribing of all relations within patriarchal capitalist society. The grubbiness of the culture business is perhaps best rendered in Georges's conversation with his congenial, sympathetic producer, who has become aware of the videotapes. At the heart of the conversation seems to be the producer's fears about any possible liability, yet what catches one's attention most are the piles of books casually stacked about in the office, not unlike the display of books as accoutrements in the home of Georges and Anne, and the backdrop of false-front books providing the set for Georges's chat show. Georges's "hosting" of culture obviously gives him an added measure of class stature and class license that will empower his cruel treatment of Majid when he angrily confronts his boyhood friend.

Sheer noise as emblem of the final breakdown of the semantic code becomes a controlling notion of *Code Unknown*. The noise is the drumming (a cultural expression both primal and constrained) of the deaf schoolchildren, who can communicate through this physical action, but the suggestion seems to be that communication happens only at an atomized, insulated level, an act of communion within a minisociety at the margins of a larger, vicious civilization, a situation not unlike that depicted at the end of *Blowup,* wherein Thomas seems to find solace by joining the symbolic games of the mime troupe. Thomas apprehends his ultimate isolation far more than the children of *Code Unknown.* The marginalization of culture itself becomes a concern of *Code Unknown,* with culture glimpsed as a transitory solace from social breakdown. The rhythm and blues street artist, whose exemplary performance goes unnoticed by the key characters just as they are about to unleash the terrible chain of events representing this film's vision of social collapse, is a key moment. Rhythm and blues—one of the liberatory music forms of the world, evolved from the experience of slavery and the betrayal of Reconstruction in the United States—is shown here to be ripped utterly from any social/historical context, having no function as a "reminder" to the racists whose fury is soon unleashed on the Other. The social world that music is supposed to celebrate, certainly the case with older rock and rhythm and blues, is here thoroughly atomized, with lives converging but ultimately broken into discrete, alienated units.

*Time of the Wolf,* the postapocalypse film that preceded *Caché,* is exceptionally spare and bleak, its worldview sharing something in common with Ingmar Bergman's *Shame* on the matter of the utter frailty of human institutions. High culture has a very fleeting role in this film, suggesting that whatever comforts it once offered have no bearing on the world the West finally constructed. The point is made efficiently enough by the just-audible strains of a Beethoven string piece on a cassette player, the batteries of which are rapidly wearing out. Culture is represented in this film through some of its primal myths, such as the story of child sacrifice—a narrative central to the Bible—used to revivify a nation. Here the myth is thoroughly deconstructed, as a naked, vulnerable boy stands in front of a bonfire on a railroad track in the film's penultimate scene. Nothing can be redeemed by the sacrifice since nothing has had authentic existence; Haneke makes the apocalypse that causes the narrative's crisis deliberately vague, as if to suggest that humanity itself has long ago produced the apocalypse by its casual cruelties and assumptions, its taken-for-granted emptiness.

Raymond Williams's famous notion of the dominant, residual, and emergent elements of culture has special application to an understanding of Haneke's project. For Williams, residual elements of culture, which we might suggest here to be the classical past, have a potential for melding with the progressive elements of the emergent (an authentic popular music and the avant garde) in an opposition to dominant culture. While Haneke avoids valorizing either "high" or "low" culture, avoiding the neoconservative traps of protecting the "canon," it seems apparent that he foresees no felicitous synthesis of the residual and the emergent in a civilization that grinds all culture into submission, awaiting the demands of corporate capital and patriarchal civilization. The utter monstrousness of the current society is being well charted by Haneke, with such precision that his prescription for a way beyond it is slowly becoming manifest.

## *Notes*

1. Robin Wood, *Sexual Politics and Narrative Film* (New York: Columbia University Press, 1998), 27–28.

2. Christopher Sharrett, "The World That Is Known: An Interview with Michael Haneke," *Kinoeye* 4, no. 1 (2004). An abbreviated version of this interview appeared in *Cineaste* 28, no. 3 (2003): 28–32.

3. Christopher Sharrett, "*La Pianiste* and The Horrors of the Middle Class," *Kinoeye* 4, no. 1 (2004); Sharrett, "The Piano Teacher," *Cineaste* 27, no. 4 (2002): 37–40.

4. Sharrett, "World That Is Known."

5. Ibid.

*The Time of the Wolf* (2003): The "border form" in Haneke's vision of Europe.

Rosalind Galt

# The Functionary of Mankind
## Haneke and Europe

In an interview with the American independent film website *IndieWire*, Michael Haneke said, "As a European filmmaker, you cannot make a genre film seriously. You can only make a parody." Asked why this was, he replied, "Because the genre film, by definition, is a lie. And a film is trying to be art, and therefore must try to deal with reality. It cannot do this by means of lies. If films are just business, then you can lie. You can sell the lie with a good conscience."[1] This claim that a European filmmaker cannot make a genre film is, on the face of it, highly prosaic. It could not articulate more clearly the cliché of the elitist European in the face of American popular culture. Indeed, it is haunted by a series of binaries that have structured European cinema since at least 1945: Europe versus America, authorship versus genre, seriousness versus superficiality, truth versus lies, meaning versus profit, art versus commodity. In tracing the discourses that have constrained the idea of European cinema, Thomas Elsaesser describes "a mostly dualistic and invariably antagonistic perception of the relationship between European cinema and Hollywood." This scheme, he continues, "is as incontrovertible in its dualism as it seems self-evident in confirming cultural prejudices."[2] Haneke, it would seem, speaks entirely within this logic.

But if the rhetoric of European auteur cinema is well worn, it is not unchanging. The 1960s heyday of modernist art cinema is long gone, and, in the post–Berlin Wall and post-Maastricht continent, the cultural locations of cinema—and indeed of "Europe"—have experienced transformation. One marker of these changes is the rise of "serious" genre cinemas that travel beyond the confines of national popular networks: we might think of Spanish horror films.[3] Equally, the terrain of "art cinema" has shifted, both in the commodifying practices of the film festival and arthouse circuits and in the recent history of scholarship analyzing art cinema as a mode of cultural production.[4] Thus, in a sense, Haneke's words sound like an echo from an older European film culture, a determined invocation of an aestheticopolitical formation that is no longer dominant. And yet, Haneke is one of Europe's most contemporary directors, engaging questions of immigration, EU enlargement, terror, and environmental catastrophe. If his films are to be read in terms of authorship, then the auteur "Michael Haneke" undoubtedly speaks about Europe today. What interests me in Haneke's words, then, is not so much their explicit argument but their rhetorical form: the fact that he speaks "as a European filmmaker."

What does it mean to speak as a European filmmaker today? By naming his speaking position in terms of the European and the filmmaker, in terms of the filmmaker from Europe, Haneke not only owns a particular aesthetic and geopolitical identity but also articulates an always already recognizable space of privilege. (For example, his statement implies that it is, or should be, self-evident why a European filmmaker cannot make genre films seriously.) He speaks as an auteur, an artist, an inheritor of the European cultural and intellectual heritage. This inheritance forms a ground from which he can speak, and from which his words are not merely the ideas of an individual but intervene in a history of continental thought. Thus, for Haneke to speak as a European filmmaker demands that we listen to him in a certain way. The position of the European auteur requires a discourse of modernist European art cinema, and Haneke's articulation thus claims a truth and a continuing relevance for *this* version of European cinema.

In the contemporary context, this position is fraught with contradiction. Given that Haneke's work often attempts to rethink Europe in terms of its colonial and marginal others, what does it mean for him to speak so resolutely from a place of cultural centrality? The inheritance that defines a European filmmaker in terms of intellectual seriousness and artistic value is also one that has historically policed the boundaries of its claim to universality quite rigorously. Thus, while the content of Haneke's filmic speech—the articulation of the films themselves—includes an explicit critique of "Europe," the position from which he articulates this critique maintains a strong association with European power and privilege. This tension is not a new one in thinking Europe: my title comes from Edmund Husserl's characterization of the European philosopher in *The Crisis of European Sciences and Transcendental Phenomenology*.[5] As Jacques Derrida points out, this philosopher is committed to universal reason, but what makes him European is his access to speaking universality.[6] The same tension is at work in Haneke's interviews and in his films, where he can speak with authority about others (other people, other films) precisely because of his European status.

We might read articulations of European identity in films by many directors, but what makes Haneke a compelling case study is the extent to which his work renders visible these contradictions. His continuation of modernist art cinema as an oppositional practice demands that we readdress the authorizing claims of this cinematic mode: its connection of a politics of form to a politics of location; its use of European cultural criticism to ground cinematic value (for example, Bertolt Brecht, Theodor Adorno); the transnational address that has always been a defining feature of art cinema and that takes on new significance in the context of the New Europe; and the claims on European identity as a bulwark against American popular culture. His films make clear at the formal level the foundational Eurocentricity of art cinema. At the same time, their international funding speaks to the economics of contemporary European film. The exigencies of EU and television funding might undermine Haneke's opposition of European art to American commerce, but more interesting than simply undercutting his position is to consider how this cultural economy subtends both the developing concept of the European art film and the very questions of "Europe" (the transnational, immigration, borders, ethnicity) that Haneke addresses.

There are, therefore, two possible approaches to thinking Haneke and Europe: the way in which Haneke's films stage the question of Europe textually and the position of Haneke as auteur, as European filmmaker. In other words, there is the Europe *of* which Haneke speaks and the Europe *from* which he speaks. My aim in this essay is to place these Europes up against each other, to explore the tensions that they create. In starting from the problem of speaking "as a European filmmaker," then, I hope to open up Europe as a question that includes but also exceeds representational politics, that looks to the institutional significance of cinema in Europe, and that enables us to analyze the location of Haneke as a contemporary European filmmaker.

## Representations of Europe: Staging Collectivity

In 2003, Gayatri Spivak considered how the discipline of comparative literature had been reinventing itself since the fall of the Berlin Wall.[7] Her contention, that literary scholars have attempted to think both comparatively and theoretically about the world, is not irrelevant to European cinema in the same period. To illustrate her argument, Spivak reads texts that "stage the question of collectivity." And, she continues, "I have chosen difficult, even mysterious texts, for the question is often too easily answered in the heat of identity politics, in the classroom, in the media, in electoral politics, in war and peace, everywhere."[8] This formulation is doubly useful for reading Haneke's films as texts about Europe, for these too pose questions that can be too easily answered. Questions of immigration, multicultural Europe, violence, and postcoloniality offer a surface-level legibility. And, unlike Spivak's case studies, Haneke's films do not seem especially mysterious in what they have to say on these matters. However, as comparative texts, films such as *Code Unknown* (2000), *Time of the Wolf* (2003), and *Caché* (2005) exceed their own narration of European themes, moving beyond the answerable to stage the space of European collectivity in the form of a question.

*Code Unknown* is the least mysterious of Haneke's European-themed films. From the beginning, it announces itself as a narrative about the New Europe, with a famous sequence in which the son of African immigrants gets into a fight with a white French teenager over the latter's treatment of a Romanian beggar. After a shopkeeper complains about loss of business, the black man is taken away by the police and the Romanian woman deported, while the white boy is free to go on his way. This scene literally narrates the problems of the expanded European Union from the perspective of the prosperous West, proffering racism, economic migrancy, immigration laws, and consumer capitalism as the issues at stake in this tableaux-form misuse of public space. As the narrative continues, it opens out onto a series of loosely connected scenes, following each of the protagonists of this initial encounter and their social circles fragmented by class and race.

The film's overt discourse on Europe is left-liberal, often in a rather didactic fashion. When Romanian Maria returns home, we hear that her friends work as gardener and nanny for a couple in Ireland. That the economic disparities within Europe oblige east Europeans to do menial work in the west is stated rather than engaged cinematically in any depth. The film presents the situation as self-evidently problematic, the brief conversation relying for its effect on not much more than liberal guilt on the part of the audience. This naming of "social problems" perhaps explains Fatima Naqvi's unease; she complains, "There is something glibly multicultural about this French-German-Romanian co-production, as it presents us with representatives from 'target' groups."[9] The film's elaboration of globalized spaces in Europe is similarly forced: Maria's grandson tells her, "When Lica and Mr. Rioara delivered the calf, Uncle Nelu gave instructions on his mobile phone from Rome."

If the film's account of east-west relations lacks subtlety, its staging of the former Yugoslavia is even more direct and yet also more ambiguous. As in many of Haneke's films, the Balkans, and specifically the countries involved in wars in the post-1989 period, form a crucial subplot in *Code Unknown*. Here, Georges is a photojournalist who has recently spent time in Serbia and Kosovo. His photographs of war zones and dead bodies enter Anne's Parisian life, suggesting both the interrupting force of political violence and the exploitative spectacle of the Western media. These contrasting interpretations are given in the film, staged as a debate in which Georges argues with a female friend about the ethics of such images. Outside of this prepackaged ambiguity is the critique made by Naqvi in regard to Haneke's earlier "glaciation trilogy," that the Balkans function not as a real place but as a metaphor for Europe's Other.[10] This troublesome shorthand continues in *Code Unknown* and beyond, suggesting less a reminder of the continent's political shortcomings and more a facile and instrumentalizing rhetoric of Balkanism.[11]

It is when we move beyond the films' overt thematization of Europe that we find a more complex staging of continental collectivity. Elsaesser suggests a similar move when he reads Lars von Trier's *Dogville* (2003) as a European film. He argues that what matters is not that a film tells European stories but that it stages ideologies pertinent to Europe (in his example, the migrant or stranger).[12] For Haneke, I would suggest, the key structuring terms are the border and citizenship. These terms have been central to the post-1989 debate on Europe, opening out as they do not only on pressing political issues of EU enlargement and immigration but also on critical theory's engagement with ideas of sovereignty and ethics. One scholar who combines both modes of inquiry is Étienne Balibar. In 1999's *We, the People of Europe,* he argues that a shift is taking place in the conditions of possibility for representing Europe: "All of this proves that the notions of interiority and exteriority, which form the basis of the representation of the border, are undergoing a veritable earthquake. The representations of the border, territory, and sovereignty, and the very possibility of representing the border and territory, have become the object of an irreversible historical 'forcing.'"[13]

Haneke's films take place in the same geopolitical space limned by Balibar: a Europe doubled by the fall of Euro-communism, distorted and re-formed internally by war and turned into a metaphoric fortress, its shape, definition, and center of gravity repeatedly revised over the course of twenty years. How, in this instability, can cinema do more than just picture social change with verisimilitude? (Look, mother, a Romanian!) Many films of the 1990s and 2000s tell border stories. *Code Unknown* is joined by *Last Resort* (Pawel Pawlikowski, 2000), *Frontières* (Mostefa Djadjam, 2001), and *Lichter* (Hans-Christian Schmid, 2003). But politically oriented modernist cinemas demanded not just that we tell different stories but that we tell stories differently; we cannot adequate radical social transformation merely by adding new faces to the same old structures. Thus, Haneke's most European films do not simply depict social conditions but rather figure Balibar's historical forcing in action. At a formal level, they encode exterior and interior, the violent rupture of borders and edges, and the impossibility of inscribing European territory in any secure or centered fashion.

Consider, for example, the final shot of *Time of the Wolf*. A traveling shot taken through a train window, it depicts at the visual level simply a flat, possibly French, landscape and by implication the movement of a train through it. But the structural position of this shot in the film prevents any direct denotative meaning. Placed within the postapocalyptic space of the narrative, the shot might imply rescue, or at least the continuation of civilization. Even if she selects this optimistic reading, the spectator will be entirely uncertain who, if anyone, inhabits this landscape, to what country it "belongs," and who might be in the position to view it from the train. And this interpretation depends upon a determined spectatorial labor, for the shot is not really located within the narrative, or even definitively within the diegesis. It does not represent any of the film's previous locations or characters. Only the fact that the protagonists are living at a train station ties the shot to what came before. Thus, the ending of the film is radically severed from any narration of Europe, and yet it bespeaks Balibar's representational earthquake. Here, the material ground of Europe—its territory, its sovereignty, its future—is held in dislocating limbo.

If we follow Balibar's argument in parallel with *Time of the Wolf*, it becomes clear why the border is so important. Contextualizing his discussion in both European and global terms (the European Union, terrorism, racism, and immigration), he says, "Not by chance, in these two sets of problems, the traditional institution of borders, which I think can be defined in the modern era as a 'sovereign' or nondemocratic condition of democracy itself, mainly works as an instrument of security control, social segregation, and unequal access to the means of existence, and sometimes as an institutional distribution of survival and death: it becomes a cornerstone of institutional violence."[14] The border lurks in the depths of European democracy, underwriting the rules and regulations of human movement, promising rational control, but its essentially nondemocratic form emerges in the racism and Eurocentrism that Balibar insists we read as immanent, not exceptional. In *Time of the Wolf*, we might likewise hope to isolate (to place on the other side of a border) the racists who accuse the foreigners of stealing a goat and who use epithets like "Polack de merde." But this superficial staging of European racism is a red herring: all of the film's survivors are on the wrong side of an unseen border. They are controlled, segregated, and their access to the barest means of survival limited, but the source of this violence—indeed the source of the narrative's disaster—is deliberately withheld. By abstracting the border form, Haneke insists on its structural centrality.

This abstraction is important, transforming the too-easy answers of the multicultural narrative into a formal figuration of Europe. Many critics have noted Haneke's reluctance to limit his settings to the national. Catherine Wheatley points to the nameless state of *Time of the Wolf* (where most characters speak French, but the location is never named) and to *The Piano Teacher* (2001), which is set in an impossible Francophone Vienna.[15] I will return to these linguistic strategies later, but for now, what is significant is how the films denationalize their diegetic worlds, demanding that we read them not as real places but as figures of the European polity. In these films, it is not that it does not matter where the setting is but that it matters a lot that it cannot be specified. The question of Europe is not an accretion of national concerns but a structure of borders that can only be glimpsed within the material places that must articulate it. Like Trinh T. Minh-ha in *Reassemblage* (1983), Haneke attempts not to speak about Europe but to speak near it.

This strategy works without friction whenever the real place lacks resistance, for instance in *Time of the Wolf*'s non-France. But this mode of figuration becomes difficult—indeed dangerous—when the weight of actual borders exerts its own pressure on the text. We can see this friction in both *Code Unknown* and *Caché,* two films that explicitly address the relationship of the European center to the margin, the inheritances of west European culture, and the construction of borders in geopolitics and subjective relations. Both films are set in Paris, and yet both seek to overwrite the locality of their narrative spaces. Elizabeth Ezra and Jane Sillars respond to the film's address when they describe *Caché* as unfolding "in a European city." This is true but reads oddly since the setting is immediately recognizable as Paris. Their rhetorical point is that critics have been too eager to "limit its exploration of colonial culpabilities to its French setting."[16] Like *Code Unknown, Caché* attempts to articulate the implication of all of Europe in political violence.

In both cases, however, this doubled signification has troubled some readers. I have mentioned the potentially instrumentalizing use of the Balkans in *Code Unknown*. The freighted history of west European representation of the region makes it hard to use it figurally without reiterating this quasicolonial mode of thought. Indeed, as the film of Haneke's that most directly speaks "about" Europe, it may also be the least successful in analyzing it. Its narrative of multiculturalism is precisely the discourse on Europe that is unable to grasp the inadequacy of ventriloquizing the West's Others. Thus, the overt narrative on immigration and race actively resists the film's more radical impulses.

*Caché* suggests a more productive iteration of this problem. Writing on the film, Paul Gilroy expresses discomfort at the unearned mileage Haneke gets from actual events, and Patrick Crowley demonstrates the irreducibility of the film's engagement with a material French history.[17] Haneke has claimed that "the film's main theme is not Algeria," and in the same interview he says that he knew little of the French massacre of Algerians in 1961 and that the specificity of the history had "never even crossed his mind" when making the film.[18] There is a faux naïveté here—I find it hard to believe that Haneke really knew so little about the events he researched for the film. What is clear is that it is important for him to downplay the national specificity of the history so that the text's figuration of European violence can come into view. But the weight of the Algerian massacre fights back against the film's attempt to abstract it, for example in the scene of Majid's death. No matter how abstracted by impossible camera angles and ambiguous narration, the horrific image of Majid's body in death cannot help but figure the unseen bodies of other Algerians and the political violence that destroyed them. It is this tension, I think, rather than any mild narrative ambiguity, that creates the film's effect of political and ethical difficulty.

Ultimately, for Haneke, the border leads to the question of citizenship. His European films interrogate what it means to belong in European space and who has access to this collectivity. *Time of the Wolf* envisions catastrophe as a space without citizenship, while *Caché* and *Code Unknown* critique the tying of citizenship to nationality, locating the international city as a place where belonging, the right to be in the world, is negotiated. To return to Balibar, we might say that Haneke stages the possibility of *droit de cité*, a concept of citizenship that is located neither in blood nor birth but in how and where one lives. Not only an antiessentialist account of the citizen, according to Balibar, *droit de cité* is more importantly derived from the lowermost, elaborating political rights from the treatment of the excluded. Here, Majid might ironically become the ultimate figure of the European citizen. The open (but only just) possibility of such a citizenship is the question that echoes through Haneke's European films.

## *Through West European Eyes? Haneke as European Filmmaker*

I want to turn now from the Europe about which Haneke speaks to that from which he speaks: how does his self-identification as a European filmmaker shape his cultural status?[19] The first element of this location is surely authorship. To speak as anything at all, Haneke must claim the position of auteur, of the kind of filmmaker whose personal statements express a unique artistic perspective. To be sure, we would expect any filmmaker being interviewed to construct a subject position for his or her work, but Haneke is one of a handful of contemporary European directors whose work is consistently discussed in all critical registers within an authorial discourse. For example, *Filmmaker* magazine describes him as having "an elevated position in the ranks of the European auteurs," while Alexander Horwath bases his analysis in a claim that Haneke is interested in continental philosophy.[20] Horwath does not merely draw textual connections between Haneke's films and the concerns of philosophy; by anchoring his reading in Haneke's personal interests, he recenters critical analysis around the figure of a legitimizing author. European critical thought is relevant to the films because Haneke thinks it is.

The category of the auteur has been dominant in postwar conceptions of European cinema, not least in what Steve Neale characterizes as the "overwhelming association of Art Cinema as a whole with a set of individual names." Linking this Romanticist view of the expressive artist to the institutions of European cinema, he argues that such name directors "are readily mobilised in marking and conceptualising what is held up as a basic difference between Hollywood and Art Cinema: that the former is the realm of impersonal profit-seeking and entertainment where the latter is the realm of creativity, freedom and meaning."[21] So far, Haneke functions in exactly the same way as canonical European filmmakers such as Michelangelo Antonioni and Ingmar Bergman, and indeed, critics frequently compare Haneke to this generation of auteurs.[22]

But his difference from these art cinematic names is that Haneke is not understood as a European filmmaker in the sense of coming from a European country (the way Antonioni is Italian and Bergman Swedish), but rather he is understood as "European," speaking from a transnational continental perspective. We can trace the process by which he became a European director quite accurately: his earlier, Austrian-made films are not generally considered to be European, although they are, obviously, made in Europe. To take just one exemplary formulation, Mattias Frey's biographical essay says, "*Fragments* indicates the beginning of Haneke's transition: he is no longer solely an Austrian director, but a European director as well."[23] There are precedents for such continental identification; Elsaesser isolates a thread of directors who have been considered European rather than national because of their background (Jean-Luc Godard as Swiss-French), their experience of relocation (Jean-Marie Straub and Danièle Huillet, Peter Greenaway), or their habit of making films in other countries and languages (Wim Wenders).[24] Nonetheless, I want to explore how Haneke's Europeanness bespeaks something particular in the history of contemporary cinema.

Most striking is the eagerness with which critics have embraced the idea of Haneke as Euro-auteur. While Elsaesser's examples certainly ring true, it is just as common to categorize Greenaway as British or Wenders as German as it is to read about them as European filmmakers. But Haneke is not only described in passing as European: the idea focuses much of his critical reception. For instance, Martine Beugnet asks whether it is Haneke's "hybrid identity as a director" that enables his films' formal detachment.[25] Haneke's transnational citizenship is argued to enable or reflect the thematic content of his films, a self-sustaining structure that often underwrites ideologies of authorship. But what story does his hybrid identity tell? It begins from the impossibility of nationality. While most directors are defined in terms of their citizenship, Haneke's films do not often speak to Austrian concerns (*The Piano Teacher* is an exception). To some degree, the ease with which his national identity disappears is happenstance: since few spectators could name a single Austrian director, it becomes hard to place his work within a national film tradition. But the lack of national identity continues into his Francophone films: although those films were shot in Paris with largely French casts, few would characterize Haneke as French.

Writing in the *Village Voice,* David Ng describes Haneke as dividing his time between Paris and Vienna, and this life detail evokes the proper name of Haneke's story: he is a cosmopolitan traveler, able to inhabit many European spaces at once.[26] Unlike his characters, he is neither limited by national enculturation nor marginalized by immigration. He can avail himself of the advantages of the French film industry, but he needs make no request for a new identity. Haneke the auteur evacuates the specificity of his birthplace and residence, just as his films ask us not to think about exactly where they take place. This cosmopolitan European figure contrasts markedly with the lowermost and the excluded that his films represent. Indeed, we might read these figures as mutually constitutive, two sides of the coin of transnational European identity today: the displaced person who loses his original identity and has no access to another versus the cosmopolitan who transcends the national and can be at home anywhere. To adapt my reading of Balibar, if the transformation of borders and citizenship is the defining issue for today's Europe, then this is not only a question for the characters in Haneke's films but also for the changing status of the European filmmaker.

If Haneke as auteur combines the rhetoric of the European cinema canon with that of the EU cosmopolitan, he is likewise located within a contemporary iteration of the European art cinema. The terms "art cinema" and "Europe" are not inextricably linked: from its inception art cinema included non-European directors like Satyajit Ray and Ozu Yasujiro, and among Haneke's contemporaries, many of its most celebrated practitioners come from East Asia (for example, Hou Hsaio-hsien, Wong Kar-wai, and Jia Zhangke). But there is a strand of art cinematic discourse that has tied the form closely to Europe, defining its aims in opposition to Hollywood. Thus, Steve Neale's influential early account of art cinema as an institution studies "the role played by what has come to be called 'Art Cinema' in the attempts made by a number of European countries both to counter American domination of their indigenous markets in film and also to foster a film industry and a film culture of their own."[27] Likewise, Andrew Tudor's sociological study argues, "In some part the rise of the artmovie was a consequence of European attempts to resurrect national film industries after the Second World War and, in so doing, to resist Hollywood domination."[28] Neither of these writers exclude non-European films, but in focusing on the institutional structures of art cinema, they make clear its historical imbrication in economic and ideological definitions of European culture.

Haneke, then, speaks as a European art cinema director, drawing on historically entrenched ideas about European film as a counter to Hollywood. And indeed, his films fit closely with the major definitions of art cinematic form proposed by Neale and David Bordwell in regard to 1960s and 1970s cinema. Thus, Bordwell argues, "The art cinema motivates its narratives by two principles: realism and authorial expressivity."[29] Neale lists as elements of emerging national art cinemas "realism, humanism, lack of spectacle, lack of excess in style and technique, and so on."[30] Each of these terms could be mapped onto Haneke's work with ease: the simple cinematography and editing that pointedly reject excess, the critique of spectacular violence that runs through Haneke's oeuvre, the strong authorial voice that shades so often into didacticism. Even humanism, which might seem a stretch for films like *Funny Games* (1997 and 2007), can be inferred in Haneke's concern for the effects of violence, the perversion of what must, after all, be human underneath consumerism's distorting effects. Linking these accounts is realism, understood here as both a concern for the social realm and the openness of form that asks spectators to read the image actively. John David Rhodes has analyzed Haneke's long takes in relation to neorealism, and in this ur-form of European art cinema we find a precursor for Haneke's complex mixture of narrative ambiguity and coercive morality.[31]

However, while realism is a defining quality of art cinema, it is reimagined under the auspices of modernism as an expression of political, psychic, or social realities that cannot be adequately by purely mimetic forms and that define the experience of modernity. The real in modernist art cinema is that which can only be grasped by antirealist modes of representation, characterized by Bordwell and others in terms of narrative ambiguity, reflexivity, and the breaking apart of classical spectator relations. Haneke's films use these forms insistently, refusing the spectator the comforts of classical narrative. In the opening sequence of *The Piano Teacher*, Erika tells her student to lift her hands from the keys quickly to produce an effect of coldness as the music starts and stops. The scene is intercut with the opening credits, the music stopping abruptly with the cuts to black. Thus, as it opens, the film reflexively comments upon and explains to the spectator (in case she is as slow as the student) its own aesthetic rhetoric. A similarly disjunctive irruption of authorial reflexivity occurs early in *Time of the Wolf*: when Anne asks a neighbor for help, he says, "You really don't know what's going on? Or are you just acting stupid?" Here, the spectator is addressed alongside Anne. We do not know what is going on, because the event has happened before the narrative begins. We are temporally excluded from knowledge, and yet, it is our fault. We should have known. We are acting stupid.

The extent to which Haneke speaks in the language of modernist art cinema can be surmised from his adoption of its themes. As a representation of the conditions of modernity, Bordwell gives as examples of the real problems addressed by art cinema "contemporary 'alienation,' 'lack of communication,' etc."[32] These concepts are reiterated over and over in the scholarly literature on Haneke. Christopher Sharrett, for example, associates Haneke with "the legacy of artistic modernism," citing as an example his "interest in the alienating features of contemporary urban life."[33] And Roy Grundmann opens a list of "the director's preeminent thematic concerns" with "the alienation of the individual in the modern world, people's inability to communicate."[34] At this historical remove, these themes take on a necessarily clichéd aspect: Bordwell highlights their accretion of typicality not just by using them as his examples but by putting them in scare quotes. To address alienation in the 1990s and after is to evoke a well-worn history of modernist representation.

Haneke's advocates are well aware that his forms are far from original. Grundmann, for instance, admits that the ideas are quite clichéd but argues that Haneke has sought new and defamiliarizing ways to address them.[35] But why use such a clichéd representational practice in the first place? To address this question is to consider the institutional location of the European art cinema inheritance today. What is at stake in Haneke's repetition of European art cinematic forms is, precisely, the sedimentation of cultural knowledge that accrues to a (particular) European audience. Repetition signals not a lack of originality but a codification of spectatorial borders. D. I. Grossvogel inadvertently makes this point clear when he argues that American audiences want to render *Caché* transparent, whereas French ones, trained by the history of Brecht and European art cinema, were happy for the film to stay obscure.[36] Thus, the spectator needs to be trained in the European intellectual tradition to read correctly. Haneke's insistence on such a historically located art cinematic form attempts to construct an audience in terms of proper (that is, Eurocentric) enculturation.

The third term around which Haneke's status as European filmmaker circulates is "industry," the national and transnational institutions within which he works. As is the case with many contemporary filmmakers in Europe (and beyond), Haneke's productions are funded by several national and international bodies. *Code Unknown,* for example, drew from French, German, Romanian, and EU funding sources, while *Time of the Wolf* included French, German, Austrian, and EU coproduction partners. How do we read the significance of this mode of production? Clearly, the complex requirements for budgeting any major production contradict the fantasy of European filmmaking as operating on a higher plane than the crass commerce of Hollywood, but what do the structures of European coproduction actually tell us about specific practices?

One possibility is to read Haneke's authorial cosmopolitanism in light of this mode of production. *Funny Games* (2007), for instance, received substantial backing from the French Centre National de la Cinématographie (CNC) on the basis that it was a "film d'initiative française." Haneke's ability to apply for *Funny Games* as a majority French film, rather than in the much more limited majority foreign category, places him in a privileged relationship to France's influential cinematic infrastructure.[37] Clearly, French funding in this instance does not correlate to any obvious textual identity, as the film is set in the United States with an international Anglophone cast. But if funding sources do not direct aesthetic choices in any simplistic way, they do, nonetheless, define the parameters within which production choices are made.

Writing on contemporary coproductions, including *Caché*, Elsaesser argues that the European Union increasingly sees films in similar terms to other high-tech industries, in which European cooperation is necessary to compete globally. Thus, "the European Union is actively promoting films that pool funding and transfer talent between different European countries through channels provided by the EU. Without their content being necessarily multi-cultural or trans-national, these national-international films help to make cinema part of the process of European Union integration."[38] The prime objective, for example, of the Council of Europe Eurimages fund, which has funded every one of Haneke's films since *Code Unknown,* is to support internationally coproduced films that "reflect the multiple facets of a European society whose common roots are evidence of a single culture."³⁹ Here, not only Haneke's overt transnational themes but the authorial persona that draws so explicitly from a European artistic and intellectual heritage mesh seamlessly with the cultural policies of his backers. The opposition to Hollywood is no longer framed, as it was in the postwar decades, in terms of European national cinemas: Haneke's "European films" exemplify the development of the coproduction into an emerging form of Europeanness.⁴⁰

A key aspect of this Europeanness is language. Mark Betz has richly analyzed the linguistic modes of 1960s and 1970s art cinema, during the crucial period of both decolonization and the early development of European economic cooperation. Betz proposes, "The dialogue tracks of art films are thus a rich site of contestation and are symptomatic of larger economic, political, and cultural forces in Europe in the 1960s and 1970s."⁴¹ Haneke's films, I would suggest, are well placed to extend this analysis of language into the 1990s and 2000s. For Betz, both casting and the choice of which language to release a film in (often via dubbing) inscribe ideological tensions between the national and the international. These tensions remain in force in the EU era, although often to somewhat different effect. Casting remains a main function of capital investment, with Haneke's use of French stars such as Isabelle Huppert and Juliette Binoche guaranteeing sales in a way that Austrian actors could not. These stars signify a promise to a traditionally Europhilic audience, one for whom Frenchness underwrites a discourse of art cinematic quality and cultural capital reminiscent of the 1960s. The power of this internal hierarchy is undimmed, as anyone who has ever curated or taught French cinema can attest.

Casting French actors as leads overdetermines language, and indeed all of Haneke's so-called European films have been released in French. Again, this choice speaks to the dominance of France not only in film funding but as the privileged language of *international* European cinema. *The Piano Teacher* is particularly telling in this regard, for here the advantages of casting Huppert in the lead and having a French dialogue track override any naturalistic desire to have language match geography. The film is set in Vienna, and yet all the characters speak French; even the television broadcast is in French. Moreover, only the three main leads are French speakers: all of the supporting characters are played by German-speaking actors dubbed into French. For Betz, this "reduction of a film's polyphonic profilmic event into a univocal sound track . . . nevertheless leaves as trace of its international production context the unsynched images of the mouths and voices of an international community of actors."[42] In 1960s art cinema, this dissonance forms a trace of a largely invisible coproduction regime. But in *The Piano Teacher*, the mismatch of voice and body corresponds to the much more noticeable mismatch of language and location. The effect is far from seamless, and yet it is not minimized: coproduction is writ large, or rather spoken loudly, across the body of the film.

In other films, the linguistic mixture is narrativized more openly, with non-French actors speaking in their own languages, without dubbing. This practice, according to Betz, often had to be shoehorned into 1960s films that had received foreign funding in return for the use of an actor but that really did not want an international storyline. By contrast, Haneke uses Romanian quite deliberately in *Code Unknown* and *Time of the Wolf* to stage transnational issues of racism and EU integration. While there is a direct narrative logic to the use of Romanian in both of these films (subtitled in *Code*, ambiguously identified and left incomprehensible to non-Romanian speakers in *Wolf*), this shift in the use of multiple languages also signifies at the historical and institutional levels. While the Romanian characters say one thing about contemporary transnational Europe, the actors themselves bespeak the geopolitics of the European film industry: the entry of some east European countries to the economic spaces of European production (via cheap studios and labor) and to the cultural spaces of European art cinema (via the success of east European, particularly Romanian, films and actors at film festivals). While these films address the difficulties of Europe textually, their production structure reflects its official rhetoric.

What each of these extratextual factors (authorship, art cinema, production) point to is how firmly Haneke is embedded within the institution of European cinema. And, in both its historically dominant and contemporary forms, this institution enables Haneke to take up a uniquely privileged speaking position. Gilroy's critique of *Caché* is again elucidating. He complains that investigations into Georges's subjectivity are clichéd and that only when the Majids of the world are presented as equivalently complex characters will we have made real progress in representing modernity.[43] Gilroy identifies a racist cultural structure, in regard to which no amount of liberal white European films can stand in for a genuine change in the conditions of representation for postcolonial subjects. One might retort that the complaint is unfair, as this entire structure is surely not Haneke's fault. Indeed, it is not, just like it is not Georges's fault that the police killed hundreds of Algerians. Nonetheless, as *Caché* tells us, fault is not the same thing as responsibility, and European responsibility before the other must be faced.[44] Haneke does not speak naively; both in interviews and in the films themselves, he presents himself as an auteur who addresses these questions. And yet, he continues to position himself as a white, west European artist, laying claim to the seriousness and depth of subjectivity that this speaking position grants him (and denies to others).

To be clear, I am sure that Haneke intends no bad faith. I do not doubt that he supports Europe's migrant workers, racialized others, and so on. But this is not enough. By speaking so unquestioningly in the language of European superiority, the superiority of the European cultural heritage, the superiority of the serious European who understands universal matters, he nonetheless demands to retain Eurocentric distinction. A different conception of European identity is possible, but Haneke's binary logic of Europe versus America prevents its development. As Elsaesser asks, "How long can European cinema flatter itself as the plucky David against Goliath Hollywood? When will it have to measure up to, or renegotiate its identity vis-à-vis Asian cinema, Australian cinema, or Indian cinema?"[45] In demanding that we continue to view European culture only in contrast to Hollywood, Haneke constructs politics along the lines of a Eurocentric modernism, limiting not only the possibility of other influences but precluding the challenges of a non-Eurocentric worldview.

## *Conclusion*

By way of conclusion, I would like to return to *The Piano Teacher*, a film that addresses topics quite different from the politics of Europe. Unusually among Haneke's films, *The Piano Teacher* focuses on gender and sexuality, issues that might seem like a detour or a distraction from an analysis of his geopolitics. And yet, I would contend that in this treatment of sexuality, we find the kernel of Haneke's politics, and the beginnings of a resolution to the tension I have outlined in his relationship to Europe. The film centers on Erika, a successful pianist and secret sexual submissive. Her clumsy attempts to initiate a BDSM relationship with a student leads to her violent emotional and professional downfall. The film was generally received as a bold and serious treatment of a challenging subject, but, as with Haneke's earlier films, Erika's "perverse" behavior functions less as a psychological exploration of transgressive sexuality and more as a figure for social dysfunction. Erika is commensurate with Haneke's other figurations of modernity gone horribly awry: the killers in *Funny Games* or the suicidal family in *The Seventh Continent* (1989).

By making Erika into a metaphor for what is wrong with society, Haneke forecloses on non-normative sexuality as a place from which a potentially engaged critique of the normative might emerge. The film gestures toward such a critique by making "normal" masculinity the source of the film's most abusive act of violence, but this rhetoric gains its effect from the supposed irony that the straight man is worse *even* than the masochistic woman. The film condemns patriarchal masculinity, but it builds its case on an assumption that Erika's sexuality is self-evidently damaged. This is a position that almost all of the film's critics have endorsed. In the most telling example, Robin Wood identifies BDSM as alienated, capitalistic, and "seriously wrong," comparing its structures of desire to George W. Bush's neoimperial domination.[46] For Wood, BDSM is one of the violences that Haneke uses to condemn modern society; it represents the opposite of a loving sexual relationship in the same way that consumer culture is the opposite of real social relations. This argument and the film (whose position I think it accurately telegraphs) assume a severely limiting sexual politics, enacting an a priori exclusion of sex-positive and queer feminisms.

Some of this attitude derives from Elfriede Jelinek, the author of the novel on which *The Piano Teacher* was based. Her writings advocate a feminism that equates marriage with capitalist exploitation and goes on to adduce pornography and sexual perversion as symptomatic of this abuse. Jelinek has much in common with Haneke politically: her feminism demarcates the same 1970s-era political landscape as Haneke's modernist radicalism. There is much to recommend in the way this politics attacks the ideologies of the family, modern consumer culture, capitalist exploitation, and so on, but the narrow view of sexuality characteristic of that strand of feminist thought makes clear the importance of what is not there, what cannot be imagined in this system. The logic of *The Piano Teacher* delegitimizes any articulation of sexuality outside the hegemonic position of the "European filmmaker." The place from which Haneke speaks excludes so much, places so much on the side of wrong, that it restricts the locations from which political speech can come. Cleaving to the European intellectual tradition, even in its more radical forms, demands that those who demur are suffering false consciousness or are failing to grasp the seriousness of the situation. And yet, just as feminism has developed a less univocal account of sexuality, likewise a contemporary politics of the image can offer more than a retreat into the false universality of Euromodernism.

One feminist theorist who has taken on these questions is Kaja Silverman, who argues that political cinema has for too long been understood only in relation to Brechtian distanciation. Positing the centrality of identification with the other to both life and politics, she contends firstly that it is impossible to escape identification and enter "the rarefied atmosphere of pure rationality" and secondly that we should not want to, because identification has "potential importance as an agency of psychic and social change."[47] In other words, both the Marxist/feminist film theories of the 1970s and the modernist European cinemas of the same period articulated identical understandings of aesthetics and politics. It is this inheritance that Haneke articulates today. But both film theory and film practice have moved on, and for Silverman, "the alienation of the viewer from the filmic screen cannot by itself constitute the primary goal of a political cinema."[48] In a passage that might have been written as a plea for Erika, she says:

Nevertheless, it seems to me that a political cinema for today must be one which, rather than lamenting the identification at the center of the cinematic experience, seizes upon it as a vehicle for taking the spectator somewhere he or she has never been before, and which discourages the return journey. Central to this project . . . is the idealization of bodily coordinates within which the viewer is not accustomed to finding him—or herself, and which have been routinely devalued at the site of the cultural screen.[49]

Just as contemporary sex-positive and queer feminisms are excluded by *The Piano Teacher*'s mobilization of the submissive woman as metaphor, so Haneke's European-themed films present excluded and marginal European subjects as figurations of social wrongs rather than as agents for radical change. A political perspective on Europe requires more than speaking about the other, no matter how responsibly: it demands a practice that opens the imaginative space of European identification to those other subjects, forms, political and aesthetic formations, and, yes, genres that the name Europe has historically disprized.

## *Notes*

1. Scott Foundas, "Michael Haneke: The Bearded Prophet of *Code Inconnu* and *The Piano Teacher*," IndieWire, www.indiewire.com/people/int_Haneke_Michael_011204.html (accessed March 21, 2008).

2. Thomas Elsaesser, *European Cinema: Face to Face with Hollywood* (Amsterdam: Amsterdam University Press, 2005), 487, 492.

3. For example, Alejandro Amenábar's *Open Your Eyes* (1997) and *The Others* (2001).

4. Elsaesser, *European Cinema*, 82–107; Mark Betz, "The Name above the (Sub)Title: Internationalism, Coproduction, and Polyglot European Art Cinema," *Camera Obscura* 46 (2001): 1–44; David Andrews, "Towards an Inclusive, Exclusive Approach to Art Cinema," (paper presented at the Society for Cinema Studies Conference, Philadelphia, March 8, 2008).

5. Edmund Husserl, *The Crisis of European Sciences and Transcendental Phenomenology*, trans. David Carr (Evanston: Northwestern University Press, 1970), 17.

6. Jacques Derrida, *The Other Heading: Reflections on Today's Europe*, trans. Pascale-Anne Brault and Michael B. Naas (Bloomington: Indiana University Press, 1992), 75.

7. Gayatri Chakravorty Spivak, *Death of a Discipline* (New York: Columbia University Press, 2003).

8. Ibid., 26.

9. Fatima Naqvi, "The Politics of Contempt and the Ecology of Images: Michael Haneke's *Code inconnu*," in *The Cosmopolitan Screen: German Cinema and the Global Imaginary, 1945 to the Present*, ed. Stephan K. Schindler and Lutz Koepnick (Ann Arbor: University of Michigan Press, 2007), 237.

10. Ibid. It might be relevant to note that Mattias Frey, writing on the film, describes Georges as a journalist in Bosnia, when in fact he is in Serbia and Kosovo. Of course, this is a simple mistake that anyone could make, but it might not be stretching a point to see it as symptomatic of how the West sees the Balkans as one big war zone, precisely a metaphor, rather than as specific places with different histories. Mattias Frey, "Michael Haneke," *Senses of Cinema*, www.sensesofcinema.com/contents/directors/03/haneke.html (accessed March 20, 2008).

11. For a historical discussion of Balkanism as a west European rhetoric, see Maria Todorova, *Imagining the Balkans* (Oxford: Oxford University Press, 1997).

12. Elsaesser, *European Cinema*, 171–73.

13. Étienne Balibar, *We, the People of Europe: Reflections on Transnational Citizenship*, trans. James Swenson (Princeton: Princeton University Press, 2004), 5.

14. Ibid., 117.

15. Catherine Wheatley, "Secrets, Lies, and Videotape," *Sight and Sound* 16, no. 2 (2006): 32–36.

16. Elizabeth Ezra and Jane Sillars, "Hidden in Plain Sight: Bringing Terror Home," *Screen* 48, no. 2 (2007): 215.

17. Paul Gilroy, "Shooting Crabs in a Barrel," *Screen* 48, no. 2 (2007): 233; Patrick Crowley, "When Forgetting Is Remembering: Haneke's *Caché* and the Events of October 17, 1961," in this volume.

18. Michael Haneke in Dominik Kamalzadeh, "Cowardly and Comfortable," *Sign and Sight*, www.signandsight.com/features/577.html (accessed April 5, 2008).

19. Elsaesser, *European Cinema*, 494. Elsaesser says, "the dualistic schemes outlined above for the relation Europe-Hollywood can have no objective validity or disinterested status: they are heavily Eurocentric and self-interested. They view the overall picture through West European eyes."

20. "The Director Interviews: Michael Haneke," www.filmmakermagazine.com/directorinterviews/2008/03/michael-haneke-funny-games-us.php (accessed April 5,

2008); Alexander Horwath cited in Roy Grundmann, "Auteur de Force: Michael Haneke's Cinema of Glaciation," *Cineaste* 32, no. 2 (2007): 6.

21. Steve Neale, "Art Cinema as Institution," *Screen* 22, no. 1 (1981): 36.

22. To give a brief sample, Leonard Quart compares Haneke to Jean-Luc Godard and Antonioni in "Code Unknown," *Cineaste* 27, no. 2 (2002): 36; Amos Vogel compares him to Alain Robbe-Grillet and Wim Wenders in "Of Nonexisting Continents: The Cinema of Michael Haneke," *Film Comment* 32, no. 4 (1996): 74; Paul Arthur compares him to Rainer Werner Fassbinder in "Endgame," *Film Comment* 41, no. 6 (2005): 28; and Christopher Sharrett compares him to Alain Resnais, Bergman, and, again, Antonioni in "The World That Is Known: An Interview with Michael Haneke," *Cineaste* 28, no. 3 (2003): 28–29.

23. Frey, "Michael Haneke."

24. Elsaesser, *European Cinema*, 486.

25. Martine Beugnet, "Blind Spot," *Screen* 48, no. 2 (2007): 227–28.

26. David Ng, "Memories of Murder," *Village Voice*, December 6, 2005.

27. Neale, "Art Cinema as Institution," 11.

28. Andrew Tudor, "The Rise and Fall of the Art (House) Movie," in *The Sociology of Art: Ways of Seeing*, ed. David Inglis and John Hughson (New York: Palgrave, 2005), 133.

29. David Bordwell, "The Art Cinema as a Mode of Film Practice," *Film Criticism* 4, no. 1 (1979): 57.

30. Neale, "Art Cinema as Institution," 26–27.

31. John David Rhodes, "Haneke, the Long Take, Realism," *Framework* 47, no. 2 (2006): 17–19. Also see Rhodes's essay "The Spectacle of Skepticism," in the present volume, for a more extended discussion of the long take in Haneke's cinema.

32. Bordwell, "Art Cinema," 57.

33. Sharrett, "World That Is Known," 28.

34. Grundmann, "Auteur de Force," 6.

35. Ibid., 6.

36. D. I. Grossvogel, "Haneke: The Coercing of Vision," *Film Quarterly* 60, no. 4 (2007): 41.

37. *Funny Games* had 56 percent French funding, 32 percent German, and 12 percent Italian according to the CNC. Other majority French productions they funded in 2006 include *Julia* (Eric Zonca), *Dante XXI* (Marc Caro), *La fille coupée en deux* (Claude Chabrol), and *Bamako* (Abderrahmane Sissako). Directors of the majority foreign films funded made up a roster of contemporary auteurs, including Denys Arcand, Manoel de Oliveira, Youssef Chahine, Krzysztof Zanussi, Carlos Reygadas, and Emir Kusturica. Centre National de la Cinématographie, "Films d'initiative française agréés en 2006," and "Films à majorité étrangère agréés in 2006," www.cnc.fr (accessed April 6, 2008).

38. Elsaesser, *European Cinema*, 507.

39. Council of Europe website, www.coe.int/t/dg4/eurimages/About/default_en.asp (accessed April 6, 2008).

40. Clearly, the coproduction itself is not a new form. What has changed is that whereas, as Mark Betz has pointed out (Betz, "Name above the (Sub)Title," 7–8),

film audiences and historiographers alike used to ignore coproduction and assign European films to a single nation, today's EU production regime tends toward thinking of films as European.

41. Ibid., 7.

42. Ibid., 30.

43. Gilroy, "Shooting Crabs," 234. I am not sure I agree with Gilroy's reading of *Caché* in its broader argument: I see more value in the rhetoric of obliquity than he does, and I find his interpretation of the death of Majid as white fantasy unconvincing. Nonetheless, his account of what he finds troubling in the film prompted me to think further about why, exactly, I find its enunciative source to contrast with its textual politics.

44. In *The Other Heading*, Derrida asks how a European cultural identity can enact responsibility "for itself, for the other, and before the other" (16).

45. Elsaesser, *European Cinema*, 493.

46. Robin Wood, "'Do I Disgust You?' or Tirez pas sur La Pianiste," *Cineaction* 59 (2002): 57. See also Grossvogel, "Haneke," 39.

47. Kaja Silverman, *The Threshold of the Visible World* (New York: Routledge, 1996), 84–85.

48. Ibid., 85.

49. Ibid., 102.

*Code Unknown* (2000): Anne irons.

Scott Durham

# Codes Unknown
## Haneke's Serial Realism

### *From the Glaciation Trilogy to* **Funny Games:** *The Impasses of Realism*

No filmmaker has more self-consciously confronted the limits of realism in postmodernity than has Michael Haneke. In the films of his "glaciation trilogy"—*The Seventh Continent, Benny's Video,* and *71 Fragments of a Chronology of Chance*—these limits impose themselves as the simultaneous necessity and impossibility of confronting the social reality of his material directly. This confrontation is necessary because the emblematic events of Haneke's films—serial killings and collective suicides, inexplicable irruptions of violence, seemingly torn from today's headlines—are just the sort of reality a postmodern public imagines will awaken it from its dreams of undisturbed consumption. But it is precisely because these same personages and events also "come out of the media" that they are not directly representable by realism as classically conceived.[1] Nor can they, given their social reality as media images, be adequately addressed solely in terms of Bressonian or Brechtian formal strategies of fragmentation and distanciation, inherited from the modernist canon.

We will explore the extent to which Haneke's films move beyond a dialectic of form and content in exploring the possibilities of a serial realism for reimagining postmodern sociality. But first we shall examine what leads Haneke to hesitate between two equally unsatisfactory alternatives, each of which initially appears as a negation of the representation of such events by mass culture.

The first involves elaborating an alternative form for representing the act of violence, without either offering it as a readily consumable image, or explaining it by the hidden pathologies of its perpetrator and thereby framing its otherwise inexplicable rupture of the established order as a reassuringly isolated exception.[2] Among the narrative techniques through which this aesthetic is elaborated is the use of sound to represent offscreen acts of violence to which the spectator is denied "visual access" (as with the killing of the son in *Funny Games*).[3] This technique, as in the work of Robert Bresson, underscores the importance of what withholds itself from visibility.[4] Haneke's disjointed presentation of the space of violence also sometimes serves (as in the devastating close-ups of flopping fish that slowly die amid the other remnants of the shattered familial interior in *The Seventh Continent*) to make visible the incommensurability of the causes of the act with its effects, both upon its victims and on the milieu whose identities and relations its violence disintegrates. But at other moments, a series of close-ups, even as it enumerates the fragments of the world to be disassembled, can also make visible their nonlocalized relations to one another over time. Thus, in *The Seventh Continent*, a series of close-ups of the ordinary gestures of hands counting money early in the film anticipates a later series of close-ups of the extraordinary (if equally methodical) gestures of the father's hands flushing money, a few bills at a time, down the toilet. The constitution and combination of such series in Haneke's films decenters the origins of the violent event, making it appear less as a unique catastrophe than as the most extreme variant of an ordinary regime of repeated routines.

Thus the questions raised by the destruction of the family's lives and property in *The Seventh Continent* are not those posed by the news coverage generated by such events ("What was unique about this father and this family?" "What could have motivated them to commit this extraordinary act?"). Haneke's treatment poses different questions: To what extent do the gestures that annihilate a family and its property (which are every bit as deliberate and routine as were the habitual actions that might otherwise appear as their antithesis) repeat the gestures that reproduce the family and maintain its property?[5] To what extent does the form of this apparently extraordinary death express the truth of the ordinary form of life from which it emerges?

Such formal devices can be understood as expressions of a fragmentary and decentered realist aesthetic, reshaping the formal components of realism in accordance with the fragmented content of postmodern life itself.

The elaboration of this aesthetic does not, however, take place in a vacuum. Because its content has already passed through the "mainstream cinema" and television, it initially appears as a negation of their forms, which "pretend," in Haneke's words, "to be showing the totality of reality" (whereas, in fact, "it's just fragments").[6] This tension is reflected in the form of the work itself. For even a film valorizing an aesthetic of the incomplete and the fragmentary can come to depend upon the unity of the consumable image it seeks to undermine, if only as a necessary foil.

This is most striking in *71 Fragments of a Chronology of Chance*, which depends upon the young student's climactic massacre of the others at the bank to bring its otherwise dispersed narrative lines together. In Haneke's initial presentation, the various strands knotted together by this event are (like the puzzles that, throughout the film, the frustrated student can never quite assemble into a single whole) dispersed into discontinuous series. The divergence of the stories of the adopting parents, the incommunicative couple, the Romanian boy, and the other characters is punctuated by brief cuts to black, marking their distance from one another (a distance that is a function of their belonging to distinct social classes, ethnicities, and milieux). Their parallel narratives are united only in the image of their deaths.

The film's climactic murder-suicide is likewise rendered in Haneke's austerely elliptical style, moving from the overhead shot of the killer's car from which we hear, after a moment, the pop of the unseen student's suicide shot, back to the seemingly interminable close-up of the blood seeping from the torso of one victim, before finally showing us the dead student through the windshield. But Haneke prepares the convergence of these characters, from their various parallel worlds, upon the bank—like debris from unrelated celestial collisions, destined to be drawn together by the gravitational force of the black hole into which they will all vanish at once—with a pitiless inexorability suggesting that their fortuitous encounter is no less fated and foreseeable for being absolutely contingent.

Indeed, it is the sense of a fatal necessity imposed upon these lives from outside that lends this scene, which so carefully eschews any appeal to sentimentality, its unexpected pathos. And yet this powerfully tragic effect is itself called into question in a parodic epilogue, showing us the representation of this same event on the evening news. Here its disparate elements are neatly summed up and packaged for us by the newscaster as the spectacular image of an anomalous "act of insanity," alongside the stories of war from Sarajevo and the alleged sex crimes of Michael Jackson. To be sure, Haneke is mocking the arbitrary unities imposed by the narrative forms of network news. But he is also implicitly acknowledging that his own disassembly of these unities presupposes and depends upon them. For they occupy, in our mental representation of the otherwise unrepresentable event, the empty center around which its fragments orbit. The afterimage of the film's concluding televisual narrative, having been prepared by innumerable such news broadcasts, retrospectively reveals itself to have been so deeply burned into our retinas as to exclude the possibility of our seeing any alternative vision that does not include it.

This suggests the necessity of a confrontation of the postmodern realist with the media themselves. This confrontation is iconically staged by Haneke in those moments when the viewers discover, between themselves and a preexisting social content, a layer of previous screenings of media images. Such foregrounding by Haneke of the seriality of postmodern representation has often been characterized as Brechtian. And indeed, if we consider the most notorious of such reflexive images in Haneke—the moment in *Funny Games* where Anna manages to shoot the killer Peter, only to have her heroic act undone when Paul, the other killer, having found the remote control, rewinds the action—this sudden reversal of fortunes might seem to follow Bertolt Brecht's example in offering a parodic restaging of the happy ending viewers presumably demand.[7]

But Haneke's device for staging this critique—a media device (the remote) endowing one of his characters, within the diegetic frame, with a godlike power over their fictive universe (a power that should be exercised only "remotely," from outside)—does not, like the queen's implausible pardon of Macheath in Brecht, lead us to reflect on the distance between media (which manipulate our expectations of a happy ending) and a contrasting social reality preexisting its media representations. For the only reality referred to by *Funny Games* is that of the media themselves.

What is foregrounded in *Funny Games* is not a distance between the forms of social life and the forms of its representation but the Baudrillardian Möbius strip that leads from the "fictions" of the media to the media themselves as a social and institutional power. The media thus appear in this film as the ultimate perpetrators of its violence—a violence inflicted, as Paul's repeated winks and nods remind us, with the tacit consent of the consumers of its images. In this light, the killers appear within the diegetic world of the film at once as "artifacts" of the media and as their delegated representatives within that subsidiary world.[8] In *Funny Games*, the violence of the characters is secondary to a primary violence of the media, from which it derives.

But this means that we have come full circle. We have moved from alternative forms of representation that resist reductive and easily consumable media images of violence to a direct confrontation with the power of those media themselves. But when the media reappear, in a self-reflexive fiction, as an "explanation" for the violent events of the film itself, the "thesis" of the alternative film risks becoming a readily consumable media object in its own right. What, after all, could be more of a media cliché than the pop-psychological claim that the media are the cause of all our violence—that they have made us cold, incapable of affective communication, indifferent to the suffering of others, and so on? But if Haneke's "Brechtian" interrogation of mainstream media permits itself to be thematized in this way, as a readily assimilable content, it is in this impasse that we find ourselves. A dialectic of realism, having led us from a questioning of the reified forms imposed on its content by the mainstream media to a parodic critique of those media, has resulted in the thematization of the media as yet another reified content, which turns out to be as readily consumable as the objects of Haneke's original critique.

## *Toward a Serial Realism: Convergent Series in the Glaciation Trilogy*

All of this would seem to support a reading of Haneke's work as a negative or suspended realism, divided between its Bressonian and Brechtian poles: the first devoted to the representation of the forms of everyday existence in postmodernity (a new form of content, demanding a new form of expression), the second emphasizing a critical reflection on postmodernity's "culture of the image" (an already existing form of representation, embedded in real social institutions and practices). Yet neither of these can make a claim to truth except as a negation of the inadequacies of the other.

But a reading of Haneke's realist project in terms of an opposition of forms of social content to forms of representation obscures the extent to which the two are parallel expressions of a reality common to both—a reality in light of which they would be neither opposed nor reducible to each other. For Haneke's glaciation trilogy also explores the formal precondition of their coexistence: the fact that the practices of everyday existence, the images inseparable from them, and the worlds they constitute and represent are formed by series of repeated elements. Haneke's elaboration of a postmodern realism makes visible the constitution of these series of repetitions as such (without presupposing a difference in kind between social contents and their representations). But he will also explore the different ways in which such series are themselves embedded in overarching series (as when series of gestures, images, and affects become, on another level, themselves elements in series of social practices or worlds) and articulated in different narrative forms of seriality—each with its own distinct way of imagining social relations.

We have seen how Haneke's use of the close-up isolates the gestures of everyday existence in order to make them visible as elements of a series. But how is such a series formed, and how is it linked with others? In the section of *The Seventh Continent* previously discussed, Haneke breaks up the activity of shopping into a series of mechanical gestures—hands grasping products from the shelves, hands loading and unloading the cart, hands paying at the register, and hands reshelving the products at home—which, together, make visible all that is unbearable in their repetition. The world of the first part of the film—the world that the collective suicide later attempts to destroy—is the bloc (or overarching series) composed of the local convergence of such series: shopping, working, housekeeping, in all their intolerable repetitions of the same.

It is true that there are sometimes affective outbursts against the tyranny of this repetition—as in the scene where *The Seventh Continent*'s Anna breaks down in the car wash—but, like the machinery of the car wash, which inexorably continues even as Anna goes on weeping uncontrollably, this juxtaposition of intense negative affect with habitual repetition only serves to underscore how intolerable and unchangeable is the form of life against which Anna's tears can only helplessly protest. It is only the little girl who attempts to flee this world, as in the episode of feigned blindness by which she disrupts her school's routines. But every line of flight she might pursue is brutally cut off by her teachers and her parents, until she herself succumbs to the suicide machine.

This world may be described as "one dimensional," in Herbert Marcuse's sense, as there is no autonomous realm of utopian fantasy or critical resistance that can oppose it. If negation is to gain a foothold within it, it will only be on one condition: that it extend its repetitions, doubling them in a serial structure where destruction appears as the equivalent of reproduction. Whence the great irony of the film, touched upon earlier: the preparation and enactment of the suicide itself are composed by analogous series—disposing of the property, flushing the money, breaking the consumer goods—which are at once the continuation and the inversion of the first, as all the series, converging at the point of death, collapse into one another.

And so it is in Haneke's early films—in each, there is a fatal event upon which all the series constitutive of its world converge. Such a violent event, even as it negates that world, is also the supreme expression of its closure. For it confronts us with the inexorability of its series' repetitions and the apparent impossibility of imagining anything beyond them. It occupies the point where the overdetermination of their repetitions appears as necessity. This means, first, that the cause of the event cannot ultimately be attributed to a single term (the killer) or to a quality in which all the elements of the whole participate (the violence inherent in the media). On the contrary, in the fatal event, its constituent series appear as elements determined by a structure. In Haneke, that event becomes the form of appearance (in Althusserian language) of "the determination of the elements of a whole by the structure of the whole."[9] This aesthetic effect of "structural causality" is all the more powerful the more these series proliferate, and the more their difference or distance from one another (in geographical, social, or affective terms) is accentuated, provided that the necessity of the relationship between these distinct strands can still be convincingly maintained.

It is in this light that the role of media images in Haneke's early films is best understood. Such images mediate between a structure composed of relatively autonomous series on the one hand and the fatal necessity of their relation on the other. For such images have the virtue of traversing the greatest possible spatial distances across their repetitions, as when, in *71 Fragments,* they bring the series of images of war in Kosovo into contact with those of random killings in an Austrian bank. And if Haneke's use of such media images emphasizes the incommensurability among series—for the "here" of television news seen on the screen is always incommensurate with the "elsewhere" of its representations of war—it also renders visible how these incommensurate series relate to one another within a single global system.

Such images can also serve to encompass the greatest possible affective difference, between the automatism of acts—like those by which a pig and a girl are killed by the same gun in *Benny's Video*—and the repeated screenings of those same acts by viewers who alone can extract from their displaced repetitions their potential affective power. The immediate effect of a series of gestures composing a criminal act before the camera is thus shown to be incommensurate with its delayed effects on a series of such viewers. We shall explore, in our discussion of *Code Unknown,* how the displacement of affect, even as it establishes the relationship between series, can also serve to underscore the impossibility of grasping the full significance of the event in any one of its iterations (as the affect produced in one series finds expression only in another). But in *Benny's Video,* as in *71 Fragments,* these series ultimately converge. Benny's parents—having experienced, as viewers of the video of the girl's killing, the horror of a crime in which they had no immediate involvement—are themselves fatally drawn by their viewing into a machinery of surveillance and criminality, which far exceeds the import of a single act of violence. We get a sense of the complexity of this machinery when we see, along with the police and Benny himself, the tape of the empty bedroom from which the parents' voices can be heard from the next room, reasonably discussing the gruesome dismemberment of the girl's corpse by which they will cover up the crime. This effect is only intensified when, at the film's conclusion, we find ourselves viewing the parents' arrival at the police station—along with Benny's departure—on a surveillance monitor.

What is at stake in this narrative is not an opposition of the reality of acts to the representational fictions of media images, whether "live" or "recorded." For while the series of acts and the series of viewings are incommensurate with each other, they are also mutually implicated in a complex apparatus where each member of a series of viewers (Benny, the mother, the father, and the police) finds him or herself in a different relation to the image of an act. But each viewing also leads to yet another act (murder, cover-up, surrender) that is recorded in its turn. As we move between these series, the criminal act retrospectively appears less contingent, more comprehensible as part of an inexorable progression. What had seemed most perverse and inexplicable in the original passage from spectatorship (the video of the pig's slaughter) to the act (Benny's murder of the girl) becomes inevitable when it is elaborated in the calculated actions of the parents, whose very reasonableness generates a horror of its own. By the time we see the documentation of the parents' crime by the police, culminating in their surrender at the station (as seen through the indifferent eye of the surveillance camera), both the glacial regularities of bourgeois life and the acts of violence that only seem to interrupt them appear equally enveloped in the regularities of social surveillance in which such anomalies are regular enough to also have their place.

Such is Haneke's first serial method, which elaborates a realism of convergent series. It first breaks down the domains of social practice (including the creation, circulation, and viewing of media images) into its constituent series of repetitions. Then it shows how these distinct series converge with one another, producing, through the repetition of apparently contingent and incommensurate elements, a graspable image of the social totality as a structure of repetitions. In the image of the act of violence, this system of social relations appears as a fatal necessity, through which the structure proclaims its determination of its elements. It is thus that the films of Haneke's glaciation trilogy achieve their grim perfection.

## Code Unknown: *Divergent Series in the Global System*

Haneke's reinvention of serial realism, in *Code Unknown: Incomplete Tales of Several Journeys* and *Caché*, depends on his willingness to sacrifice this apparent perfection, along with its effect of totality. Indeed, *Code Unknown* turns the narrative strategy of *71 Fragments*—where, through the violent act, divergent series converge—on its head. In *Code Unknown,* the pivotal event—the brief interracial scuffle between a young black man (Amadou) and a young white man (Jean) over the latter's mistreatment of a Romanian panhandler (Maria), ironically leading to Amadou's arrest and to Maria's deportation—is neither necessary nor climactic. Inconclusive in itself, its parallel worlds do not converge upon a common fate. On the contrary, if the random encounter at the beginning of *Code Unknown* initially brings its narrative strands together, the fates of their various protagonists will be determined by the disjunction among divergent series circulating in a global system.

To be sure, this event brings together on one Parisian street representatives of a number of social groups: Amadou, a young teacher and the assimilated child of African immigrants who—due to his race but also to his indignation at an injustice—is criminalized by the authorities; Maria, who, having left post-Communist Romania, fails to fulfill the dream of prosperity in the Parisian metropole but will nonetheless return to it; Jean, the drifting son who has as yet found no alternative to a hopeless life of isolation and economic hardship with his father on a dying family farm; and, finally, Jean's brother Georges, a photojournalist covering the disasters of a European war, and his partner, Anne, a sympathetic and emotive actress.

But what is missing from the parallel narratives of this collection of "outsiders" of French society is, as the title suggests, the "code" in terms of which they might be interpreted as telling a single, global story, rather than an "incomplete story" of disconnected voyages. Indeed, Haneke makes the absence of such a code felt in the narrative of each individual—and thus shows how each story is incomplete, not only as an image of the social whole, but even in its own terms, as the story of a single character. For it is precisely the inability of Haneke's characters to "transcode" (to borrow Fredric Jameson's term) between the symbolic forms governing distinct series of social practices that shapes their fate more than any material obstacle.

We see this first in the failures of Haneke's characters to master the codes that would allow them to pass among subsystems in global space. In *Code Unknown,* the distance between Romania and Paris is not significantly greater than that separating Paris from rural France, provided that the traveler has the requisite cultural capital to move between them. But a character's ignorance of even the most trivial of codes can make the smallest distance insurmountable. Thus, if Haneke begins the action of the film with Jean's otherwise trivial failure to escape the street to Anne's apartment because of a change in her security code, it is to foreground how access to codes of various sorts serves as a proxy for social differentiation. Whence the apparently privileged position of Georges relative to Maria and Jean, who move fruitlessly between the metropolis and its internal or external peripheries, and from manual labor to unemployment, without ever cracking the codes that would allow them to escape from the series of repetitions to which they are seemingly condemned. For Georges, like the "symbolic analysts" celebrated by Robert Reich, is sufficiently adept at switching between codes to profit from his ability to negotiate the passage from one subsystem to another.

From this perspective, one might expect Georges to play a key role in mediating between the incommensurate worlds that compose the global system. But the value of the knowledge accumulated by Georges, in his own repeated journeys between periphery and center, is limited by his incapacity to express what he has experienced. "I tried writing you several times, but I gave up," he acknowledges in voice-over as we see photographs of war from the former Yugoslavia: "I didn't know what to say." Indeed, despite Georges's insistence to his insulated Parisian friends that, for him, war is "lived experience" (*l'expérience vécue*) and not merely theory, the photographs he sends do not communicate his experience of war as affectively lived to a peaceful France. On the contrary, the series of individually shocking images composes, in the aggregate, a general equivalent of war, in which each image of disaster is, as Georges's friend Francine suggests, exchangeable for all the others. No doubt what might be viewed, from the perspective of classical realism, as Georges's representational failure—his apparent inability to integrate the affective reality of his individual experience as a witness of war into the images he circulates—is not the fault of Georges as an individual but of the codes of journalism as an institutional practice. But it is perhaps for that very reason that this unexpressed affective reality is expressed indirectly in his nominally private life with Anne in Paris. It is, in any case, in this direction we are led by Georges's remarks on the crunch of adjusting to each return to "civilization"—a difficulty in shifting between zones of the global system that returns, with all the force of a repressed symptom, only after a delay. The intensity of his conflicts with Anne thus appears as a symptom of his incapacity to integrate the affective charge of the collective disasters he has witnessed into a coherent individual narrative, let alone a global one.

The subject of Georges's conflict with Anne—her indecisive response to the cries of the girl she has heard from a neighboring apartment, who dies later in the film—reverses this representational problem. For the circumstances of the girl's life and death will remain, to the end, unrepresented, unfolding in an out-of-field accessible to Anne (and to us) only through her cries, whose affective power is, however, only magnified by their passage from one closed space to another, without any further communication. Yet Anne herself performs an analogous affect earlier in the film. In an audition, her character, like the girl imprisoned in the family cell, is cut off from the world by her killer and is obliged to display before the camera's gaze the disbelief, terror, isolation, and powerlessness before her tormentors that presumably informed the cries of the girl herself. Anne exhibits here, as in the other performances interspersed with her story, a power to be affected that eludes Georges. This series of pure affects, performed by the actress as professional demonstrations of her expressive power, are among the most memorable moments in *Code Unknown*. But whereas Georges represents social actuality without working through its affects, in Anne's performances such affects appear only as theatrical effects, as staged emotions, unanchored in the narrative representation of any social cause.

Georges and Anne thus confront, from opposite poles, the severing of the representation of social actuality from the affective power that might otherwise permit it to be imagined (in Georges's language) as someone's "lived experience." In this, each may be productively read as exemplary of two opposing perspectives on the role of affect in postmodernity. Georges, the journalist who traffics in images of war, takes professional pride in the unflappable cool with which he transforms the disasters he photographs into commodified images. In his apparent insusceptibility to the negative affects that might once have been considered indissociable from the experience of war, Georges seems to exemplify the "waning of affect" that Fredric Jameson associates with the devalorization of subjective interiority (and even of individual experience as such) in the postmodern culture of the serial image.[10] In light of Siane Ngai's recent work, on the other hand, Haneke's foregrounding of Anne's admittedly fragmentary and isolated stagings of emotion invites us to reconsider the aesthetic and political role such "ugly feelings" might continue to play in the postmodern context, albeit in a strangely autonomous and impersonal form. For in the brief audition we have discussed, a henceforth unanchored and unattributable negative affect, divorced from the immediate experiential world of the subject who falls prey to it, not only recovers something of its former critical power of negation but also makes felt the potentiality for an as-yet-inactual collectivity that seems on the point of emerging between noncommunicating worlds. Indeed, the paradox of Anne's performance is that she is able to express the affective reality of the young girl's world, even though she is incapable of representing or imagining it, much less acting upon it.

But if Haneke might seem to stage a conflict between two opposing perspectives on the potential role of affect in postmodern culture, *Code Unknown* does not so much ask us to decide between them as it obliges us to reframe their opposition as the effect of a division of cultural labor. For if the conflict of this couple permits Haneke to stage the decoupling of images of actuality from expressions of affective experience, it is due less to the philosophical positions or psychological limits of the characters than to their respective tasks as professionals of communication: for just as it is Georges's task as a journalist to produce images representing social actuality, it is Anne's job as an actress to stage affective performances.[11]

This suggests, first of all, that each of these opposing claims has its own local truth, as the product of a distinct sphere of social practice. But each will also ultimately be revealed to be inadequate to the task of representing social experience by its incapacity to reconcile the image of social life that it produces with that produced by the other. In this light, we could see the failure of Georges and Anne to find the "unknown code" that would permit affect to be expressed within representations of social actuality as homologous to the failure of Jean and Marie to translate the experience accumulated in one zone of the global system into the language, or constitutive series, of another. Indeed, both failures seemingly confront us with the problem of narrating or imagining the divergent series of social practices (including those of communication) constitutive of the system considered as a totality, without diminishing the extent to which that totality is composed, precisely, of such divergences.

As we have seen, *71 Fragments* proposes its own solution to the problem of relating noncommunicating series, as these series converge in the act of the killer. This convergence appears only as grim necessity, in the violence through which the structure demonstrates the subordination of its elements. But the opening image of *Code Unknown* offers a contrasting emblematic figure, which serves to emphasize the interpretive and narrative dilemmas raised by divergent series considered in their distance from and incommensurability with one another—that is, in the absence of a common code.

This first image is that of a young girl alone before a wall, toward which she slowly sidles away from the camera until, having reached the wall and with nowhere left to go, she gradually sinks, in apparent fear, into a protective crouch. This image initially appears, like Anne's auditions, as the expression of a pure affect, unanchored in any narrative world that might account for it, as isolated as is the girl herself exposed before our gaze. The subsequent contextualization of her gestures—as students in a school for the deaf offer a series of interpretations ("Alone?" "Hiding place?" "Gangster?" "Bad conscience?" "Sad?") of what we learn was the girl's staging of this affect for a sort of guessing game—does not so much resolve its enigma as thematize the difficulty of situating the expression of this deterritorialized affect in a narrative world that might permit us to decode its significance. This difficulty is underscored by the appearance of the film's title—*Code Unknown*—before the children have arrived at a solution.

It is only later that we will come to realize that this performance is only the first, along with Anne's, of a series of such free-floating affects staged in the film, which pass among the subsystems of a fragmented totality without our being able to fully account for their appearance or to decode the precise nature of their message. To be sure, this image is further situated later as an element of the cultural practices of what turns out to be an identifiable subculture—that of the school for the deaf, where Amadou's sister appears with the other children and Amadou himself in a school performance. But this contextualization of the image as a mere performance does not in any way diminish its affective power, which is further deepened if we read it retrospectively as a more immediate expression of the unseen world of the abused girl than that created later by Anne's audition. Indeed, the "explanation" of this image in terms of one localizable narrative series (the social world of the deaf children) makes it all the more striking that it can nonetheless function as the displaced repetition of an affect belonging to another, seemingly unrelated, world: the unrepresented world of the dead girl.

But even as this affect that passes among social subsystems compels us to seek out the underlying structure or code that might have made its displaced expression possible, *Code Unknown* never provides us with the key to break that code. On the contrary, the urgency with which the displaced affect calls upon us to relate the parallel worlds of a serial social space to one another only renders more intense our experience of the insuperable distance between them. Thus, unlike Haneke's earlier films, *Code Unknown* resists solving the representational problem of relating divergent series and the worlds they constitute through the image of a violent event by which those series are made to converge, as it were, by force. For here, Haneke's emphasis is no longer on effects of totality, where the convergence of parallel series makes visible their fatal interrelation as moments of an overarching structure. On the contrary, this second form of serial realism—which resonates with Jameson's notion of "cognitive mapping"—is an attempt to imagine, through the interweaving of divergent series, the relations between the multiple codes and subsystems among which we pass (or fail to pass) in negotiating our place within the global system.[12] But in its insistence upon the failure to find a common code, Haneke's realism of divergent series also reminds us of the necessarily fragmentary and provisional character of such mapping, which can be pursued only by holding the image of totality at a distance. Displaced affect thus has a contradictory meaning in *Code Unknown,* where it is not only a psychological and social "theme" but also a formal device that brings its disparate series into relation. For it appears in this film at once as the form of expression that compels us to experience the passage between noncommunicating social worlds and as a symptom of our incapacity to imagine or narrate that passage.

## Caché: *Memories of Seriality*

*Caché* pursues an alternative narrative strategy, which at first seems to abandon realism for the psychological thriller. The film begins with the mystery of who is terrorizing yet another Georges and Anne (characters in Haneke, as in Beckett, being serial) by anonymously depositing a series of videotapes and drawings at their doorstep. This raises the deeper mystery of repressed memories of Georges's own bourgeois childhood—which "return" only in glimpses over the course of the film, in rapid flashbacks and dream-sequences, but to which those tapes and images presumably lead, like so many clues. At this psychological level, the film centers on Georges's unacknowledged feelings of guilt for the expulsion from Georges's bourgeois family of his foster brother and rival, the Algerian boy Majid, who, as an adult, is the first suspected author of the tapes.

This psychological focus gives Haneke the freedom to portray Majid's expulsion, without regard for verisimilitude or plausibility, in fantasmatic images of identification and separation, in which we sometimes see Majid as an abject but frightening victim, coughing up a vivid stream of blood, and sometimes as an aggressor who, still besmirched with the blood of the rooster he decapitates, menacingly approaches his next potential victim, Georges. Meanwhile, allusions to the fate of Majid's parents—Algerians working in Georges's household who never returned from the demonstration of October 17, 1961, many Algerian protestors were killed by police in the heart of Paris—also invite us to read these fantasy images as mythic figurations of a collective trauma: as emblems of a common wound linking the Algerians and the French, each of whom perhaps unconsciously imagines the other as an unacknowledged *frère ennemi*.

The juxtaposition of these two stories—one individual and one collective—thus confronts us with two "codes" in terms of which to read the film, although the first seems unsatisfactory from the outset. In itself, a *conte moral* concerning guilt for a real or imagined childhood crime—a shopworn formula inherited from the middlebrow psychoanalytic culture of the 1950s and 1960s—is unlikely to provide some new and unexpected psychological truth.[13] But the story's historical frame, by portraying Georges's apparently private memories as inseparable from a collective fantasy, offers richer interpretive possibilities. Georges, with all his privileges, imagines his own individual destiny, through a familiar mechanism of projection, as having its origins in a traumatic wound inflicted by a vengeful representative of an oppressed social group. If Georges imagines himself to be Majid's victim, as both a child and an adult, it is thus not *despite* his privilege as the son of a French bourgeois family but *because* of it. For it is only through a fantasy narrative of supposedly inexplicable *ressentiment* (of the "Why do they hate us?" variety) that Georges can legitimize his individual position against a representative of social and historical forces that appear to menace that position. Majid's dramatic suicide—in which, after luring Georges to his miserable apartment, he cuts his own throat before the eyes of his childhood rival—would thus seem at once to confirm Georges's fantasy (since it repeats its structure, as a theatrical confrontation of victimizer and victim) and to contest it (since Majid can be seen as assuming the role of Georges's victim, rather than, as Georges would prefer to represent things, the other way around).

Haneke himself has suggested that this reinscription of Georges's private memories of childhood trauma within the larger history of French colonialism is, in part, intended to raise questions concerning the repression by the French nation as a whole of its memories of the crimes of French colonialism.[14] But by representing that history solely in psychological terms, as an imaginary rivalry, *Caché* also risks imposing the forms of individual fantasy upon a political and historical content to which it will remain inadequate. Political questions concerning collective practices that exceed the scope of any individual consciousness would, in this light, seem to be rewritten as psychological and moral ones, as each victim claims to have been more gravely or unjustly traumatized by the other. Thus the question of responsibility comes to be posed in terms of mutual accusations of hostile intent, rather than structural forms of social and political practice.

But all this looks rather different if we approach Georges's fantasmatic narrative not primarily as the "return" of a repressed memory from the past, whether individual or collective, but as a narrative strategy that makes it possible for Haneke to address, through nonrealist means, the problem of representing the present. At the level of social content, Georges's investigation of the origins of the videos he receives serves as the narrative pretext for our movement through the parallel social worlds of both a remembered and a contemporary France. Most strikingly, we move between the privileged stratum to which *Caché*'s Georges and Anne belong and the working-class immigrant milieu inhabited by Majid and his son—a movement recalling Haneke's juxtaposition of the circuits traveled by Jean and Marie with that of Georges and Anne in *Code Unknown*.

But whereas *Code Unknown* could provide no figure or code through which to translate between its divergent series, in *Caché*, the separation between social spaces appears, through the lens of Georges's and Majid's remembered or imagined scenes of rivalry, as the effect of a single originary event of bifurcation. It is as if everything that distinguished the parallel lives of these individuals from each other, in all the myriad differences that distinguish the group identities and forms of life that shape them, could be traced back to an event they are fated forever to repeat. From this perspective, the moral distinctions one might draw in comparing the different versions of this shared scene of rivalry—in which, as we have seen, each in turn aggressively assumes the role of the other's victim—would matter less than the fact that the imagined or remembered scene of origins conjures up the image of a moment in which those noncommunicating series were interwoven with one another, without being reducible to one another.

If this is no longer realism, it is because Haneke, instead of attempting to represent the contemporary world, has invented a fictive point at which its divergent series appear to overlap, and from which their continuing separation in the actual historical world seems to derive. On a narrative level, the noncommunicating worlds of the two antagonists mirror each other at a distance, as the "same" remembered event is repeated on either side of the social and historical divide, thereby making each appear as a virtual double or transformation of the other. But this overlapping is also dramatized in the visual field from the first shot of the film, although we will only learn its significance later.

The long take with which the film begins initially seems to show us Georges and Anne's home from the outside, until we come to realize we have been watching with them in the interior of that home as they screen a video presumably shot earlier by the anonymous stalker. The viewer is thus confronted with the impossibility of saying whether this banal image, which represents no event beyond the series of comings and goings of Georges's and Anne's daily routines, should be viewed primarily as the object of their present contemplation in the interior or as the video memory of a point of view surveilling that interior from the outside. By introducing the mystery of the stalker's identity (which the film, hesitating between Majid and his son as the principal suspects, never definitively resolves) in this way, through the indiscernibility of outside and inside in the image, Haneke indissolubly links this enigma to the deeper mystery of the perspective differentiating the stalker's point of view from theirs. For whom, after all, might the banal routines of this successful but uninteresting couple seem worth recording in the first place? From what angle could these uneventful routines be an object of interest or desire, worthy of being memorialized in an image to be circulated, viewed, and replayed?

The story of Georges and Majid provides a fictive memory, which accounts, in narrative terms, for the persistence of this otherwise incomprehensible interest. Majid's grievance against Georges retrospectively justifies the superimposition of these incommensurate perspectives within a single shot, which is, in light of that narrative, made to oscillate between inside and outside, between present and past.[15] For what had appeared as most trivial from within the frame of Georges's interior takes on a new significance from this perspective that has, with the arrival of its videotaped image, insinuated itself within that interior as the memory of the life it contains as seen from without: as the image of a form of life that, were it not for the mythic event of their separation, could have been Majid's. And if this narrative obliges Haneke to transgress the limits of realism and pass, by way of the psychological thriller, into the realm of myth (where the origin of the difference between the noncommunicating worlds that constitute a serial society is attributed to a memory of imaginary identification, projection, and *ressentiment*), this concession must be weighed against the new effects generated by the supplementary fiction that this permits: the fiction of a series of video images that circulate, as the elements of an ultimately unattributable memory, not only between the two protagonists but between the incompossible worlds that they inhabit.

For that fiction shows us, in the serial images of the present, something more than the divergence between actually existing social worlds, but also something different, within those distinct worlds, from the mythic repetition of a traumatic past common to them both. For in imagining the emergence of a memory of the present that encompasses both of those worlds in their very separation, it creates the retrospective possibility of a passage between them. Such a passage is accessible from neither world considered as a social space, to which each character is limited in the historical (and biographical) present. But it is rendered possible in time, through the movement of a video memory that at once exceeds and envelops them both.

This is already true of images like those in the videotaped sequence of the country estate, evoking the divergent childhood memories shared from different points of view by the two individual antagonists. But it is still more powerfully the case with others—like the first shot of Georges's home or its counterpart, the mysterious images of the hallway of Majid's housing project, whose itinerary Georges, having seen these "remembered" images from Majid's life, will "revisit" in his own present—where the image "remembered" in one world becomes indiscernible from the image of the present in the other. With such images, we discover a third type of series in Haneke: it is no longer a matter of convergent series, which produce the effect of the social totality, nor of divergent series, which measure the distances between the unknotted strands of a decentered sociality. Here we discover overlapping series, where the same element or image, as it is repeated from one world to the next, appears as the memory of the one in the other. If the relationships among series elsewhere in Haneke are imagined predominantly in spatial terms—as the convergence of different domains of social practice or the divergence among different circuits in the global system—this third type of series makes a place for the time-image in his work, producing, in Gilles Deleuze's formulation, the effects of a "non-chronological time," where the past coexists with the present, like two points of view condensed into a single shot.[16] In the overlapping circuit of such a video image, each form of life coexists with a memory that doubles it, creating a virtual passage between its isolated space and, in Deleuze's evocative phrase, a "world memory," where the points of view of Georges and Majid, having been unanchored from their individual bearers, pass into one another.[17]

It is entirely characteristic of Haneke's work that its most potentially utopian fiction—a transpersonal video memory, unattributable to any actually existing individual or collective subject—appears primarily as the resolution of a problem of realism: the representation of a fragmented social space. But it is this fiction that permits *Caché* to "solve" the ultimate mystery rightly posed as unresolvable by *Code Unknown:* the coexistence of a multiplicity of worlds within the same social system, without a common code or point of view from which to represent that system as a whole. If *Caché* succeeds where *Code Unknown* does not, in producing something like the fantasmatic equivalent of that fragmented whole, it is because in its attempt to represent the reality of postmodernity, it is willing to move beyond the limits of realism itself. Thus *Caché* creates a fictive memory for a society incapable of representing its own present. But, in so doing, it not only elaborates a mythic narrative of the historical divisions that constitute that society. It also makes a place, within the limits of postmodern sociality, for the point of view of a collectivity that it is not yet capable of imagining.

## Notes

1. Michael Haneke quoted in Christopher Sharrett, "The World That Is Known: An Interview with Michael Haneke," *Cineaste* 28, no. 3 (2003): 29.

2. See the series of 2005 interviews with Serge Toubiana on the DVDs of Haneke's films (each henceforth referenced as Toubiana, interview, followed by the name of the film with which it appears), where Haneke argues that the "mainstream" media render violence "consumable" (Toubiana, interview, *71 Fragments of a Chro-*

*nology of Chance*) and that pop-psychological and pop-sociological "explanation" serves primarily to "reassure" and "calm" the viewer (Toubiana, interview, *Benny's Video*).

3. See Mattias Frey's overview of Haneke's career at Senses of Cinema, www.sensesofcinema.com/contents/directors/03/haneke.html (accessed December 18, 2007).

4. See Brian Price, "Pain and the Limits of Representation," *Framework: The Journal of Cinema and Media* 47, no. 2 (2006): 22–29.

5. Haneke characterizes the logic of this repetition in the following terms: "They carry out the destruction with the same constricted narrowness with which they lived their lives, with the same meticulousness as life was lived. . . . The sequence is portrayed as work." Quoted in Sharrett, "World That Is Known," 30.

6. Haneke is here referring to the formal structure of *Code Unknown*. Cited in Nick James, "Code Uncracked," *Sight and Sound* 11, no. 6 (2001): 8.

7. Haneke himself speaks of Brechtian "alienation" in this scene: the happy ending's disappearance with the film's rewinding—in showing the spectator "how easily he or she can be manipulated" (Toubiana, interview, *Funny Games*, translation modified)—would presumably be Haneke's answer to Brecht's subversion of our relief when the royal messenger saves the day in *The Threepenny Opera*, with Peachum's observation that "saviors on horseback are seldom met with in practice." Bertolt Brecht, *The Threepenny Opera*, trans. John Willet and Ralph Mannheim (New York: Arcade Publishing, 1994), 79.

8. Toubiana, interview, *Funny Games*.

9. Louis Althusser and Étienne Balibar, *Reading Capital*, trans. Ben Brewster (London: Verso, 1979), 187.

10. With the emergence of a postmodern culture of the simulacrum, Jameson has suggested, the anguish expressed in the cry of protest of the alienated subject of modernism against degraded or inauthentic experience gives way to an often euphoric investment in the circulation of serial images as such—images unanchored from the existential situation that gave rise to them and that thus can no longer claim to represent any subject's experience. See Fredric Jameson, *Postmodernism, or the Cultural Logic of Late Capitalism* (Durham: Duke University Press, 1991), 10–16. As Sianne Ngai has remarked, it is the loss of the critical power of "negative affect, in particular" that Jameson emphasizes here, whose force of negation is closely associated in Jameson's view with the anxieties of the alienated but "centered subject" of high modernism (whose disappearance coincides, in his account, with the declining importance of anxiety and alienation, both as critical concepts and as experiences). See Ngai, *Ugly Feelings* (Cambridge: Harvard University Press, 2005), 285.

11. For one analysis of the place of "affective labor" in postmodernity, see Michael Hardt, "Affective Labor," *boundary 2* 26, no. 2 (1999): 89–100, where it is placed alongside the "other face" of "communicational and immaterial labor": the "symbol manipulation" foregrounded by Reich (95).

12. See Fredric Jameson, *The Geopolitical Aesthetic: Cinema and Space in the World System* (Bloomington: Indiana University Press, 1992).

13. Toubiana, interview, *Caché*.

14. See Richard Porton, "Collective Guilt and Individual Responsibility: An In-

terview with Michael Haneke," *Cineaste* 31, no. 1 (2005): 50.

15. On this "image-intrus," see Taieb Berrada, "L'Intrus postcolonial maghrébin dans la littérature, le cinéma et la bande dessinée francophones" (PhD diss., Northwestern University, 2007).

16. Gilles Deleuze, *Cinema 2: The Time-Image,* trans. Hugh Tomlinson and Robert Galeta (Minneapolis: University of Minnesota Press, 1991), 99.

17. Ibid., 98.

*Caché* (2005): Hygiene and responsibility.

Patrick Crowley

# When Forgetting Is Remembering
Haneke's *Caché* and the Events of October 17, 1961

*Caché* is and is not a film about the events that occurred in Paris in October 17, 1961, when scores of Algerians were killed by police officers and auxiliaries.[1] Within the film, Georges's single reference to the events surfaces to provide a rare unambiguous narrative before receding like previous attempts to bring this obscured event to the light of public history. It is this dynamic of remembering and forgetting and its relationship to guilt that I want to examine in my reading of *Caché*.

In an interview conducted with Michael Haneke for the Austrian Film Commission, Karin Schiefer notes that "the war in Algeria, though mentioned only briefly, plays an important role in the conflict depicted in *Caché*." She goes on to ask whether Haneke meant this to be "a reference to a sore spot in French history which isn't discussed." Haneke's reply raises the matted issues of aesthetics and politics:

I don't want to call too much attention to this issue, because I don't want the film to be regarded primarily in that light at Cannes. It's only an element which supplies a framework. During preparations before shooting *Caché* I learned about this massacre in a documentary on Arte, it took place in Paris in 1961, and about 200 Arabs were shot or thrown into the Seine, and it wasn't mentioned for four decades. I made use of this incident because it fits in a horrible way. You could find a similar story in any country, even though it took place at a different time. There's always a collective guilt which can be connected to a personal story, and that's how I want this film to be understood.[2]

Haneke acknowledges that the events of October 17, 1961, offered a "fit" for the kinds of ideas he was exploring, but he also makes clear his desire for critics to move from the context of a particular event in French history and to focus instead upon an aesthetic structure, an allegory, that figures the wider notion of collective guilt. The event, the massacre of unarmed civilians, is to function as a "framework," to be forgotten in a sense, within a film that pursues Haneke's engagement with history through the production of an aesthetic form that enacts the dynamics of memory and forgetting and their implications for the present.

Haneke's interest in repressed memory goes back at least to *Benny's Video* (1992), but paradoxically, in returning to this theme through a specific historical event, the question is raised as to whether the event, in being reduced to a device, is not quickly forgotten once its function has been exhausted. One way of examining the relationship between event and its aesthetic appropriation is to rethink the relationship between historical event and its aesthetic configuration within the terms of a Hegelian *aufhebung* (sublation) where the element (in this case the historical event) is lifted to another (aesthetic) level that, paradoxically, both preserves and changes it. I want to pursue this idea of the sublated event throughout what follows.

Paul Gilroy's comment that Haneke's "overly casual citation of the 1961 anti-Arab pogrom by [Maurice] Papon's police in Paris" seems almost to find its confirmation in Haneke's view of the events as a suitable "framework." Gilroy raises the stakes beyond aesthetic success by writing that "many people involved in building a habitable multicultural Europe will feel that there are pressing issues of morality and responsibility involved in raising that history [October 17, 1961] only to reduce it to nothing more than a piece of tragic machinery in the fatal antagonism that undoes *Caché*'s protagonists. The dead deserve better than that passing acknowledgement."[3] Here Gilroy privileges morality and responsibility over Haneke's aesthetic choices. But this reading runs against the grain of *Caché*'s allegorical portrayal of guilt. Despite Haneke's comments on the need not to concentrate on the specific events of 1961, *Caché* critically raises the questions that determine the ground of Gilroy's critique.

In his interview with Schiefer, Haneke makes reference to a documentary that provided a "fit" for this representation of collective guilt. The documentary, broadcast on October 17, 2001, by the Franco-German channel, was *Drowning by Bullets* (*Une journée portée disparue*, Philip Brooks and Alan Hayling, 1992).[4] On the same day that Arte broadcast the documentary, the left-wing newspaper *L'Humanité* published the results of a CSA (Conseil Supérieur de l'Audiovisuel) opinion poll that revealed that a majority of the French public was unaware of the events. Less than one in two had heard of the police massacre. It was an event that had yet to be written into France's national narrative. Within the documentary, the voice-over comments that many French found it hard to believe in the reports of police killings because there were no images to substantiate the claims. In the absence of such images and in the face of official denials, many allowed the events to slip away from the concerns of the present. Nevertheless, the memory of what had happened was sustained by a minority that included survivors and left-wing activists, as well as immigrant and antiracist groups.[5] Brooks and Hayling's documentary was an attempt to rectify the absence of images of the events by including Eli Kagan's photographs of Algerians, which he had taken that night shortly after the police attacks, as well as a range of interviews with eyewitnesses and archival material. In this way *Drowning by Bullets* can be situated as part of a process of anamnesis operating within a general structure of (post/colonial) remembering and forgetting. *Caché* encodes this process as it traces the issue of guilt, but *Caché* is also subject to that same structural and allusive play of memory. Even as the film evokes the events of October 17, it contributes to their "forgetting" by folding the events into a signifying structure that is built upon, and entombs, those same events.

Haneke's *Caché* draws on a specific event but can also be situated within a filmic genealogy that has also engaged with that same event. *Drowning by Bullets*, for example, includes clips from two films that either directly or indirectly addressed the events and their context. The first was *Octobre à Paris* (*October in Paris*, 1961), directed by Maurice Panijel. The second was Chris Marker's *Joli mai* (*Lovely May*, 1962). Panijel's film is an effort to draw direct attention to what was a police cover-up. The film begins with reconstructions of the FLN preparations for the march and shows scenes of daily life in the Algerian shantytowns that lay beyond the center of Paris, such as Gennevilliers. This activist reconstruction drew upon the support of FLN activists and supporters who had participated in the march. Panijel's camera revisits the places where Algerians were struck down and thrown into the river Seine and into the St. Martin Canal, where bodies were found in the days following the massacre. The film was confiscated by police and has never been shown on French television. To some extent the subversive force of *Octobre à Paris* resides in its lack of diffusion and its status as an object informed by contestation.[6]

There are fewer images from Chris Marker's *Joli mai* in *Drowning by*

*Bullets,* and those that do appear are largely taken from Marker's lyrical opening shots of Paris. Nonetheless, these images and the references to Marker's *Joli mai* in the credits are invitations to return to Marker's project, which, in many ways, returns us to Haneke's concern with collective guilt and the individual forms of its manifestation. After the lyrical opening, the images of *Joli mai* are sober, grainy, filmed with a light camera, and can be situated within the cinéma vérité techniques of the period.[7] After the initial titles, we learn that "la scène se passe au mois de mai 1962, désigné par certains comme le premier printemps de la paix" (the scenes take place in May 1962, considered by some to be the first spring of peace).[8] In the streets, suburbs, and public spaces of Paris, Marker interviews Parisians about their present circumstances and the concerns of the moment. Marker prompts his subjects, sometimes provokes them, and at times sets them up, but underlying much of what is said is the unsaid of the Algerian war, which is only indirectly referenced. In this, *Joli mai* emblematically captures France at the end of the Algerian war, the coverage of which had been censured by the government and pushed toward the margins of everyday life by an ever-accelerating consumerist modernity. Within the public sphere the war was already almost forgotten. Though this dimension of Marker's film is not conveyed in *Drowning by Bullets,* Brooks and Hayling include an interview with Panijel that forms the penultimate scene of the documentary. Commenting on the silence surrounding the massacre of October 17, 1961, Panijel says that, given what happened, the French government had to "étouffer, occulter, cacher, c'est tout simple" (suppress it, cover it up, hide it, it's simple really).

The French authorities did just that. They were able to "manage" the aftermath of the events of October 17, 1961, by stalling and ultimately preventing a public enquiry. In addition, access to police archives relating to the event was not permitted until May 1998, and then only to three historians. In any case, the amnesties of March 22, 1962, introduced as a result of the Evian Accords, signed by France and Algeria in 1962, brought an end to criminal investigations into the death of Algerians in October 1961. The amnesty as an official form of "forgetting" is the subject of Dimitri Nicolaïdis's volume *Oublier nos crimes. L'amnésie nationale: une spécificité française?* This is a collection of articles that deal with the use of amnesties in France since the nineteenth century; it includes an interview with the historian Benjamin Stora, a specialist of Algerian history, who makes the case that only a formal official acknowledgment of the events of October 17 will permit the wounds of the past to close and heal.[9] Official acknowledgment of the events remains limited to certain politicians on the Left. On October 17, 2001, the mayor of Paris, Bertrand Delanöe, placed a commemorative plaque on the wall of the quay that faces the Préfecture de Police beside the Pont St. Michel, where many demonstrators were truncheoned and, in some cases, thrown into the Seine. Successive attempts to suppress the historical truth have ultimately served to energize attempts to uncover what happened. It is this dynamic of occlusion and memory, premised upon relations of power, that drives Haneke's allegory. These processes are symptomatic of a guilt denied.

As *Drowning by Bullets* makes clear, and as Haneke's film repeatedly suggests, the particular events of October 17, 1961, raised further questions regarding France's Vichy past and the treatment of Jews during the Occupation. When Georges receives a call at work, we see a range of books on a shelf. The title most easily read is *La Grande histoire des Français sous l'occupation*. Written by the historian Henri Amouroux and published in 1977, it was an early attempt to come to terms with the unpalatable truths of Vichy France when collaboration with the Nazi forces of occupation was widespread.[10] This clear reference to Vichy France, to a period that France slowly began to come to terms with in the 1970s, signifies that more general structure of guilt to which Haneke makes reference but also offers a further link to the events of October 17, 1961, through the figure of Papon.

## *Multidirectional Memory*

Papon was prefect (head) of the Paris police in 1961. From 1942 to 1945, he was also general secretary of the Gironde in Bordeaux, where he directed the Service des questions juives, responsible for the arrest and deportation of thousands of Jews. Following the end of the Second World War, he was quickly integrated into the administration of the Fourth Republic and served from 1949 to 1951 as prefect of Constantine, Algeria, where torture was so widely practiced, and this before the war of independence, that the governor general, Marcel-Edmond Naegelen, and his successor, Roger Léonard, had to issue circulars condemning the practices.[11] Papon also served in Morocco before his appointment as prefect of the Paris police in 1958. Papon's active collaboration during the Second World War only came to the light of the public sphere in 1997, when he was brought to trial in Bordeaux for crimes against humanity. As such, the figure of Papon, though not mentioned within Haneke's film, provides a direct link to the deportation of Jews, to issues of torture, and to the events of October 17, 1961, and generates a further level of complexity in the construction of what Michael Rothberg has called "multidirectional memory."[12] Rothberg's study of Charlotte Delbo's work demonstrates that while her formally complex and moving accounts of her imprisonment in Auschwitz have been the subject of critical appraisal, less attention has been paid to her writings on the Algerian war published in 1961. Rothberg's treatment draws out the impact of Delbo's use of juxtapositions and re-citations to create parallels between France's war in Algeria and Holocaust memory. This forms part of what Rothberg defines as multidirectional memory: "the interference, overlap, and mutual constitution of seemingly distinct collective memories that define the postwar era and the workings of memory more generally."[13] The work of multidirectional memory takes place within the public sphere where official public memory and counterpublic testimony overlap. Rothberg brings his article to a close by drawing on a particular scene from *Caché* to illustrate his argument. The scene in question is that moment when Anne and Georges realize that Pierrot, their son, has not yet returned home and has left no message. They panic and link his disappearance to the videocassettes and drawings they presume are being sent by Majid. The background to their conversation is dominated by a large television screen framed by shelves of books, videocassettes, and DVDs that stretch from floor to ceiling, from wall to wall. Euronews is broadcasting a report from Iraq on the lack of communication between the Allies, which is followed by a piece on the trial of U.S. Army Specialist Charles Graner for his part in the torture of Abu Ghraib detainees. The final clip of news footage is of Palestinians fleeing Israeli army violence in the streets of the Occupied Territories. Rothberg stresses the "interpenetration of different frames of reference" as well as "the concatenation of media forms [that] embodies both the vexed relationship between public and private space and between everyday life and extreme violence."[14] Rothberg argues that the return of the colonial repressed finds its echoes within contemporary forms of imperialism. And *Caché* sponsors an uncertainty that keeps memory from condensing into a fixed image or from being locked into a particular moment through its generation of a network of crimes present (television images of Charles Graner relating to torture in Iraq) that echo those of the past (French collaboration with Nazi Germany).

The domestic scene of anxiety acted out against the background of world events offers further signifying possibilities. France's imperial ambitions since the nineteenth century have been underwritten by a colonial humanist vision: the *mission civilisatrice* that would bring the light of civilization to the benighted world beyond France. In the scene that depicts Georges and Anne's anxious exchange, the books, DVDs, and videocassettes form a wall that protects and provides a cocoon for bourgeois sensibilities reaffirmed by a culture that comforts their sense of humanity through its signifiers of refined thought. Georges, as a television presenter with editorial input, and Anne, as a publishing editor, are part of a system that instrumentalizes culture so that it might be more easily consumed. Georges cuts a section from his television program in which the reviewer becomes "too theoretical." In erasing literary difficulty and the resistances of theory, Georges drains literature of any residual capacity it might have to offer critique. The blank spines of the nonbooks that form the backdrop to Georges's literary program mirror the illegible titles of the books that line the walls of his study and suggest a bleached literary tradition in which contemporary writers are edited and past writers reduced to the public oblivion of streets names and school names. In another scene, we see a close-up of Pierrot's school address on the back of a postcard he receives: Collège/Lycée Stéphane Mallarmé, 11, rue Pirandello. Rather than convey the insights into humanity once expected of literature, French and European literary culture provide the backdrop to the film's foregrounding of silence, self-censorship, the inclination to edit, the repression and distortions of memory, and the constant succession of images of contemporary imperialism that move so quickly that the subject is easily forgotten, at least within the film's diegesis. Haneke's deliberate referencing of Luigi Pirandello and Stéphane Mallarmé may have been determined by the existence of a real school and street bearing these names or by a desire to set up further intertextual traces that lead to an elsewhere that leaves behind the moral imperatives suspended within *Caché*.[15] At times, Haneke saturates his scenes with narrative possibilities that jostle for the viewer's attention: when we listen to Georges and Anne anxiously discuss Pierrot's apparent disappearance, we attend to their domestic drama at the price of listening to news of the world broadcast in the background.[16] At other times, Haneke places the spectator before the tangible and simple immediacy of the referent.

## *Majid's Death*

Like the spectator in the cinema, Georges is witness to Majid's suicide. Shot in fixed frame, Georges and Majid are face to face in the living room of Majid's drab apartment. Majid cuts his own throat, and the blood spurts violently across the wall as Majid slumps to the floor. In *Drowning by Bullets*, we hear that the French refused to believe in what happened in the absence of any images.[17] In this scene, the referent is neither absent nor mediated by the image; there is the palpable presence of an other. Gilroy reads Majid's suicide as somehow indicative of Haneke's collusion with the fantasy that the "colonial native can be made to disappear in an instant through the auto-combustive agency of their [*sic*] own violence" and, as such, "Majid's suicide becomes in effect an exclusively aesthetic event devoid of all meaning apart from what it communicates about Georges." Gilroy goes further, however, and suggests that the "aesthetic event" in some way appeals to Haneke's audience "because that horrible death can represent a flowering of their own investments in the idea that Europe's immigrants should be induced to disappear by any means possible."[18] Here Gilroy has his own crabs to shoot, but if we return to Gilroy's commentary on Majid's suicide, it is clear that his objection is based, in part, on Majid's lack of psychological depth. He is reduced to being a screen onto which white European anxiety is projected. In this respect Gilroy's observation that Majid's suicide tells us more about Georges is as accurate as it is obvious: Georges is the film's subject, and what we learn about him is central to *Caché*'s unfolding. Clearly, Majid's death in no way satisfies the fantasy of the disappearing immigrant. Neither Majid, as haunting image, nor his son, as troubling reality, go away, and Georges does not return to a sanitized, urbane culture in which the unsettling presence of otherness is placed at a comfortable distance. The shock of Majid's death is at once a signature piece of Haneke's aesthetic interest in violence and also offers an experience that is neither one of trauma nor of accommodation but that returns both Georges and the viewer to the responsibility of the gaze/ *regard*. Where Georges has little difficulty in referring to the murder of two hundred Algerians by French police, an event of which he is innocent, Majid's death implicates Georges. Here Georges is directly confronted with the blood and death of the referent. Unmediated, present, and bloody, Majid's body lies before Georges. Gilroy bemoans that Georges has no opportunity to recover an innocence through (presumably political) action, yet Georges's responsibility lies in what he does next. He goes to the cinema, to the darkened room that frames his consumption of a reality through images—images like the penultimate scene that we can read as a nightmare. This scene's view from within the interior of the dark farmyard building of Georges's childhood can be mapped onto the darkened space of the cinema. The entrance to the farm building, like the cinema screen, frames the scene of the six-year-old Majid's forced removal by social welfare officials. Georges was responsible, then, for something for which he could have little understanding (Majid's future), but faced with the end of Majid's life, he chooses to attend the cinema. Later, and only after being prompted by Anne, he informs the police.

## Le pardon

The final confrontational dialogue that we witness in *Caché* takes place between Georges and Majid's son in the lavatory of a corporate building. Majid's son has already challenged Georges in the foyer, followed him into the elevator, and pursued him to the threshold of his office before Georges accepts to hear him out in this space, a space that belongs to neither the public nor the private sphere. Though the functionality of the lavatory is unambiguous, its muted, sanitized, white decor offers the mask of hygienic space that signifies modernity's combat against unwanted human waste.[19] This is where Haneke chooses to shoot the final scene of the sharp exchange between Georges and Majid's son. At one point the latter's formal French infuriates Georges, who shouts at him to stop the pretense of politeness. Mastery of the French language had been, throughout the period of the French Republican Empire, a signifier of the colonized's successful assimilation. In this scene Georges appears to interpret it as a parody of French cultivation, whereas Majid's son sees it, as would any other French citizen, as a sign of a good education—something he received from his father and that his father had been deprived of because of Georges. At this point Georges denies any responsibility for Majid's life: "You won't convince me that I should have a guilty conscience [*mauvaise conscience*] because your father's life was sad and botched up [*bousillée*]. I'm not responsible. Do you understand that?" How can a six-year-old who felt usurped by the arrival of another boy into his family be deemed responsible for the results of his actions? For Gilroy "the relationship between the colonial past to the postcolonial present is perverted and confused by the idea that today's complacent and indifferent adults bear no more responsibility for their resignation, inertia and poisonous choices than a conflicted six-year-old."[20] The thrust of Haneke's dialogue suggests that the guilt at stake is not the result of the actions of a child but rather the legacy of the mark of the past upon the present that can provoke guilt even when responsibility cannot be wholly assumed. Georges's internal drama is not really that of trauma, or of individual responsibility, but of the inheritance of a trace that is something within him for which he is not responsible but that he needs to confront. And that is just it. Georges is incapable of doing so as an adult; his reaction to Majid's death compounds the legacy of guilt. After Georges refuses to accept responsibility for Majid's wasted life, he then asks Majid's son what he wants of him. To fight him? Majid's son refuses the bait. Georges warns him not to terrorize his family again and that if he does he will deal with him. Majid's son reminds Georges, and the spectator-as-witness, that threatening people is what Georges does very well. "Well," responds Georges "what do you want me to do, ask for forgiveness?" The question could be read as both rhetorical and pragmatic. Georges, we imagine, would be happy to be freed from his sense of guilt by an apology without depth. "From whom? From me?" Majid's son replies with scorn. Georges, for a brief moment, does not know what to say. His face is blank, lost. "What more do you want to know?" he asks. To which Majid's son replies, "Actually, nothing more. I wanted to know how it felt to have a [dead] man on one's conscience. Now I know."

It is a powerful exchange and one that raises the kinds of questions that have been circulating within the French public sphere over the past decade. In some cases apologies were made that were determined by political expediency and pragmatism. In July 2005, Jacques Chirac, then the president of France, made an official visit to Madagascar, where he apologized for France's repression of the 1947 uprising that left between ninety and one hundred thousand Malagasy dead. In contrast, in December 2005 Chirac rejected calls that France formally apologize for acts of torture committed by the military during the Algerian war of independence.[21] More recently, a number of books have been published that argue against apologizing for France's colonial past.[22] When to apologize and when not to apologize can be seen as part of a geopolitics of seeking forgiveness that emerged in the late 1990s and continues into the new millennium. Majid's son's response suggests that the crimes of the past cannot be assuaged so easily. Majid is dead; to ask forgiveness of his son seems an unsatisfactory displacement, given that only Majid can forgive. And forgive what? Haneke's film offers no easy resolutions to questions and chooses instead to leave things in suspense. The final scene in which Majid's son and Pierrot converse in front of the school could be read as a scene of reconciliation or of conspiracy and threat, neither of which can be confirmed within the film or beyond it. Haneke's decision to let the questions remain suspended, raised but not answered, preserved and negated like the events of October 17, 1961, that provided a "fit" for Haneke's shaping of guilt, has provoked a reaction to *Caché* that exceeds the director's desire to downplay the specific event and has contributed to a wider debate about France's colonial past and the politics of the present.

## Conclusion

*Caché* encodes and enacts the multidirectional dynamics of memory within its representation of guilt. Guilt and the task of construing its cause and meaning are juxtaposed and left open. In creating a tension within the film, within the viewer, Haneke folds the events of October 17, 1961, into the shadows of the mind, the darkness of the farm building, and the cinema to keep them from fading within the light of history and the overexposure of culture. Haneke's film is not about the events of October 17, 1961. Rather, it puts in play the complex relationship of memory, forgetting, and guilt that revives the after-effects of those events and lifts them into a modernist aesthetic that offers new readings of the political present, itself already half-forgotten, its relationship to its past only obliquely remembered.

## Notes

1. For the most comprehensive account of the events of October 1961, the historical context, and the aftermath, see Jim House and Neil MacMaster, *Paris 1961: Algerians, State Terror, and Memory* (Oxford: Oxford University Press, 2006). In this scrupulous work of historical research and analysis, House and MacMaster address the question of how many Algerians were killed by police and auxiliaries during the night of October 17, 1961, when tens of thousands took to the streets of Paris to protest against the curfew imposed on Algerians' right to movement and assembly between 10:30 p.m. and 5:30 a.m. The initial official report listed two dead Algerians. The Algerian organizers of the march, the French wing of the FLN (Front de Libération Nationale—the principal orchestrators of the war of independence) claimed over 200 were killed. This figure was taken up by the historian Jean-Luc Einaudi. House and MacMaster, working with a complex range of archives suggest that well over 120 Algerians were killed by police in September and October of 1961. The figure for October 17 appears to be at least 30.

2. "Caché von Michael Haneke—Interview," Austrian Film Commission, www.afc.at/jart/prj3/afc/main.jart?rel=de&reserve-mode=active&content-id=1164272180506&artikel_id=13295 (accessed November 15, 2007).

3. Paul Gilroy, "Shooting Crabs in a Barrel," *Screen* 48, no. 2 (2007): 233. Gilroy's piece forms part of the "*Caché* dossier," composed of an introduction and six articles. France's colonial past in Algeria and its implications for the present are referenced in four of these articles and given explicit treatment in Gilroy's contribution

and in Max Silverman's piece, "The Empire Looks Back," *Screen* 48, no. 2 (2007): 245–49. Haneke's oblique treatment of the events has prompted much critical discussion, far more than the television docudrama *Nuit noire, 17 octobre 1961* (Alain Tasma), released in October 2005. Fully acknowledging the dead does not always have the effect that Gilroy, understandably, views as necessary. It is this paradox of acknowledgment and concealment that continues to animate debate in France. For a French reading of *Caché* from a post/colonial perspective, see Saad Chakali, "Le spectre du colonialisme, l'actualité du néocolonialisme postcolonial," www.cadrage.net/films/cache.htm (accessed December 15, 2007).

4. Produced and directed by Philip Brooks and Alan Hayling, *Drowning by Bullets* was first broadcast in the UK by Channel 4 in July 1992. In March 1993 it was broadcast in France by France-3 and again by Arte on the fortieth anniversary of the events, October 17, 2001.

5. The poll confirms Haneke's sense that there was a general silence surrounding the events for forty years but also indicates that many knew of the events. The memory of the events was maintained largely by militants, antiracist organizations, and those who experienced the events. More widespread knowledge of what happened was mediated by novels such as Daniel Daeninckx's crime novel *Meurtres pour mémoire* (1984) and Nacer Kattane's novel *Le Sourire de Brahim* (1985). Medhi Lallaoui, a son of one of the demonstrators, published a novel that indirectly drew on the events, *Les Beurs de Seine* (1986), and later produced a documentary on the events, *Le Silence du fleuve* (1992), as well as a second novel dealing directly with the events, *Une nuit d'octobre,* which was published October 17, 2001.

6. The documentary only received a *visa de censure*, allowing it to be shown to the public in 1973 after the filmmaker René Vautier went on hunger strike. No production company was inclined to distribute it until Papon's 1997 trial for crimes against humanity. However, Panijel wanted to include an epilogue that would frame the events as a *crime d'état,* or state crime, and the impasse that followed remains.

7. See Geneviève Van Cauwenberge, "Le point de vue documentaire dans *Le joli mai"* in *Théorem: Recherches sur Chris Marker,* ed. Philippe Dubois (Paris: Presses Sorbonne Nouvelle, 2002), 83–99.

8. France had been at war almost continuously since 1939. The end of the Second World War was quickly followed by France's wars of decolonization in Indochina (1946–54), Madagascar (1947), and Morocco, Tunisia, and Algeria (1954–62).

9. Dimitri Nicolaïdis, *Oublier nos crimes. L'Amnésie nationale: une spécificité française?* (Paris: Éditions Autrement, 1994).

10. See Éric Conan and Henry Rousso, *Vichy, un passé qui ne passe pas* (Paris: Fayard, 1994), published as *Vichy: An Ever-Present Past,* trans. Nathan Bracher (Hanover: University Press of New England, 1998).

11. See House and MacMaster, *Paris 1961,* 38. During Papon's trial for crimes against humanity relating to his period in the prefecture of the Gironde questions were raised relating to his role in the massacre of October 1961. Nevertheless, the question of torture and repression also needs to be assessed as systemic or institutional rather than simply through the prism of a single name.

12. Michael Rothberg, "Between Auschwitz and Algeria: Multidirectional Memory and the Counterpublic Witness," *Critical Inquiry* 33 (2006): 158–84.

13. Ibid., 162.

14. Ibid., 182.

15. For example, in the scene where we see Georges involved in editing his prerecorded literary program, we see clips of the writers invited to comment on a recent publication on Arthur Rimbaud. There is a brief shot of Mazarine Pingeot, the "secret" daughter of French President François Mitterrand, who served from 1981 to 1995.

16. For a discussion of a similar use of the news broadcast in the domestic sphere, see John David Rhodes's discussion of *Code Unknown* in his essay in the present volume.

17. The documentary features a clip recorded on the afternoon of October 17, 1961, in which an Independent Television News (UK) journalist reports that the police had already begun to warn journalists and camera crews not to be present on the streets of Paris for the FLN demonstration to take place later that day after seven p.m. This official attempt to organize a media blackout was largely successful.

18. Gilroy, "Shooting Crabs," 234.

19. On the relationship between hygiene, decolonization, and elimination of history's trace within French culture, see Kristin Ross, *Fast Cars, Clean Bodies: Decolonization and the Reordering of French Culture* (Cambridge: MIT Press, 1996), in particular, 77–78 and 105–22.

20. Gilroy, "Shooting Crabs," 235.

21. "Algeria: Chirac Rejects 'Torture Apology,'" December 15, 2000, http://news.bbc.co.uk/2/hi/europe/1071504.stm (accessed January 28, 2008).

22. See Pascale Bruckner, *La Tyrannie de la pénitence: essai sur le masochisme occidental* (Paris: Grasset, 2006), and Daniel Lefeuvre, *Pour en finir avec la repentence coloniale* (Paris: Flammarion, 2006).

# Contributors

PATRICK CROWLEY is a lecturer in French at University College Cork. His teaching and research focus on contemporary writing and thought, addressing issues such as identity, form, and the legacies of colonialism. He is the author of *Pierre Michon: The Afterlife of Names* (2007) and coeditor of *Formless: Ways In and Out of Form* (2005). His essays on writers such as Eugène Savitzkaya, Kateb Yacine, and Edouard Glissant have appeared in a range of journals that include *Paragraph*, *French Forum*, and *Romance Studies*. His essay on contemporary Algerian cinema appeared in *Expressions Maghrébines*.

SCOTT DURHAM is chair and associate professor of French at Northwestern University, where he also teaches comparative literary studies. He is the author of *Phantom Communities: The Simulacrum and the Limits of Postmodernism* (1998) and the editor of a *Yale French Studies* issue on Jean Genet. He is currently writing two books, with the working titles *Eurydice's Gaze: Historicity, Memory, and Untimeliness in Postmodern Film* and *The Archive and the Monad: Deleuze and the Resistance to Postmodernism*.

MATTIAS FREY is a lecturer in film studies at the University of Kent. His writings have appeared in *Cinema Journal*, *Framework*, *Quarterly Review of Film and Video*, *Literature/Film Quarterly*, and *Senses of Cinema*, as well as *Searching for Sebald*, *Film and Sexual Politics: A Critical Reader* and the *Schirmer Encyclopedia of Film*.

ROSALIND GALT is a senior lecturer in film studies at the University of Sussex. She has published in journals such as *Screen*, *Cinema Journal*, and *Discourse*, and her first book, *The New European Cinema: Redrawing the Map*, was published in 2006 by Columbia University. She is currently editing an anthology on world art cinema with Oxford University Press.

CHRISTOPHE KONÉ is a doctoral student in the Department of German, Russian, and East European Languages and Literatures at Rutgers University. He holds an MA in German studies from the University Lumière of Lyon 2, France. His research interests include Weimar modernism, recent German photography, and representations of realism.

TARJA LAINE is assistant professor of film studies in the Media Studies Department of the University of Amsterdam. She is the author of *Shame and Desire: Emotion, Intersubjectivity, Cinema* (2007), and her essays on emotions and sensations in cinema have been published in journals such as *Discourse, Studies of European Cinema, New Review of Film and Television Studies, PostScript,* and *Film and Philosophy.* Her current research interests include cinema and the philosophy of mind and body.

MICHAEL LAWRENCE is a senior lecturer in film studies at the University of the West of England. He has published essays on Todd Browning and the actor Lee Kang-sheng. He is at work on a monograph on Atom Egoyan.

HUGH S. MANON is associate professor in the screen studies program at Oklahoma State University, where he specializes in Lacanian theory and film noir. He has published in *Cinema Journal, Film Criticism,* and *International Journal of Žižek Studies,* as well as several anthologies. He is currently completing a book project that links the rise and decline of classic American film noir with the advent of television.

FATIMA NAQVI is associate professor and graduate director in the Department of German, Russian, and East European Languages and Literatures at Rutgers University. Currently, she teaches courses on postwar literature and film, Vienna 1900, and the Austrian literary tradition. Her book *The Literary and Cultural Rhetoric of Victimhood: Western Europe 1970–2005* (2007) analyzes the pervasive rhetoric of victimhood in European culture since 1968.

BRIGITTE PEUCKER is the Elias Leavenworth Professor of German and professor of film studies at Yale University. She has published extensively on questions of representation in literature and film. Her latest book is *The Material Image: Art and the Real in Film* (2007). She is writing a book with the working title *Fassbinder's Performance,* as well as editing Blackwell's *Companion to Rainer Werner Fassbinder.*

BRIAN PRICE is assistant professor of screen studies at Oklahoma State University. He is the author of *Neither God nor Master: Robert Bresson and the Modalities of Revolt* and numerous essays in journals and anthologies. He is also coeditor of *Color, the Film Reader* (2006) and of the journal *World Picture.*

BERT REBHANDL writes about film and arts for newspapers like *FAZ* and magazines like *Frieze.* He teaches freelance in the film studies department at Free University. He has published a book on Orson Welles (*Genius in the Labyrinth,* 2005) and recently edited a book on Western films (*Western: Genre and History,* 2007).

JOHN DAVID RHODES is the author of *Stupendous, Miserable City: Pasolini's Rome* (2007). His essays have appeared in numerous publications, including *Log, Modern-*

*ism/Modernity, Framework,* and *Film History.* He is currently editing an anthology, *The Place of the Moving Image,* for the University of Minnesota Press. He is a founding coeditor of *World Picture* and is a senior lecturer in literature and visual culture at the University of Sussex.

CHRISTOPHER SHARRETT is professor of communication and film studies at Seton Hall University. He is the author of *The Rifleman* (2005) and editor of *Mythologies of Violence in Postmodern Media* (1999) and *Crisis Cinema: The Apocalyptic Idea in Postmodern Narrative Film* (1992). He is coeditor of *Planks of Reason: Essays on the Horror Film* (2004). His work has appeared in *Cineaste, Jump Cut, Cinema Journal, Framework, Senses of Cinema, Film International, Postscript, Cineaction, Kinoeye,* and numerous anthologies, including *American Cinema in the 1960s, a Family Affair: Cinema Calls Home, Fifty Contemporary Filmmakers, The End of Cinema as We Know It, The New American Cinema, Sam Peckinpah's The Wild Bunch, The Dread of Difference: Gender and the Horror Film,* and *Japanese Horror Cinema.* He is currently writing a book about the ideology of contemporary Hollywood cinema.

MEGHAN SUTHERLAND is assistant professor of screen studies at Oklahoma State University and a coeditor of *World Picture.* She is also the author of *The Flip Wilson Show* (2008), and her articles on media and philosophy have appeared in edited anthologies as well as journals, including *Framework, Senses of Cinema,* and *Cultural Studies.*

# Index

Abu Ghraib, 272
Adaptation, 193–95, 199, 202–03. *See also* Haneke, literary adaptations
Adorno, Theodor, 38–39, 41, 45, 204
*After Liverpool* (James Saunders), 191. See also *Und was kommt danach? (After Liverpool)*
Albers, Hans, 201
Algerian massacre, 11, 44, 74, 228, 236, 259, 267–72, 274, 276–77. See also *Drowning by Bullets* (Philip Brooks and Alan Hayling)
Algerian war, 44, 270–72, 276
Allen, Woody, 199
Amouroux, Henri, 271
animals, real deaths in fictional worlds, 63–74
Anka, Paul, 195
Antonioni, Michelangelo, 230. See also *Blowup* (Michelangelo Antonioni)
apparatus theory, 106, 110, 121
audience, direct address, 57–58, 233. See also *Funny Games;* spectatorship

Bach, Johann Sebastian, 197, 207, 210, 213–15
Bachman, Ingeborg, 193–94, 198
Bacon, Francis, 196
Badiou, Alain, 182–83
Balibar, Étienne, 225–27, 229, 231
Balkans, 161, 225, 240n. 10
Barthes, Roland, 16, 24, 25, 29, 135–36, 138, 141

Bataille, Georges, 68–69
Baudrillard, Jean, 3, 155, 162–64, 169, 170, 217, 248
Bazin, André, 7, 66, 67, 69, 92–97, 105, 106, 110; on the long-take, 88–90, 160
Beatles, the 192–93
Beethoven, Ludwig van, 219
Bénichou, Maurice, 77, 118
Benjamin, Walter, 160
*Benny's Video*, 3–6, 30, 62, 70–73, 153, 160–63, 170, 177, 214–16, 251–52. *See also* glaciation
Benton, Ted, 69
Berg, Alban, 212–13
Bergman, Ingmar, 218, 230
Berlin, 197–98
Betz, Mark, 235–36
Binoche, Juliette, 21, 76, 93–97, 235
*Blair Witch Project, The* (Daniel Myrick and Eduardo Sánchez), 111
*Blood of the Beasts, The* (Georges Franju), 69
*Blowup* (Michelangelo Antonioni), 22, 23, 218. *See also* Antonioni, Michelangelo
Bordwell, David, 68, 232, 233
Bosnia, 3, 78, 179–80
Brahms, Johannes, 208
Brecht, Bertolt, 233; Brechtian distanciation, 52, 96, 239, 245, 248–49, 264n. 7
Bresson, Robert, 17, 24, 76, 156–59,

285

Bresson, Robert (*continued*)
  196, 199, 246
Burt, Jonathan, 66–67
Bush, George W., 45, 47, 207–8, 238

*Caché*, 28–32, 44, 73–74, 97–100, 160–64, 216–18, 228, 236, 258–63; concluding shot, 97–99, 123, 152, 276; Majid's suicide, 31, 73, 100, 117, 119–20, 122–23, 164, 228, 260, 273–75; memory in, 266–77; psychoanalytic interpretation of the gaze in, 105–23
*Castle, The*, 27, 190–91, 201–3. *See also* Kafka, Franz
Champagne, John, 128
characters, recurring names of, 32–33n. 14, 45, 65, 74–77, 188n. 18, 214
Chirac, Jacques, 276
Chion, Michel, 108–9
Clark, Kenneth, 69
*Code Unknown*, 90, 93–97, 98, 107, 117, 119, 159–61, 224–25, 228, 236, 244, 253–58, 260, 263; reality and performance in, 15–26; sign-language scene, 15–16, 91, 218, 257–58
*Conversation, The* (Francis Ford Coppola), 114
Copjec, Joan, 105, 115
Corti, Alex, 194
Crowley, Patrick, 44, 228

Debord, Guy, 3, 4, 185
Delanöe, Bertand, 271
Deleuze, Gilles, 263
De Sica, Vittorio, 88, 92. *See also Umberto D.* (Vittorio De Sica)
Derrida, Jacques, 84n. 48, 223
Diderot, Denis, 28
Dijk, Maria van, 134
*Drei Wege zum See* (*Three Paths to the Lake*), 193–95
Drenica, 23
Dreyer, Carl Theodor, *Vampyr,* 114–15
*Drowning by Bullets* (Philip Brooks and Alan Hayling), 268–71, 274. *See also* Algerian massacre

*Duel* (Steven Spielberg), 117–18
Durgnat, Raymond, 66, 71

Eisenstein, Sergei, *Strike,* 67–68, 69, 74.
Elsaesser, Thomas, 221, 225, 230, 234, 237
Europe: European cinema of violence, 153; European collectivity, 224–29. *See also* Haneke, European identity
Evenson, Brian, 35–36, 38
Ezra, Elizabeth, 102n. 21, 228

family: bourgeois, 18–19, 28, 75, 100, 216, 259; and politics, 29, 238
Felix, Jürgen, 52
Fenichel, Otto, 133
*Fraulei—Ein deutsches Melodram,* 200–201
Frankfurt School, 208, 211
French New Wave, 17–19
Freud, Sigmund, 28, 128, 134, 196. *See also* psychoanalysis
Frey, Mattias, 63, 187n. 9, 230, 240n. 10
Friedrich, Georg, 133
Frisch, Arno, 71, 77, 96
*Funny Games,* 22–23, 34, 51–59, 60n. 12, 96, 108, 153, 234; audience responsibility, 51–60 (*see also* audience; spectatorship); American remake, 43–45, 58, 102n. 15; pain and representation in, 35–47; Paul's remote control rewind, 23, 36, 50, 56, 96, 160, 171, 248

Giering, Frank, 33n. 14, 96
Gilroy, Paul, 228, 236, 268, 274, 275
glaciation, 57; trilogy, 83n. 40, 154, 171, 197, 212–14, 245, 249–53. *See also Benny's Video; Seventh Continent, The; 71 Fragments of a Chronology of Chance*
Godard, Jean-Luc, 157, 192–93
Goethe, Johann Wolfgang von, 198
*Grey's Anatomy,* 43
Grossvogel, D.I., 233
Grundmann, Roy, 233
Guantanamo Bay, 45

# INDEX

Hall, Stuart, 169
Haneke, Michael: and art cinema, 2, 6, 76, 95, 221–23, 230–36; cameos, 20; compared to Hollywood/mainstream media, 43, 63–64, 108, 111, 114–15, 117–18, 120, 131, 154, 221, 247; early experiences with cinema, 156; European identity, 1–2, 8, 153, 221–23, 229–37 (see also Europe); films (see individual films); as film/media theorist, 153–64; literary adaptations, 127, 131, 146n. 3, 154, 191, 193, 199, 202–3; on the long-take, 87, 90, 92–93, 261; made-for-television features, 191–204; and neorealism, 87–100; as philosopher, 123, 193; and realism, 245–63; on television, 78, 90, 159 (see also television); on violence, 60n. 12, 63, 64, 78–79, 228; written texts: "Film as Catharsis," 155; "Terror and Utopia of Form, 156–59; "Violence and Media," 154–55, 158–59
Hegel, Georg Willhelm Friedrich, 268
Heidegger, Martin, 174–76, 181, 182, 195
Helms, Bobby, 200
Hitchcock, Alfred, 8, 20, 63, 121. See also *Rear Window; Rope*
Horwath, Alexander, 229
Huppert, Isabelle, 76, 88, 146n. 3, 148n. 36, 235
Husserl, Edmund, 223

Iraq, 45, 78, 272

Jackson, Michael, 3, 179, 247
Jameson, Fredric, 18–19, 168, 170, 175, 256, 258
Jelinek, Elfriede: *Children of the Dead*, 142–45. *The Piano Teacher*, 127–28, 131–33, 139–42, 238. See also *Piano Teacher, The*
jouissance, 132–33

Kafka, Franz, 202–3. See also *Castle, The*
Kagan, Eli, 269
Kant, Immanuel, 38

Kleist, Heinrich von, 157–58, 159
Kluge, Alexander, 153
Kosovo, 23, 225, 251
Kracauer, Siegfried, 69

Lacan, Jacques, 105–6, 108–10, 113, 115, 121, 122, 123, 128; conception of the gaze, 111–12. See also psychoanalysis
Laclau, Ernesto, 46, 175, 181, 182
Lang, Fritz, 19
Le Cain, Maximilian, 178
*Lemminge* (*Lemmings*), 195–97
Lessing, Gotthold Ephraim, 28
Lippit, Akira Mizuta, 64, 67, 77
literature. See Haneke, literary adaptations
long-take, 87, 91–92, 93–95, 107–8, 114. See also Bazin, André; Zavattini, Cesare
Lotar, Eli, 68
Lugosi, Bela, 167

Mallarmé, Stéphane, 273
Manker, Paulus, 199
Marchart, Oliver, 174, 182
Marcuse, Herbert, 250
Marker, Chris, 269–70
McGowan, Todd, 106, 111, 122
medium specificity, 7, 10, 159, 164
Merleau-Ponty, Maurice, 99
Metz, Christian, 132, 134, 135–36
Minh-ha, Trinh T., 227
*mise-en-abyme*, 109, 132, 172–73, 175–86
Mulvey, Laura, 110, 133
music, 192, 209–11, 212–13, 214–15, 218

*Nachruf auf einen Mörder* (*Obituary for a Murderer*), 202
Nancy, Jean-Luc, 182
Naqvi, Fatima, 225
*Natural Born Killers* (Oliver Stone), 4, 58, 60n. 12
Nazi: Nazism, 38, 69, 182–83, 208, 211; occupation of France, 44, 271, 272
Neale, Steve, 229, 231, 232

Nesbet, Anne, 68, 71
neorealism. *See* Haneke, and neorealism
Ng, David, 231
Ngai, Sianne, 256
Nicolaïdis, Dimitri, 270
Nietzsche, Friedrich, 169
Nüchtern, Klaus, 127

ontology, 7, 16, 21, 93, 95, 98, 158–59, 161; of the gaze, 110, 144, of television, 94, 168–70, 176–77, 186
*Ossessione* (Luchino Visconti), 92

Panijel, Maurice, 269–70
Papon, Maurice, 268, 271
Paris, 23–24, 161, 228, 231, 253–55, 267–71
*Peeping Tom* (Michael Powell), 21–22, 25–26, 30, 31
Peucker, Brigitte, 63, 101n. 9
*Piano Teacher, The*, 88, 126, 206, 227, 232–33, 235–36, 237–39; classical music in, 209–13; voyeurism in, 127–45. *See also* Jelinek, Elfriede
Pirandello, Luigi, 273
pornography, 134, 136–37, 140, 206, 210–11, 238,
postmodernism, 169, 171–74, 177, 209, 245, 245–50, 256, 263
Powell, Michael. See *Peeping Tom*
Price, Brian, 59n. 7, 187n. 16,
psychoanalysis, 31, 121, 128, 134, 142; *fort-da*, 71, incest taboo, 196, 216–17. *See also* Freud, Sigmund; Lacan, Jacques

Quart, Leonard, 91

*Rear Window* (Alfred Hitchcock), 28, 120. *See also* Hitchcock, Alfred
*Rebellion, Die* (*The Rebellion*), 201–2
reflexivity, 18, 20–23, 26, 27, 36, 106, 139, 153, 164, 170, 233, 248–49
Reik, Theodor, 31
Rhodes, John David, 119, 177, 232
Rice, Condoleeza, 207–8
Rodowick, D. N., 162–63

Roeper, Richard 42–43, 45
Rolling Stones, The 192
Romania, 254; characters from, 17–19, 236
*Rope* (Alfred Hitchcock), 108. *See also* Hitchcock, Alfred
Roth, Joseph, 194, 202
Rothberg, Michael, 272
*Rules of the Game* (Jean Renoir), 23, 66
Rush, Jennifer Rush, 3, 213

Sarajevo, 78, 247
Samel, Udo, 202
Scarry, Elaine, 37, 42
Schiefer, Karin, 267, 268
Schubert, Franz, 137, 148n. 41, 209–11, 213
Schumann, Robert, 209
Seeßlen, Georg, 140
*Seventh Continent, The*, 83n. 40, 107, 166, 171–77, 200, 212–13, 246, 250. *See also* glaciation
*71 Fragments of a Chronology of Chance*, 14, 17, 86, 91–93, 107, 134, 177–85, 247, 257. *See also* glaciation
sexuality, repressed, 128, 133, 139, 141–42, 209, 237–38
Sharrett, Christopher, interview with Haneke, 39, 60n. 12, 90, 233
Sillars, Jane, 102n. 21, 228
Silverman, Kaja, 238–39
Sobchack, Vivian, 66
Somalia, 178
Sontag, Susan, 58
Sorfa, David, 56
spectacle. *See* Debord, Guy
spectatorship, 16, 23, 25, 27, 73, 95, 138, 162; audience complicity, 51–59, 97, 105–6, 134, 137, 139, 154, 274; and torture, 36–37. *See also* audience; *Funny Games*
Spivak, Gayatri, 224
Stiglegger, Marcus, 52
*Strike* (Sergei Eisenstein). *See* Eisenstein, Sergei
Stora, Benjamin, 270

television, 70–71, 93–96, 136, 144, 156, 159, 161–62; and representations of death, 167–86. *See also* Haneke, made-for-television features; Haneke, on television
*Time of the Wolf,* 27–29, 72–73, 83n. 41, 218–19, 220, 226–27, 233, 236
*Today* (NBC), 176
*Tom Jones* (Tony Richardson), 156
Trier, Lars von, 225
Trotsky, Leon, 208
Tudor, Andrew, 232
*Twelfth Night* (William Shakespeare), 20, 26

*Und was kommt danach? (After Liverpool),* 192–93
*Umberto D.* (Vittorio De Sica), 92. *See also* De Sica, Vittorio

*Variation. Daß es Utopien gibt, weiß ich selber! (Variation. That Utopias Exist, I Know Very Well Myself ),* 197–99
Venice, 199–200
Vertov, Dziga, *Kino-Eye,* 71

Vienna, 5–6, 28, 202, 235
violence: images of blood, 3, 29–30, 32, 42, 68, 71, 73, 170, 247, 274; offscreen, 6, 41–42, 55, 63, 70–71, 94–96, 170, 246; sadomasochistic, 22, 30–31, 138–39; torture, 19, 22–23, 34, 36–47, 52, 271, 276;
Virilio, Paul, 155, 162–63

*Wavelength* (Michale Snow), 114
Wenders, Wim, 153, 230
Wheatley, Catherine, 130, 133, 227
*Wer war Edgar Allan? (Who was Edgar Allan?),* 199–200
Williams, Raymond, 219
Winnicott, D. W., 16
Wood, Robin, 139, 207–8, 238
Wyler, William, 21

Yo-Yo Ma, 207–8

Zavattini, Cesare, 92, 96, 100; on the long-take, 87–88
Žižek, Slavoj, 116, 144
Zorn, John, 39–40, 53, 216

www.ingramcontent.com/pod-product-compliance
Lightning Source LLC
Chambersburg PA
CBHW072232240426
43670CB00040B/2449